The Word in the Wind

The Word in the Wind

Sermons for the Lectionary,
Year A, Advent through Eastertide

BRUCE L. TAYLOR

WIPF & STOCK · Eugene, Oregon

THE WORD IN THE WIND
Sermons for the Lectionary, Year A, Advent through Eastertide

Copyright © 2019 Bruce L. Taylor. All rights reserved. Except for brief quotations in critical publications or reviews, no part of this book may be reproduced in any manner without prior written permission from the publisher. Write: Permissions, Wipf and Stock Publishers, 199 W. 8th Ave., Suite 3, Eugene, OR 97401.

Wipf & Stock
An Imprint of Wipf and Stock Publishers
199 W. 8th Ave., Suite 3
Eugene, OR 97401

www.wipfandstock.com

PAPERBACK ISBN: 978-1-5326-8213-1
HARDCOVER ISBN: 978-1-5326-8214-8
EBOOK ISBN: 978-1-5326-8215-5

Manufactured in the U.S.A.   06/21/19

To my wife, Linda, without whose steadfast encouragement this collection would not have been attempted, and without whose constant support it would not have been accomplished.

Contents

Copyright Notices   xiii
Introduction   xv

FIRST SUNDAY OF ADVENT
First Presbyterian Church, Norfolk, Nebraska—December 3, 1989
Isaiah 2:1–5, Romans 13:11–14, Matthew 24:36–44
"God's *Kairos* in Our *Chronos*"   1

SECOND SUNDAY OF ADVENT
Spanish Springs Presbyterian Church, Sparks, Nevada—December 4, 2004
Isaiah 11:1–10, Romans 15:4–13, Matthew 3:1–12
"Salvation for All"   5

THIRD SUNDAY OF ADVENT
Spanish Springs Presbyterian Church, Sparks, Nevada—December 13, 1998
Isaiah 35:1–10, James 5:7–10, Matthew 11:2–11
"Waiting for the 9:01"   10

FOURTH SUNDAY OF ADVENT
First Presbyterian Church, Dodge City, Kansas—December 24, 1995
Isaiah 7:10–16, Romans 1:1–7, Matthew 1:18–25
"Trust Beyond Reason, Hope Beyond Doubt"   16

CHRISTMAS EVE (EARLY EVENING)
Spanish Springs Presbyterian Church, Sparks, Nevada—December 24, 2010
Isaiah 9:2–7, Titus 2:11–14, Luke 2:1–14 (15–20)
"What Gold Is For"   21

CHRISTMAS EVE (LATE EVENING)
Spanish Springs Presbyterian Church, Sparks, Nevada—December 24, 2010
Isaiah 9:2–7, Titus 2:11–14, Luke 2:1–14 (15–20)
"Amazed Again"   29

CHRISTMAS DAY
Spanish Springs Presbyterian Church, Sparks, Nevada—December 25, 2005
Isaiah 52:7–10, Hebrews 1:1–4, John 1:1–14
"Through the Eyes of Christmas"   34

FIRST SUNDAY AFTER CHRISTMAS
Spanish Springs Presbyterian Church, Sparks, Nevada—December 26, 2010
Isaiah 63:7–9, Hebrews 2:10–18, Matthew 2:13–23
"Home, for Christmas"   40

SECOND SUNDAY AFTER CHRISTMAS
Spanish Springs Presbyterian Church, Sparks, Nevada—January 3, 1999
Jeremiah 31:7–14, Ephesians 1:3–14, John 1:1–18
"Christ Our Center"   45

EPIPHANY OF THE LORD
Spanish Springs Presbyterian Church, Sparks, Nevada—January 6, 2001
Isaiah 60:1–6, Ephesians 3:1–12, Matthew 2:1–12
"Light-Bearers"   50

THE BAPTISM OF THE LORD
Spanish Springs Presbyterian Church, Sparks, Nevada—January 9, 2005
Isaiah 42:1–9, Acts 10:34–43, Matthew 3:13–17
"From Bath to Meal"   55

SECOND SUNDAY IN ORDINARY TIME
Spanish Springs Presbyterian Church, Sparks, Nevada—January 17, 1999
Isaiah 49:1–7, 1 Corinthians 1:1–9, John 1:29–42
"Witness"   60

THIRD SUNDAY IN ORDINARY TIME
Spanish Springs Presbyterian Church, Sparks, Nevada—January 23, 2005
Isaiah 9:1–4, 1 Corinthians 1:10–18, Matthew 4:12–23
"*Sine Qua Non*"   65

FOURTH SUNDAY IN ORDINARY TIME
Spanish Springs Presbyterian Church, Sparks, Nevada—January 31, 1999
Micah 6:1–8, 1 Corinthians 1:18–31, Matthew 5:1–12
"Beatitude"   70

FIFTH SUNDAY IN ORDINARY TIME
Spanish Springs Presbyterian Church, Sparks, Nevada—February 6, 2011
Isaiah 58:1–12, 1 Corinthians 2:1–16, Matthew 5:13–20
"No Double Standard"   76

SIXTH SUNDAY IN ORDINARY TIME
First Presbyterian Church, Dodge City, Kansas—February 11, 1996
Deuteronomy 30:15–20, 1 Corinthians 3:1–9, Matthew 5:21–37
"The Point of the Game"   82

SEVENTH SUNDAY IN ORDINARY TIME
First Presbyterian Church, Ponca City, Oklahoma—February 23, 2014
Leviticus 19:1–2, 9–18, 1 Corinthians 3:10–11, 16–23, Matthew 5:38–48
"Holiness"   87

EIGHTH SUNDAY IN ORDINARY TIME
Spanish Springs Presbyterian Church, Sparks, Nevada—February 27, 2011
Isaiah 49:8–16a, 1 Corinthians 4:1–5, Matthew 6:24–34
"To Believe and to Trust"   92

TRANSFIGURATION OF THE LORD
Spanish Springs Presbyterian Church, Sparks, Nevada—February 3, 2008
Exodus 24:12–18, 2 Peter 1:16–21, Matthew 17:1–9
"The Light that Shines Brightest in All the Dark Places"   98

ASH WEDNESDAY
First Presbyterian Church, Ponca City, Oklahoma—March 5, 2014
Joel 2:1–2, 12–17a, 2 Corinthians 5:20b—6:10, Matthew 6:1–6, 16–21
"Why Lent?"   103

FIRST SUNDAY IN LENT
First Presbyterian Church, Ponca City, Oklahoma—March 9, 2014
Genesis 2:4b–9, 15–17, 25—3:7, Romans 5:12–19, Matthew 4:1–11
"Skiing Within Bounds"   109

SECOND SUNDAY IN LENT
First Presbyterian Church, Dodge City, Kansas—March 3, 1996
Genesis 12:1–4a, Romans 4:1–5, 13–17, John 3:1–17
"The Word in the Wind"   115

THIRD SUNDAY IN LENT
Spanish Springs Presbyterian Church, Sparks, Nevada—March 7, 1999
Exodus 17:1–7, Romans 5:1–11, John 4:5–42
"Wherever Jesus Is"   121

FOURTH SUNDAY IN LENT
Spanish Springs Presbyterian Church, Sparks, Nevada—April 3, 2011
1 Samuel 16:1-13, Ephesians 5:8–14, John 9:1–41
"To See or Not to See"   127

FIFTH SUNDAY IN LENT
Spanish Springs Presbyterian Church, Sparks, Nevada—March 17, 2002
Ezekiel 37:1–14, Romans 8:6–11, John 11:1–45
"Faith Debunking Futility"   133

PALM/PASSION SUNDAY
Spanish Springs Presbyterian Church, Sparks, Nevada—March 12, 2008
Isaiah 50:4–9a, Philippians 2:5–11, Matthew 21:1–11
"Through the Gates and into the Valley"   138

MAUNDY THURSDAY
Spanish Springs Presbyterian Church, Sparks, Nevada—March 24, 2005
Exodus 12:1–4, 11–14, 1 Corinthians 11:23–26, John 13:1–17, 31b–35
"The Meal of Anticipation"   144

GOOD FRIDAY
Spanish Springs Presbyterian Church, Sparks, Nevada—March 21, 2008
Isaiah 52:13—53:12, Hebrews 4:14–16; 5:7–9, John 18:1—19:42   149

THE RESURRECTION OF THE LORD (SUNRISE)
First Presbyterian Church, Ponca City, Oklahoma—April 20, 2014
Jeremiah 31:1–6, Acts 10:34–43, John 20:1–18
"The Pilgrim Heart"   157

THE RESURRECTION OF THE LORD
First Presbyterian Church, Ponca City, Oklahoma—April 20, 2014
Acts 10:34–43, Colossians 3:1–4, Matthew 28:1–10
"Whom God Raises Up"   161

SECOND SUNDAY OF EASTER
Spanish Springs Presbyterian Church, Sparks, Nevada—March 30, 2008
Acts 2:14a, 22–32, 1 Peter 1:3–9, John 20:19–31
"And Him Crucified"   166

THIRD SUNDAY OF EASTER
First Presbyterian Church, Dodge City, Kansas—April 21, 1996
Acts 2:14a, 36–41, 1 Peter 1:17–23, Luke 24:13–35
"The Guest" — 171

FOURTH SUNDAY OF EASTER
Spanish Springs Presbyterian Church, Sparks, Nevada—May 15, 2011
Acts 2:42–47, 1 Peter 2:19–25, John 10:1–10
"Ecology" — 177

FIFTH SUNDAY OF EASTER
Spanish Springs Presbyterian Church, Sparks, Nevada—May 22, 2011
Acts 7:55–60, 1 Peter 2:2–10, John 14:1–14
"Who We Are" — 182

SIXTH SUNDAY OF EASTER
Spanish Springs Presbyterian Church, Sparks, Nevada—May 1, 2005
Acts 17:22–31, 1 Peter 3:13–22, John 14:15–21
"To Suffer for the Good" — 187

ASCENSION OF THE LORD
Spanish Springs Presbyterian Church, Sparks, Nevada—June 2, 2011
Acts 1:1–11, Ephesians 1:15–23, Luke 24:44–53
"No More Good Old Days" — 192

SEVENTH SUNDAY OF EASTER
Spanish Springs Presbyterian Church, Sparks, Nevada—May 5, 2005
Acts 1:6–14, 1 Peter 4:12–14; 5:6–11, Luke 17:1–11
"God's Gift to Christ" — 197

APPENDIX: WEEK OF PRAYER FOR CHRISTIAN UNITY
Holy Cross Catholic Community, Sparks, Nevada—January 25, 2008
Isaiah 55:6–9, 1 Thessalonians 5:12a, 13b–18, John 17:6–21
"If Jesus Prayed for It . . ." — 203

List of Sources Cited — 209

Copyright Notices

Scripture quotations are from Common Bible: New Revised Standard Version Bible, copyright © 1989 National Council of the Churches of Christ in the United States of America. Used by permission. All rights reserved worldwide.

From CELEBRATION OF DISCIPLINE: THE PATH TO SPIRITUAL GROWTH, Third Edition, by Richard Foster. Copyright © 1998 by Richard Foster. Reprinted with the permission of HarperCollins Publishers. All rights reserved.

From CHRIST THE CENTER by Dietrich Bonhoeffer. Copyright © 1960 by Christian Kaiser Verlag in Bonhoeffer's GESAMMELTE SCHRIFTEN, Vol. 3. Copyright © 1966, 1978 in the English translation by William Collins Sons & Co. Ltd., London, and Harper & Row, Publishers, Inc., New York. Reprinted with the permission of HarperCollins Publishers. All rights reserved.

From CREATION AND FALL: A THEOLOGICAL EXPOSITION OF GENESIS 1–3 by Dietrich Bonhoeffer, edited by Martin Ruter and Ilse Todt, and translated from the German Edition by Douglas Stephen Bax. Copyright © 1959 by SCM Press Ltd. Reprinted with the permission of Touchstone, a division of Simon & Schuster, Inc. All rights reserved.

Excerpt(s) from SMALL CEREMONIES by Carol Shields, Copyright © 1976 Carol Shields. Reprinted by permission of Vintage Canada/Random House Canada, a division of Penguin Random House Canada Limited. All rights reserved. Any third party use of this material, outside of this publication, is prohibited. Interested parties must apply directly to Penguin Random House Canada Limited for permission.

From THE COST OF DISCIPLESHIP by Dietrich Bonhoeffer, translated from the German by R.H. Fuller, with revisions by Irmgard Booth. Copyright © 1959 by SCM Press Ltd. Reprinted with the permission of Scribner, a division of Simon & Schuster, Inc. All rights reserved.

From THE NEW OXFORD AMERICAN DICTIONARY, Second Edition. Copyright © 2005 by Oxford University Press, Inc. Reprinted by permission of Oxford University Press. All rights reserved.

From THE QUEST OF THE HISTORICAL JESUS by Albert Schweitzer. Copyright © 1968 by James M. Robinson; Copyright Renewed 1996. Reprinted with the permission of Scribner, a division of Simon & Schuster, Inc. All rights reserved.

Introduction

Scholars tell us that worshipers in the Jewish and Christian traditions have long been aided in their reading and hearing of the scriptures by the use of lectionaries in liturgical assemblies and private devotions. Indeed, Jesus himself seems to have taken the practice for granted when he was invited to read in the synagogue at Nazareth the passage from Isaiah that became programmatic for his life and ministry. Congregations and ministers who follow the custom of using a lectionary typically, or at least occasionally, number themselves among a large company of Christians who have benefited from this tradition.

There are, of course, practical advantages for using a lectionary in the contemporary church, namely the ability to coordinate the preparation of liturgy and music weeks or months in advance, and to plan Christian education curriculum that reinforces the proclamation that is made through spoken word, instrumental and sung praise, and petition. In my own years of parish ministry, I and my fellow professionals and lay volunteers in Christian nurture and other ministries have used the lectionary as a key element in helping congregations experience the fullness of scripture, as the Presbyterian *Book of Order* commends.

As the years have gone by, however, my appreciation of the lectionary has grown beyond the practical value of such a tool for planning and coordinating to center on the powerful knowledge that Christians around the world are hearing the same passages of scripture read and proclaimed on any given Sunday, and that they are praying and working through the week with these words in their minds—even if only subliminally—and hopefully on their hearts, as together the church gives witness to the gospel through the rhythms and seasons of life in the Spirit. The potential for conforming our lives more and more to God's intention, and pointing all of humankind to the purpose of creation revealed through the Scriptures heard and considered in their fullness, is a wondrous opportunity that the disciplined exploration of the Bible's manifold themes and insights offers to the whole church, united in common prayer and worship, and out of which flow its mission and ministry.

In summary, I have found the Common Lectionary (Revised), including the Psalms and canticles to be used as sung commentaries on the first reading of each set, especially to be a gift from God and a blessing of the Spirit, prepared through wise insight and careful sensitivity to the purpose of Christian worship and the needs of the church. Not intended to be an imposition upon the expositor's judgment or creativity, it nevertheless, by the working of the Holy Spirit, seems almost invariably weekly to point toward insightful texts from the written word of God appropriate to the occasion in the life of the world, the denomination, the congregation, and the individual. In my own use of the lectionary, I have felt free to depart from it on occasion, or to expand an appointed reading to be more contextually inclusive, but those occasions have been rare and in fact highlight the lectionary's general dependable utility. It also constitutes a humbling reminder that the proclamation of the Word is not about the preacher or her or his likes and dislikes or comfort and ease in the preparation of sermons. The preacher, no less than the worshiping assembly, stands to be blessed by courageous and trustful wrestling with difficult and even uncomfortable passages, some of which are found in juxtaposition with more congenial lections in the same set of designated texts. As the Reformed truism expresses it, scripture is the best interpreter of scripture.

None of the sermons collected herein was conceived or preached in isolation from the day's liturgy. Sermons neither can nor should bear all of the expository weight of worship. The selection of hymns and sung responses and instrumental voluntaries, the composition of prayers of confession and thanksgiving and intercession, the discriminating selection or composition of prayers surrounding the sacraments, and the choice of an affirmation of faith from the Christian heritage, all deserve as much care as the preparation of the sermon that will be nested within the whole liturgy. In an effort to unfold the fullness of prescribed readings and their theological and pastoral themes, it will often be appropriate that various other parts of the liturgy offer a contrast and not just a cumulative affirmation or repreaching of the sermon. Limitations of space prevent the inclusion of the full orders of worship within which these sermons were heard, but I encourage the reader at least to read the lectionary passages at each sermon's heading, and perhaps to consult the scriptural allusion index or lectionary-based use guide in a hymnal for companion devotional reading. In some cases, the date on which the sermon was preached will provide some insight to public events that were in the minds of the preacher and his congregation on the particular occasion.

Introduction

It is my hope that the inclusion of sermons from services beyond the fifty-two Sundays of the year will encourage readers whose congregations or communions do not yet observe the feast days of the church in their worship calendars to consider doing so—not just Christmas Eve and perhaps Ash Wednesday, Maundy Thursday, and Good Friday, but Christmas Day, Epiphany, Ascension Day, and All Saints' Day—so that these celebrations do not overcome or obscure, or are themselves overcome or obscured by, Sunday feast days and traditional observances such as Baptism of the Lord or Reformation Sunday. The sermons will often indicate that the observance of the sacrament of the Lord's Supper is normative in Christian worship, and that it is appropriate that each Sunday should be an encounter with the meaning of our identity as baptized people.

Finally, I wish to acknowledge my appreciation for the translators and editors of the New Revised Standard Version of the Bible, which is used throughout in this volume. They must sense a special blessing in having been the Spirit's agents in providing an honest and reliable version of the Hebrew and Greek scriptures for late twentieth- and twenty-first century, English-reading Christians. I also wish to express my gratitude for the exegetes and commentators I have consulted over the years in sermon preparation, who, perhaps even more than simply identifying what scripture *says*, have valuably cautioned what scripture does *not* say. In some cases, they have helpfully guided my own thoughts and expression, and in others, have prompted more original insights.

This is the first in a projected series of collected sermons on the lectionary texts, offered for devotional reading by laity and clergy and stimulation for the faithful work of expositors in their own settings and with the needs of their own hearers in mind. I have benefited, in my own life of faith and in the blessed task of proclaiming the gospel for communities of followers of Jesus Christ, from such offerings by countless others. The sermons in each volume will reflect the particular interests, emphases, and approaches of the featured Gospel for the respective year of the lectionary cycle, in conscious reliance upon scripture itself to shape not just the theological content of the sermon but, to some degree, literary style. The story sermons were an especial joy to write and deliver, although my practice has been to use such vehicles of exposition in a measured way (to the expressed disappointment of some parishioners).

May each of us, in every setting of the gathered people of God, be blessed in the preaching, and the hearing, of the word.

First Sunday of Advent
First Presbyterian Church, Norfolk, Nebraska
December 3, 1989

Isaiah 2:1–5
Romans 13:11–14
Matthew 24:36–44

"God's *Kairos* in Our *Chronos*"

"But about that day and hour no one knows, neither the angels of heaven, nor the Son, but only the Father" (Matt 24:36 NRSV). So Jesus spoke to his followers concerning the close of the age, impressing upon them the suddenness of its coming, describing God's searching discrimination between those who are preserved and those who are left to their doom, and encouraging the disciples to be prepared and watchful for the coming of the Lord. They should not be like the people living in the days before the flood, when all but Noah and his family were so entirely immersed in their ordinary occupations, heedless of the impending deluge, that they were swept away unprepared and unrepentant. Absorbed in the habits of the world, so busy with the routine of their lives, they had no sense of how *irrelevant* that routine was about to become. Their attention all focused on their *own* comings and goings; they failed to perceive *God's* coming. They could think only of human *chronos*, and were unable to see God's *kairos*.

The Greek New Testament uses two very distinct words to express the idea of time. English has no precise counterparts for them. The Greek word *chronos* refers to time in the sense of the clock and the calendar—time that can be measured in minutes and hours and in days and years. Our English word "chronology" comes from *chronos*, and stands for a succession of events in the order in which they occur on a calendar of twenty-four-hour days. *Chronos* is time as perceived and measured by the daily activity of human affairs, by the rise and fall of kings and empires, by the deposit of the monthly paycheck and the payment of monthly bills, by births and by deaths, by profound sorrows and intense joys. It is the perspective of the farmer who only looks down at the long furrows he is plowing in the dusty ground and never lifts his eyes to see the approaching rain clouds; it is the attitude of the scientist who studies her graphs and her test tubes but never looks out the window to see the trees budding.

In contrast, the Greek word *kairos* is used in the New Testament to mean the appropriate moment, the instant and its fullness; not a measure of hours and days and weeks, but of readiness and ripeness and suitability. *Kairos* is the word for "time" that Paul uses in our epistle reading for this morning: "Besides this, you know what time it is, how it is now the moment for you to wake from sleep" (Rom 13:11a NRSV). *Kairos* is time as *God* conceives of it, seeing all of human history as a single piece, unlimited by calendars and the cycles of human busy-ness, in which the temper of the spirit is more significant than the page of the datebook. It is a heart suddenly warmed, opening to love the person once despised. It is the perspective of the prophet who looks through the smoke rising from battlefields to envision a refashioning of weapons of destruction into tools for cultivating the earth. It is the nations embarked on pilgrimage to gather together and hear the proclamation of God's will. It is a King born in a cattle stall and laid in the straw of a manger. It is the return of the same King, once executed for speaking and doing God's truth but raised from the dead, to consummate his dominion over all creation.

Throughout the history of Christianity, there have been people who insisted that God's *kairos* was capable of being measured by human *chronos*. In spite of Jesus' declaration that not angels, not even he himself knew the day and hour when God will close history, there have been those who were unwilling to permit the times and places to remain in the knowledge of God alone. And so we in our own age are periodically treated to predictions of the end by those who correlate present-day events with their own calendars of ruin, much as has been done for twenty centuries now, emphasizing the human relish for interpreting God's judgment as destruction and doom, generally ignoring the New Testament promise of judgment as salvation and fulfillment. The Christian is called *always* to be prepared for the fullness of God's deliverance. "For," wrote Paul, "salvation is nearer to us now than when we became believers" (Rom 13:11b NRSV). As disciples of Jesus Christ, we become more convinced daily that God's purpose of salvation must be achieved. We are called to put on the Lord Jesus Christ, entering fully into the new order of existence which God creates through his Son.

To understand time in the sense of *kairos* is to relate the minutes and hours of our lives to God's purpose. It is to lift us above the matters of daily routine, of interpreting life as merely days crossed off a calendar. It is to glimpse the possibility of fulfillment of God's will within our own daily activity. It is to see that God is concerned with creation in a personal and purposeful way. It is to believe that, in spite of discouragement and disappointment in ourselves and others and in the events around us, God can break into any one of our moments with the experience of eternal life. It is to have faith that God can enter into our world, whether it be at home or at work, at school or at leisure, in the town hall or in the voting booth, and hallow the mundane with the possibility of the holy. It is to be convinced that God not only cares about each one of us his creatures, but that God intervenes to thrust his *kairos* into the midst of our *chronos*. It is to recognize the sovereignty of God even as we observe the pretentious saber-rattling of the nations, knowing that the new era which Christ promised is a qualitatively different age from the one we have measured with clocks and calendars. It is to understand even in the midst of the world's confused history that God alone is the one who can and does give enduring peace through his judging and forgiving word, and that God will finally bring history to its culmination.

Sometimes, when life's perplexities give rise to doubt, it is easy to wonder whether God has not abandoned the creation after all; whether the only meaning of life is in the routine cycles of existence summed up in the contemporary wisdom, "First you're born, and then you die." There are those pains in our life's chronology that strain our expectation of deliverance and tax our hope of salvation. When a marriage has lost its joy and has dissolved into bitter resentment, when a child seems determined to discard every moral principle that we have tried to instill, when the vigor of our youth has left us and we fear the prospect of a long decline of health, when it seems that no one is listening to our cries of despair, it's hard to rouse ourselves to expect an advent of God in our lives. But scripture tells us over and over again that it is just at such moments that God is likely to infuse our *chronos* with divine *kairos*, to shout or whisper his presence in a compassionate embrace or a friendly smile, in the loud collapse of an inhumane government or the quiet conquest of a dread disease, in the humble birth of his own Son or the glorious return of the risen Lord.

The New Testament urges us to be vigilant, always ready for Christ's advent. The call to "wake up" is a summons to be alert to this new set of realities that God is preparing. We are called to watch for the Lord's coming, not because we know *when it is*, but because we know *what it means*. The truth of God is on its way into our world. The light of God's promised deliverance is intense enough to break through the darkness of human time; the birth of Christ was its first dawning and his second coming will be the full glow of the mid-day sun. "[T]he night is far gone, the day is near" (Rom 13:12a NRSV). That is the promise. Thanks be to God.

Second Sunday of Advent

Spanish Springs Presbyterian Church, Sparks, Nevada

December 4, 2004

Isaiah 11:1–10
Romans 15:4–13
Matthew 3:1–12

"Salvation for All"

A news story on public radio a while ago focused on the increasing fragmentation of public opinion in California, and how it was becoming virtually impossible for the state legislature to govern when there was no political consensus on any major issue. The legislators, in their disagreements, were merely reflecting the disunity of the voters they represented. Since then, the problem has grown beyond California. Our own recent legislative experience in Nevada shows the same trend. And we look at what is happening in Washington and quickly realize that there is no unanimity of thought in our nation, and it is diminishing the effectiveness of all of our institutions, not only governmental, but even religious. Perhaps unanimity on the great public questions of our time would not be a good thing anyway. We need to hear diverse opinions. We need to test different approaches. But, for the first time in a long time, we have crossed over into the dangerous territory where there is no consensus about the *way* we *debate*. Our society seems to have lost the sense of community and shared goals that bound us together in the past even during times of disagreement. Individuals and factions have shown their willingness to wreck society at large and even our churches over any single issue. Two of our scripture readings this morning address the matter of unity by addressing the scope of the salvation promised by God and accomplished in Jesus Christ.

Paul wrote his great letter to the Romans at the height of his career, probably just after the mid-point of the first century. A Jew, Paul had long since adopted as his particular ministry a mission to the Gentiles—to non-Jews, people who did not live according to the law of Moses, people who ate foods that Jews considered unclean, people among whom circumcision was a revolting thought, people who were much more interested in *personal* salvation *today* than in God's ancient covenant with the nation of Israel. Most *Jews*, on the other hand, could scarcely conceive of *their* God being interested in people from any *other* nation, could not imagine *individual* salvation unrelated to the salvation of the *community*, and could not abide the notion of *fellowship* with people who violated the dietary laws and who did not number Abraham and Moses and David among their ancestors. Both Jews and Gentiles were proud people. Both Jews and Gentiles had their own histories and their own traditions and their own suspicions. To observers at the time, the ways of Jews and Gentiles must have seemed totally incompatible, and their differences must have seemed totally irreconcilable. What was true when Paul wrote to the new Christians at Rome surely became even more so a few years later, when Roman armies marched into Palestine and wrecked Jerusalem and destroyed the temple and put the population to flight. Once again, as on so many occasions, Israel had been preyed upon by another nation, and her people had been scattered to the corners of the earth.

But at the time Paul wrote his letter, the distinctions and the enmities between the Jews and the Gentiles were already there; they were the reason that some Christian leaders had thought it an absolute scandal that Paul should mount a mission to the Gentiles, and one reason why Paul frequently ran afoul of Jews living in the cities of Europe and Asia Minor in which he tried to establish churches. For *their* part, the new Christians at Rome tended to disregard the authority of the Old Testament altogether, as something that did not concern them. What had *they* to do with *Israel's* holy book, and what did *it* have to do with *them*? So Paul wrote, in the section of his letter that we read this morning, that the scriptures—what *we* know as the *Old Testament*—were written of *old* for instruction *today*, to provide hope for *both* Jew *and* Gentile, so that *together* we *all* might recognize Jesus Christ as Lord, who confirmed and fulfilled the promises given to the Jewish patriarchs, and who showed God's mercy even upon those who were *not* descended from Abraham and Isaac and Jacob. "May the God of steadfastness and encouragement grant you to live in harmony with one another, in accordance with Christ Jesus, so that together you may with one voice glorify the God and Father of our Lord Jesus Christ" (Rom 15:5–6 NRSV), wrote Paul. "Welcome one another, therefore, just as Christ has welcomed you, for the glory of God" (Rom 15:7 NRSV).

The laying aside of divisions, the putting to rest of hostility, the coming of peace and unity to all creation, was an ancient dream. The scriptures give sad witness to the enmity that infected the world on the eighth day, but they testify mightily to God's satisfaction with the peace and harmony of creation on the day *before* that. Based on their understanding of God, the prophets could imagine a world in which the enemies that they observed in *their* time would be at peace; not only would they not be fighting with *each other*, but they would respect one another, and look out for one another's welfare, and enjoy fellowship with one another. "The wolf shall live with the lamb," as Isaiah put it,

> the leopard shall lie down with the kid,
> the calf and the lion and the fatling together,
>   and a little child shall lead them.
> The cow and the bear shall graze,
>   their young shall lie down together;
>   and the lion shall eat straw like the ox.
> The nursing child shall play over the hole of the asp,
>   and the weaned child shall put its hand on the adder's den.
> They will not hurt or destroy
>   on all my holy mountain. (Isa 11:6–9a NRSV)

Imagine! Can we even do that, imagine? Or have competition and viciousness and distrust and enmity so much become the way that *we* understand the world that we think all such talk of peace and harmony and fellowship is impossible folly? Impossible, and even unwise? Some biblical interpreters think that Isaiah was specifically talking about a day in which *Israel* and her *neighbors* would be at peace. But whether Isaiah's language is a metaphor for international politics or for all of creation in harmony, for us, the grandness of the vision or the folly of the imagination remain the same, and whether we regard it as grand or foolish depends upon whether we are hopeful or cynical, people of faith in the *promises* of *God* or people who put *our* trust in *worldly* wisdom.

Peace and harmony are major themes of Advent. In the days leading up to Christmas, everyone is encouraged toward good will and optimism by Christmas cards and street decorations and all the rest. But for the *Christian*, hope for peace and harmony goes *beyond* wishful thinking to the promises of God and the *fulfillment* of those promises in Jesus Christ who lived and lives again, who came and will come again. For the *Christian*, peace and harmony are not a sentiment awakened annually on Thanksgiving and retired again on New Year's Day. For the *Christian*, peace and harmony are a practiced *certainty* because they are the will of *God*, integral to the divine purpose of redeeming all of creation and restoring it to the community of love and fellowship that is God's very *purpose* for creation. The world only *glimpses* at this time of year the abiding vision that *should guide* the church and each disciple of Jesus Christ *daily*: enmity and discord and hostility are not acceptable, because they are contrary to the will of God and to the witness of Jesus Christ. Where there is bitterness and distrust and jealousy, the will of God is being opposed, and, if it should happen among *Christians*, the *praise* that is *due* to *God* is being *corrupted*.

The church at Rome had failed to learn the obvious lesson from its very existence—that if Gentiles were now on even footing with Jews in the eyes of God because of Jesus Christ, then surely the members of their own *church* must be on even footing with *each other* in the eyes of God. Something was causing disharmony in the Roman congregation and preventing the full unity and community that ought to characterize Christians—some issue, some distrust, some difference in class or status. "May the God of steadfastness and encouragement grant you to live in harmony with one another," Paul prayed earnestly in his letter, "in accordance with Christ Jesus, so that together you may with one voice"—not in discordant squabbling but in a genuine unity of praise—"glorify the God and Father of our Lord Jesus Christ. Welcome one another, therefore, just as Christ has welcomed you, for the glory of God" (Rom 15:5–7 NRSV). Put aside your pride and your petty jealousies, whatever they might be; they are not as important as being a fellowship of believers, a family of faith with Christ as your brother and God as your Father and every church member as dear to you as your own flesh and blood. Show hospitality toward each other, bend over backwards to avoid discord, bear with one another's foibles as together you all seek to grow into the stature of the fullness of Christ who is our peace, Paul was saying. Believe that the Christ in whom you have new and abundant life is the Messiah who was *promised* to the *Jews* and *through whom* the *Gentiles* have *mercy*, under whose rule the entire creation shall be made whole and whose mission is the salvation of all. Imagine! A lamb safe in the company of a wolf! A kid resting confidently alongside a leopard! An infant uninjured as it plays with snakes! A ridiculous dream? Or the promised root of Jesse come to fulfillment in the reign of Jesus Christ the Messiah in whom you and I and every Christian have said that we put our faith?

Fanciful folly? A new nation of blacks and whites living and working side by side in peace and equality is emerging from the stinking ashes of apartheid in South Africa, without racial recrimination and without economic collapse. Preposterous absurdity? A peace treaty brought to an end the destruction of warring pride and ethnic prejudice between Christians and Muslims in Bosnia, and the perpetrators of great crimes of genocide are being brought to justice. Wishful thinking? A peace accord has held in Northern Ireland for more than ten years, bringing an end of violence between Protestants and Roman Catholics whose decades-long distrust of each other had devastated the economy and brought heartbreak to countless homes. Impossible hope? A generation of Middle Eastern warriors has finally come to see that *sharing* Palestine is the only way to avoid mutual devastation, though a younger generation of snipers and assassins and suicide bombers must still be convinced of the wisdom which came so late to their parents.

The day is coming. Its dawn in the cessation of hostilities is not yet the full noonday of harmony and community and love and self-giving, but the day is coming. Have faith, people of God, and think and speak and act hopefully and trustfully in the day of salvation that approaches ever nearer—the day of salvation for all of God's creation.

Third Sunday of Advent

Spanish Springs Presbyterian Church, Sparks, Nevada

December 13, 1998

Isaiah 35:1–10
James 5:7–10
Matthew 11:2–11

"Waiting for the 9:01"

The morning sun had just climbed over the hill on the south side of the river—the hill on which the university was nestled among a forest of bare branches—and now it illuminated the taller hill that dominated the center of town, crowned by the great cathedral that towered above the shops and offices and apartments, and the railroad platform on which a lone figure stood. Dressed in a gray wool coat, checkered blue scarf, and dark gray hat, the man began pacing back and forth, perhaps in anticipation, perhaps to stay warm, but he paused every few steps to glance eastward up the tracks. Occasionally, he grasped the collar of his coat against the cold December air that turned his breath into little white puffs. The train from the city was not due for another twenty minutes yet, but the man showed no interest, whenever he passed the door to the waiting room, of seeking refuge from the chill.

As he came back into the shadow of the station, a heavy wooden door on the side of the depot noisily slid open, and a porter dressed in the railroad's winter uniform pulled out onto the platform a cart bearing half a dozen suitcases and boxes. "Just left Brampton eight minutes late," the porter said as she passed the man. The man nodded vaguely in acknowledgment of the information. The porter dropped the handle of the cart and stood for a moment watching the man walking away from her toward the east end of the platform. She judged him to be well into his seventies, though his gray beard might have made him look older than his age. The porter had only worked at the station for a couple of weeks, but every morning since she began, the man in the wool coat had shown up about this time, pacing back and forth until the train arrived, and again later in the day when it was time for the evening train to arrive. Then he would walk up to the door of the silver and blue and yellow coach, looking intently into the faces of the passengers who stepped off onto the platform, and when they had all passed him by and the departing passengers had climbed up the steps into the coach and the conductor had closed the door, he would shake his head a little sadly, and watch the train as it pulled out on its westward journey far down the track until the red rear light disappeared from view around the curve toward Kitchener. Then the man would descend the stairs to the street level below and disappear into the morning traffic or into the evening darkness.

After her first few days on duty, the porter had asked the station manager about the man. "Been coming for as many years as I've been working here," the station manager had told her. "Meets every westbound train. Don't know who he is—never asked. He's got nothing better to do, I suppose. Maybe he just likes trains. Or maybe he's not quite right in the head. He hasn't been harassing you, has he?"

"Oh, no, sir, no," the porter assured him. "I just wondered. It seems so strange."

"Just humor him," the station manager had replied, swiveling his chair back to his desk and continuing with his paperwork.

But all those *other* days she had noticed the man, the weather had been *warmer*. Cardinals had flitted from tree to tree along the street below the tracks, children had laughed as they ran along the sidewalk to school, passengers had sat on the outdoor benches reading the morning newspaper. It had been a mild December so far, but now a cold east wind was blowing in off of the lake, and as she watched the man, low clouds pushed by the wind suddenly blotted out the sunshine and blanketed the town with a pall of somber hues. The sudden gloom moved her to concern for the pacing figure. Her friends often called her inquisitive and rather impetuous. For days now, the mystery of the old man on the platform had been growing. It had finally become too much for her. As he walked back in her direction, she resolved to satisfy her curiosity. "Are you waiting for someone, then?" she asked when he was still a ways off from her.

"What?" he looked up and around vaguely, then noticed her as for the first time. "I beg your pardon," he said in a soft brogue.

"I'm sorry, I didn't mean to startle you. I just asked if you are waiting for someone on the train."

"Yes. That is, I think so. I mean, I am hoping." He turned away from her to look back up the track, then he began his slow walk to the east end of the platform again.

"Cold, eh?" she called after him, but he apparently did not hear her.

As the man approached the porter on his return trip along the platform, he started to turn around before reaching her, but she called over to him, "Someone you know, then? A friend or a relative?"

He stopped and turned back toward her. "Someone I know? Yes. That is, we've only met once, long ago, but I know him, yes. I have followed his career very closely."

"Well," said the porter, "it will still be several minutes yet. Why not wait inside where it's warm?"

"No, no," said the man. "I must be here when he arrives. I must be ready."

The porter thought a few seconds. "I could let you know when I see the headlamp."

The man smiled a bit, raising his hand and waving it slightly. "Thank you, but . . . I'll stay here waiting."

As he started walking back east along the platform, the porter strode over to walk alongside him. "I know it's not my business—" she said, bracing herself for an affirmative gesture from the man; when it did not come, she continued. "I couldn't help but notice that you've been here every day since I've been working. And when I asked about it, I heard that you've been here to meet the westbound trains every day for several years."

"Yes, well, you see," said the man, stopping now, "I don't know exactly when he's coming. I only know that he *is* coming, and I need to be here when he arrives."

"He's coming out from the city, then?"

"He's been in the city recently, yes. And other places. I hear of him working all around—Kingston, Barrie, Peterborough."

"Perhaps you could go to meet *him*?"

"Oh, it would be hard to know where he is from day to day. And his work is too important for me to presume so much. *He* knows what has to be done, and when, and where. He'll come," said the man smiling more broadly now at the young woman and nodding. "He'll come. He *said* he would come." He looked back up the track and nodded to himself. "He'll come."

"He must be quite important to you," she said.

"Important?" the man responded as they began walking, his voice hinting some surprise at her lack of perception. "He has carried on the vision of my own work, and that of my predecessors, and made it his own. Very important work, not appreciated by everyone. But he has taken it to such new heights, has revealed its profound implications for all people. I thought I knew what it was all about, but now I know that I really understood so little." He looked at his young companion and saw that she did not at all comprehend what he was saying. He explained more simply, as in summary, "Everything will be fine when he arrives. Everything will be just fine."

"Then maybe I should be waiting for this person to come, too," the young woman said with a chuckle.

She had expected the man to laugh with her, but instead, he looked at her quite intently now. "Yes, indeed you should."

The young woman's mood of gentle mirth disappeared, and she became all sober. There was such an earnestness in the man's voice, a sense of urgency, almost, of pleading.

"But you've been waiting for him for *years*," she finally said.

"Yes," said the man. "I've waited a long while. There have been times when I almost gave up hope, but then I would receive his assurances through a trusted messenger, I would remember the promise that he made me long ago, and my hope would be restored."

The young woman looked at him, but she remained silent. He glanced up the track, and then turned toward her and spoke in a tone of close confidence. "You see, I know he will come, because I know *him*. It's not that we've conversed face to face in all these years, but I have spoken with others who have been with him recently, friends who assist him in his work, and they have told me that it is well worth the wait, not to give up hope. For a time, I doubted whether I *should* wait—the reports of his comings and goings seemed so different from what I had hoped, disappointing at first. I had expected that he would perpetuate my *own* work, continue in the paths that *I* had pioneered, adhere to the plans that *I* had made. But that was before I understood the true importance of it all, saw the real meaning—when I was younger, thinking mainly of myself, my own desires, my own ambitions; I thought that I might be able to use him to advance my own agenda. But the things that I heard *he* was interested in, the things he was *doing*, didn't seem to fulfill my plans, my expectations. He heard of my disenchantment, my disappointment, even, and sent word to me. 'Can't you understand what my work is all about?' he said. 'See how people's lives are changed, made more complete, less concerned with selfish ambitions. If you want something different, if you don't think that's important, you should quit waiting for *me* and look for someone else who is more in tune with *your* desires. But if what *I* have to offer—what you hear that I am doing everywhere I go—if *that* is what you want, be patient and be ready to meet me—I am coming.' And I grew to understand over the years that I had only scratched the surface, you see, only glimpsed through my own poor efforts and understandings the enormous scope of it all, had such a narrow conception of the work. I thought *I* was the teacher, but now I realize that *he* is the master. So," said the man, "here I am, ready and waiting to meet my master. And I fully expect him to step off of that train this morning. And should he not, then I will be here tonight, after spending the day trying to be faithful to his vision, fully expecting him to step off of *that* train. I trust his judgment about when it will be right."

The young woman looked into the man's blue-gray eyes, aged and filled with longing, and then she looked up the track. She still did not understand exactly what or whom the man was waiting for, but she had a sense that she, too, should be expectant and hopeful, though she didn't know what it was she was expecting. She *did* have hopes in her life, of course, or did *once*—her home life had not been perfect, and now her parents were divorced and her mother was sick and she seldom heard from her father. There had been bigger dreams after university, but she had to take any job that would support her, even lugging baggage carts on a cold and windy railroad platform. There had been a young man, and he had made fine-sounding promises, but, after she had given her heart and her body, he was gone. Her hope had seemed to dissolve even as her yearning had become more acute. She had been interested in banning land mines and saving the old growth forests and promoting a local rock group, but none of those things seemed ultimately satisfying. She had wanted to be a part of something bigger than her own life that would give it meaning, had wanted to surrender herself completely to something worthy of her devotion, but everything had disappointed her in one way or another. She had high hopes when her political party won the election, but now that it was in power, nothing had really changed—more economic muddle and continuing constitutional crisis punctuated every few weeks by a whiff of scandal, and, more immediately worrisome, talk from her own party about accelerating the payments due on her student loans. She wished that something could stir in her the hope and devotion that this man had.

"You really think this could be the day, then—he could really be on this train?" she asked the man.

"I fully expect it," the man said, looking east up the track and nodding. Then he added, "That is what I live for."

The young woman followed the man's gaze, and she felt an anticipation rise in her breast. Exactly *what* was about to happen, she didn't know, and she realized that this event, she had no part in arranging, had no way to make happen. For the *old man's* sake, she *hoped*, though, that *this* was the day. But no, that wasn't all of it. For some reason that she could not pinpoint, she realized that it was not for the old man's sake alone—she found herself hoping that this was the day for *her own* sake.

    They stood together waiting in silence, a man nearing the end of his life and a woman just turned an adult, watching, watching. She had looked up that track many times over the past couple of weeks, but never with the same emotion that she had now. Then, there it was—just a faint, tiny pinprick at first, but then growing in brightness as the young woman's certainty grew that it was real—the headlamp of the 9:01. She grinned and turned toward the man, and could just make out the trickle of a tear down his cheek through the blur of her own tears of joyful hope.

Fourth Sunday of Advent

First Presbyterian Church, Dodge City, Kansas

December 24, 1995

Isaiah 7:10–16
Romans 1:1–7
Matthew 1:18–25

"Trust Beyond Reason, Hope Beyond Doubt"

Biblical literacy continues to decline in our modern age. One of the casualties is the appreciation of the distinctive message of each respective book of the Bible. This is probably the time of year when the problem is most noticeable among Christians. Just where do we find the story of the shepherds and the wise men, the stable and the flight into Egypt? Some of us may be surprised to open the New Testament to Mark or John, and discover that neither of those Gospels has anything to say about Jesus' birth at all. Others of us may search in vain through Luke, looking for the wise men and Herod's order to kill the newborns, or search in vain through Matthew, looking for shepherds and the stable. A lot of us have composed our own Gospel over the years, with bits and pieces taken from each of the four Gospels and perhaps movies and devotional books and assembled all together in a fashion that we have never examined critically. "What's wrong with that?" some may be thinking. "It's all true, isn't it? What difference does it make what part of the Bible it came from? What difference does it make if the source of our pious notions isn't really the Bible at all?" The difficulty is that, in the process of making our own "Gospel", we will invariably lose the unique and important perspectives of the Bible as it has been handed down to us, and we will therefore naturally lose a large part of the truth that it conveys. We may even manufacture information that has no biblical basis at all.

On Christmas Eve, how we love to hear the familiar story from Luke's Gospel about Mary giving birth to the baby Jesus as an angel had told her. We are charmed by the heavenly host appearing to the shepherds with good news of great joy. And there, at the stable, in addition to Jesus, of course, our mental tableau highlights Mary, and the shepherds, with Matthew's wise men thrown in for good measure. The nativity story in Matthew, however, highlights another personality—Joseph. In Matthew's Gospel, it is through Joseph that Jesus' lineage is traced back to King David, and back even farther to Abraham, with whom God first made covenant. In Matthew's Gospel, it is to *Joseph* that an angel explains Mary's pregnancy. In Matthew's Gospel, it is *Joseph's* character that is held up as exemplary. It is fitting that, on this fourth Sunday of Advent, we hear the New Testament's *other* story of Jesus' birth to complement tonight's familiar Christmas Eve reading from Luke.

To all appearances, Mary deserved to be stoned to death—that is what the law prescribed in cases where a woman had sexual relations with a man not her husband, and it seemed obvious that, if *Joseph* had not been with her, someone else *had*. Imagine the shock and the shame, the tremendous heartbreak and dismay that Joseph experienced when he first heard that his wife-to-be was pregnant by another—hardly the sort of emotions that we usually associate with Christmas. All of his hopes, all of his dreams, were dashed. He was a righteous man, we are told, a man of the law. But he was also a compassionate man, unwilling to see Mary disgraced. He resolved not to make public the scandal by going to the authorities, either to charge her with a crime or to petition for a divorce. But a divorce could also be worked by simply handing his fiancée a writ in the presence of two witnesses. Apparently, that is what he decided to do—to divorce her quietly, in the presence and knowing of the fewest possible people. Could he *forgive* her? He was a man of the law; there was no possibility of forgiving a sinner. How could she have done this to him, to violate his trust and cause him shame? How could he have been so wrong about her, to suppose that she was good and pure and faithful? Better to find out now, no doubt. Better to limit the scandal. Better to let his heart mend in secret. Surely, that was the reasonable thing to do.

But then Joseph had a dream—a dream no less fantastic than the dreams his namesake of old had had. "Joseph, son of David, do not be afraid" (Matt 1:20b). Do not be afraid of the gossip. Do not be afraid of having misplaced your affection. Do not even be afraid of disregarding the law of Moses. "[D]o not be afraid to take Mary as your wife, for the child conceived in her is from the Holy Spirit. She will bear a son, and you are to name him Jesus, for he will save his people from their sins" (Matt 1:20b–21 NRSV). And Joseph "did as the angel of the Lord commanded him; he took

[Mary] as his wife" (Matt 1:24b–c NRSV). Aside from the question of what the law prescribed for adultery—and that is what this amounted to, from all reasonable appearances—any man in this room would have to admit that Joseph's behavior was remarkable. Men are vain and prideful and stubborn by nature; perhaps you women have noticed. I do not know what the Hebrew equivalent of "machismo" is, but Mary's pregnancy certainly would have offended *Joseph's*. What man here would not have been thrown into a *rage* over such news about his betrothed? What man here would have been credulous enough to accept the explanation that Joseph dreamed of? And even if he *did* accept the explanation as God's own truth, what man here would have been willing to brave the gossip, the stares, the lingering doubts that surely would follow him all of his life?

Matthew could easily have glossed over Joseph's reaction to the news of Mary's pregnancy, as Luke did. But Matthew had a particular interest in telling us about Joseph. "Do not be afraid," the angel said to Mary in Luke's Gospel. "Do not be afraid," the angel said to Joseph in Matthew's Gospel. Mary could not do anything about the fact that she was pregnant, or the fact that gossipers would reckon her the sinful mother of an illegitimate child, but Joseph could have walked away from the crisis without anyone ever knowing, or he could have been deemed a righteous practitioner of the law by exposing Mary. But Joseph didn't do either of those things. Joseph trusted God, even in so incredible an explanation and promise as came from an angel in a dream, and, we may safely assume, he became a model of faithful obedience to God from whom God's own Son found much to learn. "All this," Matthew adds, "took place to fulfill what had been spoken by the Lord through the prophet: 'Look, the virgin shall conceive and bear a son, and they shall name him Emmanuel,' which means, 'God is with us.' When Joseph awoke from sleep, he did as the angel of the Lord commanded him; he took [Mary] as his wife" (Matt 1:22–24 NRSV).

Now, the prophet to whom Matthew referred was Isaiah. Isaiah had delivered a prophecy to King Ahaz of Judah. The king had angered two of Judah's neighbors by refusing to join in league with them against Assyria. They threatened to invade Jerusalem if he refused to ally himself with them. Instead of joining with them *against* Assyria, King Ahaz had been advised by his council to seek Assyria's *assistance* against the threatened *invasion*. Isaiah had told Ahaz that the invasion of Jerusalem would not happen in any event, and therefore, Ahaz should *not* turn to Assyria. Perhaps Isaiah realized that reliance on Assyria would result in Jewish society and Jewish religion being polluted with Assyrian customs and Assyrian gods. "It shall not stand," the Lord had declared concerning the threatened invasion, "and it shall not come to pass. . . . If *you* do not stand *firm* in *faith*, you shall not stand at *all*" (Isa 7:7b, 9b NRSV, emphasis here and in subsequent scriptural quotes has been added). God even offered to give Ahaz whatever sign Ahaz chose as a proof that things would go Judah's way without any help from Assyria. Excusing his disobedience in the pious terms of not wanting to put the Lord to the test, Ahaz declined the offer. "Then Isaiah said: 'Hear then, O house of David! Is it too little for you to weary mortals, that you weary my God also? Therefore the Lord himself will give you a sign. Look, the young woman is with child and shall bear a son, and shall name him Immanuel'" (Isa 7:13–14 NRSV). So great would be the joy at God's saving Jerusalem from destruction, that a woman then with child—perhaps Ahaz's own wife—would name her newborn "God is with us."

But this king in the line of David went his own way in the matter, and the result was disaster for Judah. The promise of God's deliverance from the approaching armies seemed too incredible to Ahaz. The enemies were at the gates. The best minds in the kingdom had urged Ahaz to trust in the military might of Assyria. As logic dictated, he chose the worldly wisdom of his human advisors over the implausible promises of God. Hundreds of years later in a little Judean village, another man in the line of David received another promise of God that seemed implausible, but being a righteous man, he trusted God's promise, and so he was instrumental in protecting and raising *him* who would save his people from their sins. It defied all reason, what Joseph did—trust such an incredible promise. His hope in God transcended all the doubts that he naturally would have had about Mary and about her child. And when she bore a son, Joseph named him Jesus, which means "salvation."

The story of Christmas is a message of faith—of trust against long odds, of hope that casts out fear. That the Savior of the world should be an infant born into a carpenter's family in an insignificant little place called Bethlehem—incredible! That the Son of God should live with common people and serve their common needs and forgive their common sins—unbelievable! That the hope of the world narrowly averted a scandalous birth and a shameful label—amazing! God certainly expects a lot of us by asking us to trust and to hope—to trust beyond reason and to hope beyond doubt, to trust beyond human contracts and to hope beyond human accomplishments, to trust beyond savings accounts and insurance policies, to hope beyond the American dream and the next election, to trust beyond human senses, human logic, and human satisfactions, and to hope beyond worldly reservations, fortune, and reputation. The message of Christmas is that the promises of God are true, and that the promises of God are for you. Incredible? Unbelievable? Amazing? God certainly expects a lot of us by asking us to trust and to hope. But see what an enchanting starting place God gives us:

Now the birth of Jesus the Messiah took place in this way. When his mother Mary had been engaged to Joseph, but before they lived together, she was found to be with child from the Holy Spirit. Her husband Joseph, being a righteous man and unwilling to expose her to public disgrace, planned to dismiss her quietly. But just when he had resolved to do this, an angel of the Lord appeared to him in a dream and said, "Joseph, son of David, do not be afraid to take Mary as your wife, for the child conceived in her is from the Holy Spirit. She will bear a son, and you are to name him Jesus, for he will save his people from their sins." All this took place to fulfill what had been spoken by the Lord through the prophet:

> "Look, the virgin shall conceive and bear a son,
> and they shall call him Emmanuel,"

Which means, "God is with us." When Joseph awoke from sleep, he did as the angel of the Lord commanded him; he took her as his wife, but had no marital relations with her until she had borne a son; and he named him Jesus. (Matt 1:18–25 NRSV)

Christmas Eve (Early Evening)
Spanish Springs Presbyterian Church, Sparks, Nevada
December 24, 2010

Isaiah 9:2–7
Titus 2:11–14
Luke 2:1–14 (15–20)

"What Gold Is For"

Winter had come early to Troublesome Gulch and the entire Heartless mountain range. The snow was already three feet deep around Sam McPherson's little shack above timberline, where there were no trees to stop the wind when it came howling across the ridge and down the gulch and seemed to pick apart the gaps in the siding and even cause the single oil lantern above the table to flicker. The cold only added to the oppressive feeling of loneliness. Sam had thought of giving up many a time, but the rumor of rich strikes in the neighboring vicinity had persuaded him to keep at it, hoping that he, too, would come upon a rich vein under one of the leads he was exploring. If, by a month from now, none of his samples showed any values, he would give up and go . . . where? That was always the question that, when the month was up, caused him to add another month to his vow.

A lot of the men in these mountains had left families behind when they went prospecting in hope of a better life for themselves, intending to send for their wives and children whenever they were able to carve a working mine out of the mountainside. Sam McPherson had no wife or children, and so, perhaps, the loneliness was not as keen for him—he had been on his own since a third successive year of crop failures had made *his* one too many mouths to feed back on the family farm. But still, he missed the joys of home and kinfolk. Though specific images were fading, he sensed the loss of something profoundly important and meaningful. In his late teens, he had drifted west, finding odd jobs in the towns that were springing up on the prairies and the farms that supported them and the new trading hubs along the Front Range of the Rocky Mountains until, like so many, he had succumbed to a disease that had reached epidemic proportions in the late 1860s—gold fever. He managed to save enough money to buy a burro and an outfit, and had set out for the high country whence had flowed seductive stories of men near starvation becoming suddenly as wealthy as Croesus.

That was three years ago, and, as it had not come true for most of those who tried their hand at prospecting, so it had not come true for Sam McPherson. Now and then, he would find some fine flakes of gold, more often free silver, that had washed down a creek here or there, just enough to fan his hopes and buy some supplies. But, as the population of would-be miners had increased, easy pickings like that had become more scarce. In early October, just before the first snow fell, he had selected a lead about 200 yards uphill from his little shack, jutting out like a sentinel at the head of the gulch, and had exposed a vein of quartz after digging about twenty feet into its base, which seemed to be the likely source for some bits of gold he had discovered farther down the gulch. He had been drifting along the vein now for the past several weeks while the wind outside the mouth of his tunnel first carried away the last of the leaves from the aspen trees below his shack and then blew in snow which it mounded into deep drifts. During one storm, he had spent nearly three days inside his workings for fear that he would get lost in the blizzard if he were to try to make his way to the shack. Luckily, he had brought his burro with him that day to offer it shelter as the winds had increased, and they had kept each other warmer than either would have been without its companion. At first, Sam had kept working during the storm, but as his single day's supply of food had run out, by the middle of the second day he was becoming too weak to keep flinging his pick at the stubborn rock. After the storm subsided, he strung a rope between his shack and the entrance to the little tunnel, securing it well at both ends so that he could follow it should he experience another white-out.

Then, finally, after several more storms, one day, the vein showed some flecks of gold, more and more the farther he followed it. Usually restrained in expression, he began whooping and hollering as the vein seemed to get progressively richer. And he began to make plans to take his treasure into Mule Ear and have it assayed and weighed, and to file a claim on the basis of his discovery. So it was that Sam McPherson and his little burro Angel forced their way down Troublesome Gulch through the snow on the next day that dawned cloudless and windless. Sam had mentally calculated that, if clouds were building by the time they reached Hard Luck Creek, he and his burro would turn back so as not to risk being caught in a storm. But the sun continued to shine unimpeded, and, though the air was crisp at that elevation, the joy of his discovery kept Sam's mind off of the cold as he pushed through the thick blanket of snow and coaxed Angel along behind him. Besides carrying the sacks of rock downhill to Mule Ear, the burro was needed to haul supplies back to the shack, supposing, as Sam did, that the contents of the sacks could be converted to enough cash to purchase food and oil and other supplies to last him a good while. Still, it was slow going through the snow, so that Sam and Angel were yet a couple of miles from Mule Ear when darkness began to fall on this, one of the shortest days of the year, though he could see the lights of the little town winking from the distance through the trees. First, the assay office, then the little mining district recording office, then the stable, the saloon, the cafe, and a bed for the night. Sam had it all figured out.

But when he got to the assay office in this little whisper of civilization, Sam found the door locked and no light on in the place. The story was the same at the recording office next door. In fact, most of the storefronts along the stubby main street were dark, though here and there in the apartments overhead he could see light from a candle or lamp. By his reckoning, it was not yet five o'clock. He and Angel turned off of the main street, walking on the frozen mixture of mud and snow to the town's stable. Even the stable was void of human presence. Sam found an empty stall, ushered his burro into it, and threw in some hay as he looked for a bucket. Finding one beside a water trough just outside, he broke through the thin layer of ice that had formed on the surface of the water, dipped the bucket in, and carried it back to the stall. Now, he faced a dilemma. He hadn't considered what he would do with the sacks of ore should he find the assay office closed. For the time being, he decided to pile them in the corner of the stall and cover them with some fresh straw. That job done, he left the stable and turned back toward the main street in search of some sign of human life.

As he entered the main street, Sam turned left toward one of the saloons, from which he imagined he could hear the faint sound of a human voice. Before he could reach the door of the building, whose windows were lit brightly, the single voice became a chorus of voices joined in song. But what he thought he now heard was no barroom ballad, but a melody that stirred a faint memory from his youth back east, a memory of some event that at once triggered emotions of both joy and melancholy, though he could not, in that instant, have explained why.

He opened the saloon door into a room full of people, some seated on whatever chairs were available, others standing around the perimeter of the place, and a man dressed in black waving his arms as the people sang, "And wonders, wonders of his love." The room itself had been transformed from the last time he was in it, during a spell of Indian summer; there were ropes of pine hanging from the ceiling, and a star, crudely fashioned out of paper, was suspended from the oil lamp that hung above the middle of the room.

"Brother, come in," the man dressed in black said as the song came to an end. "Come in and join us. Follow the light out of the darkness. Come in from the cold and warm yourself at the manger."

Sam's face betrayed his bewilderment, not yet comprehending the transformation of the saloon and its clientele. Finding a vacant spot along the wall, he nestled in between two other men, and turned to the one on his right to ask, in a low voice, "What's goin' on? How come the town's shut down?"

"It ain't shut down, son," the man responded. "Don'cha know? It's Christmas Eve!" After a pause, he continued, "This here's a parson from somewhere's or other. Gonna preach at us now."

"Shh!" a stout woman seated in front of them turned with her finger to her lips.

"Sorry," Sam mumbled, the memory now forming itself more clearly in his mind as the sounds and scenes of his youth started to emerge as from a trunk stored in the attic. In the succession of days on his lonely mountain, one after another much the same, he had forgotten about Christmas, and hadn't considered that his journey to town might coincide with the holiday, although it surely must be late December. In truth, he rather wished the saloon were open for its regular business, and hoped that the cafe would welcome his patronage before the evening was over. But he had had something to eat at mid-day, and so was not yet particularly hungry, and decided that, if all these townspeople could endure being preached at, so could he. Now that his curiosity about the absence of shopkeepers and tradesmen had been satisfied, however, his mind was somewhat preoccupied with the security of the hiding place he had fashioned in Angel's stall.

The traveling minister was now embarking upon his retelling of the story of some other travelers who had entered a town late one night searching for refuge from the darkness and the cold, and had been offered only the rude comfort of a stable, with its cattle and donkeys, and of shepherds who came at the urging of heavenly messengers to see a sight at once marvelous and common. And he went on to tell of the visit of wise men from beyond the eastern horizon some days later who brought gifts of gold—Sam's thoughts quickly turned again to Angel's stable—and frankincense and myrrh, whatever those were. Gold, he knew about, and the value that human beings placed on it—even to the point of leaving family and the comforts that even a menial job on a farm or in a city could offer in order to make one's fortune. The "best use gold could be put to," the preacher was now saying—offering it to God's Son, using it for God's purposes. And so anything we have in life is best spent on the things that matter to Jesus, the poor little child who had to be born in a stable because he was not wanted elsewhere, life from the virgin womb of a young mother, watched over with anxious concern by her husband, serenaded by choirs of angels and worshiped by poor shepherd boys. So God showed he loves us, the preacher said, and wants us to care for and love each other, especially those who feel forgotten. "Set your hearts not on the riches that come from the mines, shored up by timbers deep in the depths of the earth, but on the riches that come from following the rich vein of faith constructed on the timbers that formed the cross, through which we have life sprung eternal from the depths of the tomb."

Some of the few women in the place were crying now, and most of the men were obviously lost in sober thought. And Sam began thinking about the family he had left—wondering how his mother and father and younger brother and sister were getting along without him, and their neighbors who plowed and planted and harvested, who went to church on Sundays and, it dawned on him, were probably at church also on this very night. And Sam shed a tear for himself and for all of those who found themselves distant from home.

The sermon eventually came to its conclusion, and another song of Christmas was sung, and the minister led everyone in the Lord's Prayer, whose words came easily to Sam's lips from daily repetition at the insistence of his mother in childhood but which he had not thought to recite now for almost three years. To his surprise, the bar showed no signs of reopening after the service. To his *greater* surprise, he was not particularly thirsty for what it had to offer. He was getting hungry, and hoped that the cafe would open for business, but even more so, the assay office. He turned again to the man on his right. "Do you know if the assay office will be opening up? And the recorder's office?"

"There's the assayer, right over there," the man replied with a nod across the room. "Why don'cha *ask* him?" Which Sam did, walking up to the man, not the same one with whom he had dealt the last time he was in Mule Ear.

"Hadn't planned to," the middle-aged man said, "it bein' Christmas Eve and all. But, then, won't be open tomorrow, cause of it's bein' Christmas."

Sam looked dejected, and the man reconsidered. "Tell you what," he said. "My wife over there'll be expectin' me to come along with her for dinner now. But I'll be over after supper, say, in an hour. An' I'll bring along Lucius Pierce—he's the district recorder—so you can get your claim filed and not worry about it. That is, of course, if your ore's any good." He paused. "You needin' a place to eat?"

"I don't want to be no bother," Sam said. "I'll see what I can get at the cafe."

The assayer now appraised Sam. "Suppose you were countin' on convertin' your goods into cash tonight?" he asked.

"Well, yes, but I'll make do, somehow."

"Here," the man said, digging his hand into his pocket and producing a quarter. "We'll call it an advance. See you in about an hour. The cafe ought to be open again any time now. Pret' near ever'body in town wanted to come hear the parson."

"Thanks ever so much," Sam said. Before going to the cafe, however, he went back to the stable, where he found the proprietor and made arrangements for Angel's care overnight, and to cast a casual glance at the straw in the corner of the stall to make sure that his bags were still well hidden—the straw that might also have been *his* bed, had the assayer not agreed to open his office. As he was leaving the stable, he heard what sounded like a sneeze from the stall in the far corner of the building. Nervous about his ore, he took a few steps back toward the location from which the sound had come. "Anybody there?" he demanded. There was no answer. Probably one of the other animals, he thought, continuing toward the stall and peering into its darkness. Then, chiding himself for being overly suspicious, he left the stable in search of supper.

The assayer was as good as his word, and after conducting a fire assay on the contents of one of the sacks Sam had retrieved from Angel's stall, said, "That's all I can do tonight, but I'll open up again the day after Christmas." He went to his safe and exchanged the gold for some cash, which he counted out into Sam's hand. "Not exactly a fortune, but your ore's rich enough to prove your claim." He nodded toward the claim office. "Lucius'll take care of you."

"Thank you," Sam said, turning toward the door. Then he paused and turned his head back toward the assayer. "And Merry Christmas."

The assayer looked at Sam over the rim of his glasses. "How old are you?"

"Twenty-two," Sam answered, stretching to his full height.

"How long you been out here, up on that mountain?"

"Three years," Sam replied.

"You're stayin' in town tomorrow, then?"

"Reckon."

"Nobody should be alone on Christmas. You come over for Christmas dinner with us, why don'cha? Yellow house on Pine Street—next street over. Only yellow house there. About noon. O.K.?"

"Thank you. But these are the only clothes I got." He looked down at his patched knees and his muddied boots, and became self-conscious that he hadn't bathed in many weeks.

"Hotel's got a bathtub," the assayer said, "and they can wash your clothes tonight if you want." He produced another quarter. "A Christmas gift."

Sam smiled in reply, then added, as he accepted the coin, "That's mighty kind."

The cash Sam had received for the contents of his first sack of ore was adequate for his hotel bill and meals while in Mule Ear and for a few supplies, but he would need to convert the contents of his other sacks to cash in order to purchase the food that he needed to see him through the worst of the winter. So, indeed, he needed to remain in town through Christmas Day, when the stores were closed anyway. On his way to check on Angel Christmas morning, he took a detour to the train station, which served the newly constructed narrow-gauge railroad, curious to see what time the trains arrived and departed. He would like to see a steam engine again, pulling cars full of people and goods along the track. Even though it was Christmas, the chalk letters and numbers on the blackboard facing the platform showed an eastbound departure at 11:45 a.m. For a moment, he considered, and then shook away the temptation.

Angel uttered a little bray of recognition, and Sam scratched the burro's ears. "'Fraid you wouldn't recognize me in clean clothes an' smellin' nice," he whispered.

Then he heard another sneeze. There was no doubt this time. He shut the gate to Angel's stall and walked toward the sound. It was still dark in that corner of the stable, but he could make out a crouching figure in the back corner of the otherwise vacant stall. "Who's there?" he asked. "I can't see you, but I know you're there."

After a few seconds' hesitation, the figure stood up, stiffly, and the dim light caught his face. It was a young face, not yet bearded, under a tousle of hair mixed with straw. "I wasn't hurtin' nothin'," a voice mumbled.

"You work here?" Sam asked. There was no answer. Sam asked a different question. "What are you doin'?"

"Just sleepin'." Then he added, "Please don't tell no one."

"How old are you?"

"Sixteen."

"What're you doin' in Mule Ear?"

"Pannin' for gold, mostly. Till the creek froze over."

"How long you been here?"

"Since summer. The harvest wasn't lookin' so good."

"You got family?"

"Back on the farm." Tears started forming in the boy's eyes, and in Sam's, too.

Sam's mind traveled back to his own family's farm, and Christmases that, even during hard times, were happy. And he remembered the words of the preacher.

"There's an eastbound train at 11:45. You get on it, an' go back to your folks." Sam thrust his hand in his pocket and pulled out the money he had received the previous night from the sale of his gold.

The tears started trickling down the boy's face. "Thank you," he said. "I'd like to go home." Then he asked, "Why you doin' this?"

Sam answered with two simple words: "It's Christmas."

Christmas Eve (late evening)
Spanish Springs Presbyterian Church, Sparks, Nevada
December 24, 2010

Isaiah 9:2–7
Titus 2:11–14
Luke 2:1–14 (15–20)

"Amazed Again"

The year that Disneyland opened, when I was a young child, my parents took me there. None of us knew exactly what it would be like, but my parents had read and heard enough about it to think that it was a place they wanted to take their little boy. I had seen some of the Disney animated movies by then, and I watched the Mickey Mouse Club on television, and Davy Crockett, and I had some sense that Disneyland would be a wonderful experience for a kid. And of course, it was—it surpassed any expectations that I might have had, based on whatever my mother and father might have told me about it. Of course, they hadn't *really* known *themselves*. It was advertised as being beyond any amusement park they had ever visited, far exceeding even Lagoon, our local amusement park a few miles north of Salt Lake City, near Bountiful. It was certainly an amazing vacation, and we brought back home movies and brochures and ticket stubs that are still family treasures. And my mother, for my fifth birthday later that year, made a cake that was really five *separate* cakes—each one decorated as a part of Disneyland: Main Street, Fantasyland, Tomorrowland, Adventureland, and Frontierland. Wish I knew what happened to my little artificial coonskin cap.

I have been back to Disneyland several times during my life, and, of course, each time, something has changed, or has been added, and it is still a fun experience despite the crowds and the price, and I experienced great joy when my wife and I introduced *our* children to Disneyland. But it has never been quite the same as that *first* visit, so fresh, so magical, so surprising. If someone offered me the opportunity to return to Disneyland *tomorrow*, I would jump on it—well, maybe not *tomorrow*, Christmas Day, but the *next* day. But I am aware that, enjoyable as it would be, it would not, *could* not, be quite the same thrilling experience as it was fifty-five years ago. Not *boring*, certainly not boring, but not quite as *amazing* as the first time. Of all the wonderful trips on which my parents took me, that one was certainly very special.

It may be that for some of us, perhaps many of us, Christmas is rather like that—as we have grown older, it has become for us, over the years, not quite as exciting as the year before, not exactly old hat, necessarily, but predictable, practiced, and because of the preparations for the family celebration or parties with friends or trips to visit relatives, *even* a bit of a *drudgery*. Now and then, I hear some people say that they wish Christmas would be over already, and, as commercial as it has become, a gluttony not only of food but of such crass materialism, adding to the pressures of trying to meet others' expectations of open houses and gift-giving and greeting card writing, I understand how the holiday can be less *enjoyable* than it is *burdensome*. And, for some people, facing illness, or estrangement, or the death of a loved one, or joblessness, or poverty, all of the seasonal rituals of our culture can mock our childhood wonder and amazement at angels and shepherds and mother and child. The secular habits that have grown up around Christmas don't do much to convince us that *old* news is still *good* news—that, at the core of all the feasting and spending and wrapping and hustling and bustling is a truth wonderful and amazing beyond any other: that God, one night long ago in a very ordinary place and in a *way* seemingly very ordinary too, became human, bending heaven to kiss the earth with the dearest expression of love that humankind has ever known, ripping open eternity for every one of us to step through and be enfolded in God's embrace.

Familiarity does not always breed *contempt*, but it certainly can lead to taking something—or someone—for *granted*. Never having lived in southern California, I find it difficult to imagine, but people who grew up in the area tell me that it's true: Disneyland, though they enjoyed visiting it from time to time, was just sort of always "there." I guess, for some residents of the Reno area, Lake Tahoe has just sort of always been "there." There are certainly a lot of local residents who, though they have the opportunity, don't go up to the lake very often, while some folks from out of state make a point of traveling many miles to enjoy it as often as they can. The locals are proud of it, perhaps, but don't all behave as if they are still "amazed."

If that has become our experience of *Christmas*, I think we need to spend a little more time pondering in our hearts the story that we *think* we have come to know so well—and not just the part about angels and shepherds and mother and child, but the full gospel of which that is merely an opening scene. Martin Luther once said, "The more firmly one believes in something, the more he wonders at it and the more he rejoices at it."[1] Is our belief that Jesus was the incarnation of God so firm that it is a source of endless wonder and rejoicing?

> In that region there were shepherds living in the fields, keeping watch over their flock by night. Then an angel of the Lord stood before them, and the glory of the Lord shone around them, and they were terrified. But the angel said to them, "Do not be afraid; for see—I am bringing you good news of great joy for all the people: to you is born this day in the city of David a Savior, who is the Messiah, the Lord. This will be a sign for you: you will find a child wrapped in bands of cloth and lying in a manger." And suddenly there was with the angel a multitude of the heavenly host, praising God and saying,
>
> "Glory to God in the highest heaven,
>   and on earth peace among those whom he favors!"
>
> When the angels had left them and gone into heaven, the shepherds said to one another, "Let us go now to Bethlehem and see this thing that has taken place, which the Lord has made known to us." So they went with haste and found Mary and Joseph, and the child lying in the manger. When they saw this, they made known what had been told them about this child; and all who heard it were *amazed* at what the shepherds told them. But Mary treasured all these words and pondered them in her heart. The shepherds returned, glorifying and praising God for all they had heard and seen. (Luke 2:8–20a NRSV)

Those who heard the testimony of the shepherds that first Christmas believed, at least, that something very extraordinary was coming to pass in the guise of a very ordinary event. They were "amazed." The word "amazed" is one of the most common words in Luke, and in Matthew, Mark, and Acts as well. It appears forty times in those four books alone. In Luke, it describes the reaction of a great diversity of people to the things that Jesus said and did and brought about, and the things that were said *about* him, and in Acts the things that his *followers* did in his name. And that *amazement* led to *belief*—and from *there* to *wonderment* and *rejoicing*. That God would come

---

1. Quoted in Schweizer, *Good News According to Luke*, 52.

to us in the form of a baby! That God would care for us enough to feed us, to forgive us, to teach us, to befriend us! That God would love us enough even to *die* for us, having taken upon himself all the weight of human sin in the hatred and rejection and persecution and torture Jesus endured! That God would have power enough to raise Jesus from the grave to life again, testifying in the most dramatic way that everything Jesus said and did was the very word and deed of the holy one, the almighty one, the everlasting one who set the stars in the sky and keeps the planets from colliding! That God would honor the poor so emphatically! That God would identify with us so completely in our weakness and dependence! That God would so hallow our *own* experiences of being hated and rejected and persecuted and oppressed! That God would refuse to permit death to have the final word over us, but, rather, life eternal with him!

Can we pick through the tinsel and bargains and parties and gift-wrap enough to see the face of the baby Jesus, and listen to his soft cooing, without distraction from the competing images and sounds, to believe the miracle, and wonder at it and rejoice? Not just because another baby is born to another poor couple in another obscure village—for even the most faithful of obstetricians, childbirth must eventually become rather routine—but because of what scripture testifies about Jesus when he had grown to adulthood, preaching and teaching, healing and feeding, dying on the cross and rising again from the tomb, so that we too may rise with him to eternal life and all of creation be restored to wholeness? "To walk rightly in the Word of God," John Calvin wrote, "is never to cease to be amazed."[2] And the Word of God is preeminently Jesus himself.

There is no easy antidote to the spiritual anesthetic that our culture and our calendars and our own preoccupations may have worked on some of us over the years to render Christmas less meaningful, less exciting, less welcome in our lives. But for those who make a practice of reading the scriptures, of praying that our perspective and priorities may be aligned with those of God, and of showing to others the same kindness and generosity and mercy that Christ showed to all whom he encountered, we can expect to be amazed again and again. We can expect to be amazed every time we listen with the shepherds to the tidings of the angels, and are willing with them to set aside the daily busyness and follow them to the stable to find a child wrapped in bands of cloth and lying in a manger and look with them at this tiny gift of newborn life. And, in amazement, we will understand what it means that this is the Messiah, the Lord, sent for us, for you and for me. No matter what we are facing in our lives (and some of us are

---

2. Quoted in Schweizer, *Good News According to Luke*, 52.

facing trials that are very serious indeed), no matter what society around us values (and some of its values are far from the selfless love that scripture counts as the highest virtue), no matter how many December twenty-fifths we have crossed off the calendar (and some of us have seen eighty or ninety or more), the potential, the hope, is that we each *can* and *will* be *amazed* yet *again* this holy night, and that the amazement will sustain or perhaps kindle for the first time an abiding wonder that causes us to rejoice all of our days, and in all of our words and works. And the wonder and the rejoicing will be all the more profound because our belief is *undiminished* by those trials, by those competing values, by those many years in which, after all, we have enjoyed the manifold blessings of God.

Our *need* is always *urgent*. God's *answer* is always *true*. Our *yearning* is always *deep*. God's *grace* is always *sufficient*. A Savior has been born for us. Come now, yet once more, to hear the story, to receive the gift, to sing the praise, to taste the goodness, to light the hope, to worship the worker of our salvation, and, once again, to be amazed.

Christmas Day

Spanish Springs Presbyterian Church, Sparks, Nevada
December 25, 2005

Isaiah 52:7–10
Hebrews 1:1–4
John 1:1–14

"Through the Eyes of Christmas"

Of all the places that the writers of the Christian Gospels looked for insight to interpret and explain who Jesus was, and his significance, no other source proved to be so important and helpful as the collection of prophetic writings we know as the book of Isaiah. For in these writings, the longest single book in the Bible—except for Psalms, and of which the Gospel writers also made good use—the purpose of God, the ways of God, and the need of God's people for a savior, are described perhaps more poignantly than anywhere else. The first half of the book of Isaiah tells about the wrongs that the people had committed, and how God would bring judgment upon their failure to worship rightly, and upon their greed, their abuse of the poor, their failure to do justice, their mistreatment of the foreigner. Then comes a section addressed to the people after the ax had fallen—after the Babylonian army had conquered Judah and destroyed Jerusalem and dismantled the temple and the people had been marched off to exile in pagan Babylon. These are chapters of assurance, of encouragement, of promise that the God who brought Israel into being had not abandoned his people, would not abandon them, but would restore them to their homeland that God had prepared specially for them and favored with prosperity until they turned away from God and his commandments. Finally, in the book of Isaiah, there is a section written for the people after they returned to Judah from their exile and found that rebuilding their society was not going to be an easy task.

For nearly twelve chapters, the book of Isaiah has been moving toward the declaration in today's reading, the Old Testament lection appointed for Christmas Day:

> How beautiful upon the mountains
>   are the feet of the messenger who announces peace,
> who brings good news,
>   who announces salvation,
>   who says to Zion, "Your God reigns."
> Listen! Your sentinels lift up their voices,
>   together they sing for joy;
> for in *plain sight* they see
>   the return of the Lord to Zion.
> Break forth together into singing,
>   you ruins of Jerusalem;
> for the Lord has comforted his people,
>   he has redeemed Jerusalem.
> The Lord has bared his holy arm
>   before the eyes of all the nations;
> and all the ends of the earth shall see
>   the salvation of our God. (Isa 52:7–10 NRSV)

Another part of Isaiah declares the heavenly commission to the prophet to bring words of assurance to the exiled people of Judah, those who were paying the price for their sins and the sins of their nation by having their fields laid waste and their cities destroyed and they themselves taken away from their homes and their livelihoods and their temple to faraway Babylon: "Comfort, O comfort my people, says your God. Speak tenderly to Jerusalem, and cry to her that she has served her term, that her penalty is paid, that she has received from the Lord's hand double for all her sins" (Isa 40:1–2 NRSV). And today we read that the messenger had been faithful to deliver those words as God directed, that the message of comfort had indeed been proclaimed to God's people, and more than just an announcement to the Israelites—the entire world, *all* the nations, have witnessed the victory of God.

And yet, what was the visible evidence of God's victory? How was God's return in "plain sight"? What would a visitor to Jerusalem in those days have seen? God riding in triumphal procession on a powerful warhorse? Surely not. Such a sight would have been unthinkable anyway, and a mixed blessing at best, since it was thought that anyone who looked upon God would die. All the peoples of the world flocking in pilgrimage to Zion? There is no historical record that anything like that ever occurred. As empires rose and fell around the ancient world, no earthly authority ever acknowledged

Jerusalem as the center of the world or the *temple* as its capitol. Bricks and stones miraculously raising themselves up to reconstitute the city's imposing walls and grand buildings that had been so devastated by years of siege and purposeful destruction? The archaeological evidence is that most of Jerusalem was still in ruins many years after the Israelites returned to their city from exile in Babylon, and the Bible itself suggests that it took a supreme effort of will to begin reconstructing the city walls and the temple, and required much coaxing and cajoling. Isaiah makes it sound rather like the return to Israel was much the same joyful and hopeful occasion that these people's *ancestors* had experienced many centuries *earlier* when they escaped slavery in Egypt and came up out of the deserts of Sinai and crossed over the Jordan into the promised land.

But other parts of the Bible suggest that the return to Judah was a pretty discouraging prospect. The people were returning to fields that had overgrown with a lifetime's worth of weeds, were coming back to houses whose *roofs* had fallen *in* and whose *walls* had fallen *down*, were reentering cities that bore *some* resemblance, at least, to New Orleans and Biloxi and the other towns devastated by Hurricane Katrina, whole neighborhoods empty or simply disappeared, only in *this* case, it was destruction not by the forces of *nature*, but by force of *arms*—the Babylonian soldiers of King Nebuchadnezzar had broken down the walls and laid waste the temple and made the place generally uninhabitable. Most of the population had been away for seventy years. No one had repaired Jerusalem in the meantime. The joy of homecoming must have been nearly overwhelmed by the daunting prospect of what it would take to make Israel once again a home at all. "Break forth into singing, you ruins of Jerusalem" (Isa 52:9a NRSV)? "[F]or the LORD has comforted his people, he has *redeemed* Jerusalem" (Isa 52:9b NRSV)? "The LORD has bared his holy arm before the eyes of all the nations; and all the ends of the earth shall see the salvation of our God" (Isa 52:10 NRSV)? All those assurances must have seemed like a joke when the exiles finally arrived at their destination. Whatever songs of rejoicing there were must have given way to not a few curses. And the *feet* of the messenger who proclaimed that God has resumed his residence, his people must have considered not *beautiful* at *all*, but merely dirty and callused and bruised and bleeding.

Was God simply being cruel? Was Isaiah totally blind to reality? Or is the Bible here declaring a truth which is confirmed not by *sight*, but by *faith*, a faith that requires *commitment* and depends upon *cooperation* and even prompts *sacrifice*? The prophet is testifying here that appearances *can* be, and often *are, deceiving*. Truth is not a matter of what *we see*, but what *God proclaims*, not *our words*, but *God's Word*. The redemption of the people of Israel from their long night of subjugation, he was declaring, was indeed God's own victory—and a mighty one—over the sinful habits of his people, over the destructive cruelty of pagan empires, over the hopeless despair of those who continuously bewailed, "We will never see Zion again!," over human resignation to oppressive fate, over the faithless skeptics who assured their listeners that God either couldn't save them or had forgotten about them. This victory wasn't just a matter of *military strategies* and *international politics*. It was the wondrous working of *God*. But it required *faith* to *detect* it. Without faith, and without commitment, cooperation, and sacrifice, the reality would be nothing more than what it appeared to human eyes. As they read the headlines of the local newspaper, as they watched television reports showing block after block of devastation, acre upon acre of barrenness, or whatever their equivalent of newspapers and television newscasts might have been, it would have been easy to feel more grief than hope.

So, too, the average person of Jesus' day might not have been very impressed with the claim that he was the Son of God, indeed, according to John's testimony, the very *Word* of God, the *truest expression* of God's creating, sustaining, and reconciling power. Notwithstanding century upon century of artistic imagination, the Bible itself does not suggest that Jesus was other than ordinary in appearance, not dashingly handsome, not unusually muscular. His earthly *end* was certainly not impressive—executed in the same way as a criminal or a runaway, abandoned by all but a handful of his friends. And his earthly *beginning* was certainly not impressive, either—born, according to Luke, in a stable, given a respectable birth only by the kindly gesture of Joseph, Mary's fiancé, to go ahead and marry her in spite of the biological facts. The zoological surroundings might not have discouraged a handful of shepherds who stepped in out of the cold that night and were charmed at the sight of a baby lying in a manger. But could, would, monarchs and philosophers who had traveled over long distances to greet a newborn king really have supposed they had found the one they were seeking when they came upon a humble family living in a humble house in a humble village?

That, of course, remains, even *today*, life's most crucial question: Do we, peering into the manger, watching a man dying on a cross, glimpsing through the testimony of the old, old, writings a figure who ate with the disreputable, healed the untouchable, forgave the notorious, and befriended the dishonorable, see the glory of God, light shining in the darkness, the very Word of God through whom all things were made? The scriptures testify that the Word becoming flesh is the decisive event in human history and the whole history of creation, changing forever God's relationship to humanity and humanity's relationship to God and therefore the relationship of human being to human being. In Jesus the Christ, we see, hear, and know God himself, visible and dwelling among us, "pitching his tent" among us, in the literal translation of John's text. But the scriptures quickly admit that "[h]e was in the world, and the world came into being through him; yet the world did not know him. He came to what was his own"—the world and its inhabitants whom he was instrumental in creating,—"and his own people did not accept him" (John 1:10–11 NRSV).

Christ is a gift from God, and the most important gift. Christmas is a gift from God, too, and a welcome one. Annually, with its emphasis on good will and generosity and happiness, Christmas is the exception to the *world's* methods and expectations. In a culture of provable facts and undeniable figures, Christmas encourages a suspension of disbelief and skepticism—a brief one, anyway. To the degree that we can free ourselves of the social and commercial pressures to buy, buy, buy, and can appreciate it as a holiday in *every* sense of the word, Christmas points toward the peace and joy that *could* be ours *every* day of the year, if we would just allow ourselves to accept fully and unreservedly God's gift of Christ.

I've heard of people who leave their Christmas decorations up all year long, indoors as well as out, and I think it's not just a matter of aesthetics—that they like sights and sounds and smells that have become traditional at Christmastime—but they want a year-round reminder that the world, or at least their own lives, *could* be infused with good will and generosity and happiness, *can* be infused with good will and generosity and happiness. "[T]o all who received him," the scriptures testify of Jesus the Christ, "who believed in his name, he gave power to become children of God, who were born, not of blood or of the will of the flesh or of the will of man, but of God" (John 1:12–13 NRSV). The lives of all who received him, and of all who receive him today, bore and bear the marks of being God's children: hopeful, loving, forgiving, faithful, even if standing in a field of weeds, even if surveying the ruins of a ruined culture, even if reading daunting reports of corruption and warfare and scandal and abuse.

What about you? Tomorrow, December twenty-sixth, will Christmas be over and packed away for another year? Will you return to the *habits* of the world, repeating the *gossip* of the world, relying on the *wisdom* of the world, counting on the *rewards* of the world, conforming to the *expectations* of the world—which, after all, is a way of confirming that Christmas is and will *remain* only an *exception* to life, an *aberration* from the calendar, an *anomaly* from custom, a *suspension* of reality, a *disregard* of truth? Will you in fact be like those who were freed to come back from Babylon to Jerusalem and reckoned it all despair, and like those who looked into the manger and then up at the cross and reckoned it all waste and nonsense?

Or will *you* be like the humble shepherds who looked into the face of a baby weak and gentle and helpless, and discovered salvation, and returned to their humdrum tasks singing praises to the Most High, and like a Roman centurion thirty-some years later who looked into the face of a dying man convicted for daring to live out what the scriptures command and who praised the Most High saying, "Truly this man was God's Son!"? Do you see in Jesus Christ God in plain sight? Can you look at life, at your fellow men and women, at your work, at your family, at the stranger passing on the sidewalk or living under the bridge or picking through the ruins of a house destroyed by earthquake or mortar round in some far-away country, and give witness with your thoughts of hope, with your words of love, with your deeds of compassion, to the victory of God that began in a stable one night long ago? Can you declare with the prophet every day of the year and every moment of the day, "The Lord reigns"? Can you see the world, and your life *in* it, through the eyes of Christmas?

First Sunday after Christmas

Spanish Springs Presbyterian Church, Sparks, Nevada

December 26, 2010

Isaiah 63:7–9
Hebrews 2:10–18
Matthew 2:13–23

"Home, for Christmas"

One of the most popular secular Christmas songs of a former era, and one still heard frequently in shopping malls and on the radio this time of year, is "I'll Be Home for Christmas." The phrase originated in the early days of World War I, when soldiers stationed in military camps stateside and on the battle lines in Europe at first thought the war would be over quickly, and they would return to their families in time for the holiday. It wasn't, of course, and so they couldn't. But the sentiment those words captured is a timeless one, true for just about anyone who finds him- or herself distant from loved ones and the familiar holiday sights and sounds and smells. And during World War II, when the next generation found itself at war in Europe and throughout the Pacific, Kim Gannon and Walter Kent wrote the song that was made famous by Bing Crosby. It rang true for countless soldiers, sailors, and airmen who were separated from their families by miles and by the call to dangerous duty.

For all of the quaint or exotic charm of Christmas traditions in a foreign land or the regional customs of a far-away posting, when you are distant from well-known surroundings at Christmas not by choice, but by necessity, nothing about where you are quite matches up to the imaginings of how things are back home. For most of us, no other time of year is filled with such nostalgia. No other holiday draws us so instinctively back to the place where everything seems familiar and normal. No other celebration defines quite so clearly what it means to be home.

This Christmas, as for many Christmases past, there are many millions of people around the world who don't *have* the option of being at home—and I don't mean just people stuck in European airports, or even military personnel in places like Iraq and Afghanistan. I am speaking of refugees, from Sudan to Gaza, from Somalia to Indonesia. All of them have one wish—to be home again. But for reasons political or religious, or because of natural disaster, or fear of disease, or fear of soldiers, or because they are simply driven by hunger, these people have had to flee their homeland or have been deported, and can be at home today only in their dreams.

The letter to the Hebrews speaks of the Son of God being able to identify completely with his brothers and sisters because he has been "perfected" by being subjected to the same sorts of sufferings that you and I endure. To many people in ancient times, it was inconceivable that a divine being could be subject to suffering, could feel physical pain or emotional abuse, could die, and so the claim of Hebrews is a bold assertion indeed. And yet, that suffering that Jesus endured was absolutely necessary for him to be effective as our Savior. It is because he has been there, because he is like us in every respect, because he has been tested by what he suffered, that he is able to be our Savior. He has shared fully our human experience of frailty, vulnerability, temptation, pain, and eventually even death. In every way that is significant, he became one with us. Only by enduring the depths of human suffering could the guarantor of our salvation become perfected—consecrated—for this very work of salvation, our great high priest doing everything necessary to close the gap between God's *holiness* and our *un*holiness, so that we might dwell forever in the heavenly home God has opened to us. Throughout it all, Jesus remained faithful and obedient. Even as he appeared to the disciples after his resurrection, he bore the scars of the cross, the scars of human suffering and death.

The Gospel of Matthew signals to us from the beginning that the Messiah, this son of David and son of Abraham, will not be privileged to be *immune* from life's hardships and unfairness. He was very nearly born out of wedlock, saved from that stigma only by virtue of the unusual sensitivity of his mother's betrothed, Joseph, who followed *exactly* the Lord's command delivered to him by an angel in a dream. And, after Jesus was born, he would have been slaughtered along with all the other infant boys in Bethlehem by the order of the jealous King Herod, had it not been that Joseph was visited *again* by an angel in a dream and he followed exactly the command to take the child and his mother by night and flee into Egypt. Finally, when Herod was dead, "an angel of the Lord suddenly appeared in a dream to Joseph in

Egypt and said, 'Get up, take the child and his mother, and go to the land of Israel, for those who were seeking the child's life are dead.' Then Joseph got up, took the child and his mother, and went to the land of Israel" (Matt 2:19–21 NRSV). But even *then*, it was too dangerous to return to *Bethlehem*. "[W]hen [Joseph] heard that Archelaus was ruling over Judea in place of his father Herod, he was afraid to go there. And after being warned in a dream, he went away to the district of Galilee. There he made his home in a town called Nazareth" (Matt 2:22–23a NRSV).

In the story as Matthew knew it, Jesus had been born in Bethlehem because that was Joseph and Mary's hometown. So, he assumed, they had been there all along, and Jesus was undoubtedly born in a regular house. There would have been no need to seek out an inn, no need to have settled for a stable. They only traveled to Nazareth, later, because it was too dangerous for them to return to Bethlehem, which was in the region where Herod's son now ruled. Having been refugees first in Egypt, the little family now became refugees in Galilee. And from then until his death on a cross, Jesus would never have an earthly home, would always be living on foreign soil, so to speak, no matter where he was, and thus was always without a place to call his own, dependent solely on the goodness of God.

As in so many cases, it is important not to *confuse* the stories told by the different Gospels. If we mix into *Matthew's* account the tradition as *Luke* knew it—a difficult journey from a hill town in Galilee to Bethlehem for a brief but momentous appointment with angels and shepherds in the discomfort of the stable, and then an arduous return home to Nazareth—we will miss the important theological point that Matthew is conveying. From the very *beginning*, Matthew wants us to know, Jesus experienced the *same* sort of suffering as much of humankind for whom he is the Savior. We need to attend to what Matthew, uniquely among the Gospels, is saying here. Perhaps it helps to know that scholars believe he was writing especially for Christians of Jewish background who themselves had been displaced because of antagonism toward Jesus. Most likely, the congregation for which Matthew wrote his Gospel was located someplace in Syria, perhaps Antioch, composed of believers who had been forced out of their synagogues in Judea and shunned by their families and fired by their employers and scorned by their friends, years before the Romans entered Jerusalem and destroyed the temple and forced many to flee. Now these Christian refugees were living far from home and everything that was familiar and routine, striving to maintain the traditions of their faith and culture but finding that, try as they might, it was all very different, rather as their ancestors had experienced hundreds of years earlier when they were exiled in Babylon. Their convictions that Jesus was the long-awaited Messiah who fulfilled the prophecies of the Jewish scriptures had caused them to be persecuted by their Jewish rabbis and their Jewish relatives and their Jewish neighbors. It was ironic, it was bewildering, it was cruel, it was heartless. But it was their reality—*faithfulness* to the king of *heaven* meant, for them, *homelessness* in the *world*. Many of these new Christians must have thought that this wasn't what they had bargained for. And what sort of God, what sort of Savior, would allow them to be so abused and mistreated for his sake? What had they done wrong? Was their allegiance misplaced? Had they been duped?

Matthew very likely recited all of the geographical details as a way of signaling that the life of the Son of God *himself* was destined from *birth* to be a life of homeless wandering, such as would also be the destiny of his *disciples*. So these followers of Christ who had gathered in Antioch, or wherever, were not experiencing anything that their Lord had not suffered before them. "A disciple is not above the teacher, nor a slave above the master," Matthew quotes Jesus as saying later in his Gospel, in a somewhat different context; "it is enough for the disciple to be like the teacher, and the slave like the master" (Matt 10:24–25a NRSV). To hear about *Jesus'* homelessness was meant as an encouragement for their *own* present experience as refugees. Something of *Jesus'* nomadic life, made necessary by his obedience to the call to be faithful to God, would be reflected in the experience of Jesus' *disciples*. But so would God's dependable care for Jesus *also* be experienced by Jesus' followers. And if *death* should come because of their loyalty to Jesus, their Lord's own *resurrection* was their guarantee that God would be faithful to raise them, *too*, to eternal life in a heavenly home, where they would forever be beyond the worry of rejection and oppression, the discomfort of exile and asylum, the disappointment of human fickleness and the pain of popular scorn. For their true home was no longer a *place*. It was no longer a *building*. It was no longer a memory of *childhood*. It was a *person* with whom they had the most intimate relationship—the living Lord with whom they feasted regularly on bread and wine, whose presence they felt giving them courage to meet the challenges of the day and hope for eternal life beyond any current disappointment, blessing surpassing any present suffering. Had not their own Lord and Savior experienced the very same thing?

I don't know whether your Christmas celebration this year matched your expectations, whether it fulfilled your dreams, whether it happened in the place where you normally gather with those who are dearest to you, whether you were surrounded by all the sights and sounds and smells of cherished tradition. Wonderful as that would be for the Christian, that is not the most important thing about the good news that God has sent us a Savior, one who shares our flesh and blood and, by his sufferings, brings his sisters and brothers—God's many children—to glory, as Hebrews says. For the Christian, to be home for Christmas or any other time is simply to be at the side of Jesus Christ, the wanderer, who goes wherever people need to be fed, to be healed, to be forgiven, who is susceptible to being ridiculed in any street, scorned in any town, turned away from any village, whose life even as an infant was perceived as a threat by a tyrannical king, whose death on a cross as an adult was perceived as a scandal by those who measured right by the exercise of might and by those who champion law and denounce grace. For the Christian, to be home for Christmas is to *empathize* with the refugees living with little in the way of worldly comfort and who can look only to God for security and provision, shelter and food, friendship and consolation, the suffering ones who have no home as the world defines it, and to *minister* to any and all who feel or are treated as aliens in a world that offers little compassion for the weak and abused, that bullies whenever it suspects its power is threatened, that doesn't scruple trampling the innocents whenever it thinks its privileges are jeopardized. Perhaps, in fact, it is those who are feeling the most like world-weary wanderers this Christmas who are most likely to understand that being *home* for Christmas is not so much about a *place* as a *person*, not so much nursing a *sentiment* as answering an *invitation*.

By telling us how the holy family was made to wander from Bethlehem to Egypt to Nazareth, the Gospel of Matthew urges us to come home for Christmas. Matthew summons us to respond to the news of the birth of a Savior by yearning not for an ornamented tree or an aroma-filled kitchen or stockings hung on the mantle above a crackling fire or even the embrace of family and friends, but by yearning instead for the one who knows our hurts before they happen, the one who suffers our rejections before they occur, the one who experiences even death before we do, the one who has destroyed the power of anything to defeat God's loving purpose of eternal fellowship with each of his children, including you and me. No matter where we are on the globe, no matter how distant from the holiday celebrations we *remember* and no matter how distant from the holiday celebrations we *dream* of, if we are showing ourselves to be sisters and brothers of Christ, caring for others as *he* cared for them, forgiving, healing, feeding, comforting, befriending the sin-burdened, the sick, the hungry, the bereaved, the lonely, because we believe the one born in Bethlehem was, is, the Messiah, Lord and Savior of all, it is clear that we, in fact, are *also* children of God, and have discovered what it truly means to be home for Christmas.

Second Sunday after Christmas

Spanish Springs Presbyterian Church, Sparks, Nevada

January 3, 1999

Jeremiah 31:7–14
Ephesians 1:3–14
John 1:1–18

"Christ Our Center"

As I sat down a few days ago to write this morning's sermon, out the window of my study I could see airplanes descending on their final approach to the airport, like every day, could see the cars and trucks as usual across the valley traveling north and south on Pyramid Way, could hear the familiar sounds of my children running up and down the stairs, could hear the mail truck laboring up our block and parking in the familiar spot from which our letter carrier makes his rounds of mailboxes. People were coming and going like almost every other day of the year, commerce was flowing, along with personal messages both momentous and trivial, vacations and business trips were beginning or ending. I had just come home from the post office, past the Christmas tree recycling depot near the high school; the fenced enclosure was already well filled with the discarded tokens of the holy day. In other words, Christmas was over, and things seemed pretty much back to normal just a few days after our celebrations of Christ's birth.

Listening to some people talk in the post office and the stores, there was even a *hunger* for things to get back to "normal," as if Christmas had never even happened, except, of course, for the unwanted evidence of credit card bills and tighter waistbands. Even in the church, we often hear a sigh of relief, in the final days of the calendar, that the season of pageants and music programs and family craft nights is done with, that the special services and extra orders of worship that disrupt the routine are behind us.

Celebration means exhaustion for a lot of us, and when the celebrating, or at least the *buying*, begins well before Thanksgiving—well before Advent, the traditional period of expectancy and preparation—Christmas itself can be a sort of anti-climax, a finish line to be crossed, so that we get anxious to hustle away the decorations even before Christmastide is over, maybe even begin to box them up and store them away before Christmas Day has ended.

What is it in us that is thrilled and excited by holiday celebrations, on the one hand, but then is so eager to return to life as usual, which is to say, life as it was *before* the celebration? The planes, the cars, the household sounds, and even the delivery of the mail gave no suggestion this past Monday that, just the Thursday night and Friday before, we had testified to the miracle that God has come into our world in the flesh and blood of Jesus. To put it a bit cynically, God's annual intrusion into our culture's consciousness had left hardly a footprint on the world's agenda, except a new record against which to measure *next* year's shopping spree. Or were there enduring moments of wonder as, for the first time, a young child peered innocently over the side of a pasteboard manger? Were there lingering moments of reflection as modern angels singing "Gloria" coaxed a tear down the cheek of an adult who remembered how his or her parents used to sing a bedtime song about shepherds sore afraid on a hillside and then offering jubilant praise in a stable? Were there surprising moments of gratitude when someone long burdened by a sense of sin suddenly realized that Christmas is not a sentence of doom for our failures, but the dawn of hope for a new beginning?

Who can resist the charm of Luke's story of the shepherds and the manger? Who can hear it without painting a mental picture that can be revisited time and time again? But it is more difficult to fathom the profound words of *John's* Gospel that tell us why Christ's birth was so *important*:

> In the beginning was the Word, and the Word was with God, and the Word was God. He was in the beginning with God. All things came into being through him, and *without* him not one thing came into being. . . . And the Word became flesh and lived among us, and we have seen his glory, the glory as of a father's only son, full of grace and truth. (John 1:1–3b, 14 NRSV)

Charming as it is, a lot of us file the story of the shepherds and the manger away with the *other* stories that charm us, arrange it amidst the other annual interruptions of our workaday life, like birthdays and wedding anniversaries. But if we really *ponder* the opening words of the Gospel of John, we have to understand that Christmas is not just an annual nudge to be a little more generous and a little less judgmental. Our Christmas Day celebration should be an annual witness to the day two thousand years ago on which all of history changed forever, which demands that human priorities must be completely reordered, *after* which *nothing* could ever be the same as it was before. Christmas is the abnormal, extraordinary, unusual day on the calendar that declares that we should no longer think of *any* day as normal or ordinary or usual. That first Christmas, the most amazing miracle happened that could *ever* happen, and the most important event. That first Christmas, God entered the world to walk among us and alongside us. That first Christmas, *the Word of God became flesh.*

In a series of lectures on the nature and meaning of Christ, reconstructed from the notes of his students and published under the title *Christ the Center*, German theologian Dietrich Bonhoeffer said, "Christ the Word is truth. There is no truth *apart from* the Word and *by* the Word."[1] That, by the way, was in 1933, the same year in which Adolf Hitler was named chancellor of Germany and began his systematic campaign to call a wicked *falsehood* the only truth—to redefine evil as good, to replace the word of love with the propaganda of hate, to wrest the lordship of history from God in Jesus Christ and twist the course of history to serve the purpose of the devil.

But, of course, no human hell can swallow up God's heavenly purpose—the purpose of salvation that God revealed as a grand design to gather together all things in Jesus Christ. And in an inevitable process that no politician, no army, no nation can thwart, either by orchestrated insanity or by unspeakable atrocities, either by rampant materialism or by a steady diet of amusement, *everything* is coming into its proper place arranged around and having its only real meaning in Jesus Christ, the Word of God. The world may be too preoccupied with its busyness to acknowledge the truth. Dictators and business tycoons may ignore it. Shoppers and moviegoers may not realize it. Scholars and tramps may be unaware. But everything is being brought to a focus in Christ, and as far as God is concerned, Christ is the center of the entire universe and all of history. Nothing has significance apart from Christ—no fact, no object, no thought, no emotion, no deed. No institution has significance apart from Christ—no government, no school, no economic system. No relationship has significance apart from Christ—no friendship, no marriage, no employment, no rulership. Only as they are focused through the lens of the truth of Jesus Christ are *any* relationships *genuine*, are *any* institutions *worthy*, are *any* facts, objects, thoughts, emotions, deeds *important at all*. Because *only in Christ* are they seen in the light of the truth of God's *purpose* for all of creation, and the light of the truth of

---

1. Bonhoeffer, *Christ the Center*, 49 (emphasis added).

God's *destiny* for all of creation. *Only in Christ* are heaven and earth joined in the redemptive fellowship of the creatures with their Creator. *Only in Christ* are human pride and fear and jealousy and greed and hatred overcome by and through the ultimate truth—the Word of God, revealed to us in the very person of Jesus Christ.

All of us, to some degree, show by what we do and think and say on December *twenty-sixth* that we suppose there are *two* universes, that we suppose we can operate in *two* realms of existence, that we believe in *two* truths, if you will—the truth of Christmas, and the truth of the rest of the year. Shocked by a truth that he had worked hard to ignore, Ebenezer Scrooge announced near the end of Charles Dickens' masterful tale that he was going to keep the spirit of Christmas throughout the entire year. And perhaps we can even imagine that he did, as a fictional character. But a hundred messages from the culture we have built—what we think of as the realities of business, the requirements of school, the duties of family life—tell us that it is the message of *Christmas* that is not quite *real*. It is a toasting of virtues that we can never attain, a championing of a hope that we spend the rest of the year unraveling, an idolizing of what we can never be. "Let's get back to business," "Let's return to normal"—those sayings suggest that it is the Word of God lying in a manger that is the fantasy, a gentle falsehood, and that it is everything *else* we do and say and think that is *real*, that is *true*—money-making, amusement, seduction, war. Doesn't it seem these days that Christmas is an annual pause in things as usual, and then it's back to outwitting the competition, foreclosing mortgages, and spreading gossip? In other words, back to truth as Madison Avenue tries to define it, as Wall Street tries to define it, as Hollywood tries to define it, as the Pentagon tries to define it, as you and I try to define it in our self-interest and our self-concern? Maybe even the truth as King Herod tried to define it in his pride and his jealousy?

But Madison Avenue, Wall Street, Hollywood, the Pentagon, our self-love—none of those is the Word of God. None of those is the rightful focus of our existence and of all creation, the world and everything that is in it. None of those can reveal to us the true purpose of life, and our part in it all—what is expected of us, and how we should show gratitude for what we have been given. Jesus Christ is the Word of God, the light, the revelation, the truth that stands above and judges every fact and object and relationship. Jesus Christ is the focus, the hub, the pivot around which all of history turns. Jesus Christ is the norm, the standard, the measure of significance and worthiness and goodness of every human thought, word, and deed. Not just a teacher, his very life and death and resurrection are what God wants us to learn. Not just an example, he himself is the way and the truth and the life. Not just a character in a charming story that we like to recite once a year, he is *the* person whose birth, whose life, whose death, and whose *continuing* life have real importance for every race, for every nation, for every generation. No event of history is truer than Christ—not storm, not war, not conquest, not recession. No threat to human existence is truer than Christ—not disease, not hunger, not injustice, not oppression. No enemy of human hope is truer than Christ—not pain, not divorce, not unemployment, not even death.

The Word of God, which is Christ, existed before time was, and will exist even after history comes to an end. All creation came into being in and through him. All things have meaning and worth and destiny only in relationship to him. Everything out there that competes for our attention and our allegiance is only secondary to the truth of God that *is* Jesus Christ, the Word of God that became flesh to live among us that first Christmas so long ago. And whether they are aware of the truth or not, whether they acknowledge the truth or not, whether they honor the truth or not, every person and every event that ever *was* revolves around him. He is the meaning, he is the focus, he is the center.

You and I say that we know that truth. You and I have seen the miracle of the manger. You and I must never think that Christmas is a diversion, an interruption, an abnormal suspension of our daily reality. God coming into the world in Jesus Christ is the one truth, the one reality that should be our focus in life. We must never allow all the competing claims of all the other days of the year to deceive us or distract us, to misdirect us or mislead us. We must allow our lives to be ruled by the truth of Christmas, so that Christ, the Word of God who was in the beginning with God, remains the center on which our life, like all of history, is focused. For "[a]ll things came into being through him, and without him not one thing came into being. What has come into being in him was life, and the life was the light of all people" (John 1:3–4 NRSV). Praise God. Amen.

Epiphany of the Lord

Spanish Springs Presbyterian Church, Sparks, Nevada

January 6, 2001

Isaiah 60:1–6
Ephesians 3:1–12
Matthew 2:1–12

"Light-Bearers"

I lived in Richmond, Virginia, for three years. And being interested in history as I am, it was a wonderful place to go to school—so much of our textbook past happened within a couple of hours' drive of Richmond. Many of us first think of Richmond as the capital of the Confederacy, of course, and figures like Jefferson Davis and Robert E. Lee come to mind. But it was also the home territory of Revolutionary War figures like Thomas Jefferson and Patrick Henry. And even before America was a *nation*, the area was an important center of colonial agriculture and commerce. Today, you can still tour many homes and plantations that date from colonial times, and I took advantage of that opportunity to the extent that my study schedule and my budget would allow, visiting the stately mansions looking out over the James River and scattered along the fall line from Richmond north to the Potomac.

The architecture of the old plantations was fascinating, and those responsible for preserving the homes have done their best to furnish the houses with period décor, sometimes even displaying pieces that were actually owned by the inhabitants of the houses more than two centuries ago. Something that today's visitors notice is the abundance of mirrors in these old houses—nearly every room has at least one, and usually several. Most of us have mirrors in our bathrooms, of course, and perhaps on a dresser or even hanging in a front hallway for primping and for checking our appearance before we go out of the house or when we come in, but nothing like the number of mirrors that you see in these old plantation houses. Our first assumption might be that our ancestors were hopelessly vain creatures, forever powdering their wigs or rouging their cheeks.

But the explanation that the guides give for all the mirrors is that it wasn't a matter of *vanity*. It was a matter of *light*. Long before the invention of the electric light bulb, the rooms were all illuminated by candles. And since light multiplies when it is reflected, just a few candles could be used to light up an entire room if it had enough mirrors, hung in just the right places. It wasn't simply a matter of economy, this getting the most out of every candle. It was also a matter of practicality—lighting dozens of candles for a single room when just a few could be made to suffice would have been a tedious job. So there were a lot of mirrors in these houses to reflect the candelabras and chandeliers, and even the sconces usually had polished metal plates behind them so that the illuminating quality of the candles hung on the walls would also be enhanced.

Light is an important theme of the Bible. It is one of the Bible's favorite ways for expressing the glory of God and the advent of God in human form. The word "epiphany" is related to the Greek word for "light." More specifically, it means "to show to." This day on the calendar—January sixth—is the day the church annually celebrates Christ's being revealed as the world's light. It is the day on which we traditionally read the story from Matthew about the wise men—most likely not kings, but astrologers—following the light of a great star in the heavens to the house in Bethlehem where the baby Jesus was. More generally, it is the day on which we proclaim anew the unveiling of God's glory in the person of Jesus Christ, which means the revelation and discovery that Jesus was the Son of God, the Messiah promised by God and foretold by the prophets.

Matthew draws our attention to the fact that it was not the scholars of the Bible, not the religious leaders of Israel, who first came to worship Jesus as the new-born king of creation, but *foreigners, pagans*, *Gentiles*, whose search for truth and salvation brought them to the infant in Bethlehem, where the Jewish scriptures had foretold the Messiah would be born. Everyone in Jerusalem heard about King Herod's visitors from afar who had come looking for the Messiah. But far from coming *themselves* to pay homage to the Messiah in Bethlehem, a mere five miles from Jerusalem, the *scribes* and the *priests* didn't even bother to seek him out. And *Herod's* only interest in where the child was, the wise men learned in a dream, was his jealous intent of clinging to his throne by murder.

But the light had come into the world, and, as prophets had promised of old, the light was the light to which all nations would come, and which would make of Israel a light to the Gentiles. Already it was happening: it was *Gentiles* who came bearing gifts fit for a king—gold and frankincense and myrrh. And they brought them *not* to the earthly king *Herod*—a cruel despot who held his throne only by murderous intrigue and by threats of violence—but to *Jesus*, an infant innocent and gentle. Jesus fulfilled the prophecies of the Jewish sriptures, but he *also* fulfilled the longings of the Gentiles' hopes. And what the wise men came *seeking* they found *not* in the secrets of stars and planets, but in the very earthly event of *childbirth*. All the glory of God was lying in a crib. And he was the light of the world. The wise men were but the first installment of what the scriptures declared: "Nations shall come to your light, and kings to the brightness of your dawn" (Isa 60:3 NRSV).

Epiphany is a reminder that Jesus Christ came for all people, not just those in the inner circle of the spiritual elite who can recite the names of the books of the Bible flawlessly and who can quote a verse for every occasion. In fact, when they set out on their quest, the wise men most likely had never even heard of the Jewish scriptures. They followed a star and a yearning—a sign from God that anyone who was interested might have seen and pursued, a yearning for salvation from the fearful demons and remote principalities that haunt our past and bind our present and doom our future. Epiphany is a reminder that God's finest gift to us calls for *our* giving *our* finest gifts in *return*—that *our* abundance, like the gold and frankincense and myrrh of the magi, is used properly when it is laid at the feet of King Jesus, when it is brought forth in praise and offering. Epiphany is a reminder that Christ came to create community—to break down walls of race and nationality, even religion, as it was then understood, and to introduce a *new* way of relating to one another, through *him*; the wise men from the East join the lowly shepherds in the New Testament's pageant of adoring faithful who meet in worship at the crib of a baby, and find there the Savior of us all. And in their acts of praise and devotion, God glorifies their witness to all the succeeding generations.

Long before the birth of Christ, the Old Testament prophets celebrated God's nature as light—God "in whom is no darkness at all" (see 1 John 1:5 NRSV)—and they recognized that God's glory is displayed when God manifests that nature by self-disclosure, self-giving, self-revelation of the great divine love that lies behind the great divine purpose. The prophets said that one day within history, people of every nation would come to where God could be found—*they* talked in terms of a temple of *stone*—not only to *learn* of God, but to have *fellowship* with God. In passages like today's reading from Isaiah, they gave witness to the transforming and illuminating effect of life in God's presence. But no matter how many people came to it, and no matter what truths were spoken there, the temple was a mass of stone, lifeless, cold, and hard, built by sinful hands, embellished and enlarged even at the direction of such a godless tyrant as King Herod. "Come to him," wrote a follower of the crucified and resurrected Christ, to "a living stone" (1 Peter 2:4a NRSV)—the very presence of God not contained in walls of rock, but alive, sensing, rejoicing, generous, sympathizing, vulnerable, triumphing over everything that would make *us* cold and lifeless and rigid and unfeeling. "Come to the light"—not a place, but a person, known not in lonely speculation but within a community of faithful action. "Arise!" said the prophet of old. "Shine!" Share in the glory of God, and reflect it all around you. God is revealing all the love and mercy and peace and hope of heaven. And with wise men who traveled from afar seeking after that light, you and I are witnesses that it is Jesus, the Christ, the light of the world. The true light that enlightens everyone has come into the world. In him, everything is revealed—all is clear: the reason for the law, the patriarchs, the prophets, the exile, all the history of the Old Testament is illuminated by the birth of a babe in Bethlehem, and the crucifixion of a man on Calvary, and the resurrection of God's perfect servant from the tomb. The light shines in the darkness, and the darkness did not overcome it.

If this light is inherently for *all* people—and the story of the wise men and so many other passages of the Bible shows that it *is*—then those upon whom the light has shined have a duty to *share* that illumination, to *reflect* that revelation, to *bear* that light out into all the world's dark places. It is not a private possession, only for the few who are like us or who meet our standards or who are already perfect in their own eyes. If, through God's grace, we have been blessed with the gift of Jesus Christ, then we are called to be *stewards* of that grace, *each one of us*, to give witness to the light that has illuminated *our* lives, not by casting *judgment* upon the world that God loves and walked through and blessed in the person of Jesus Christ, but by showing forth Jesus Christ. If, through God's grace, we have experienced that light in *our* lives, then we must invite *all* people into the community of which Christ is the center, this long-foretold gathering of people in the very presence of God, where race, class, nationality, language, gender, condition pose no barriers, where past sins are forgotten and deemed irrelevant, where we are accepted simply by our answer to the invitation, not by any deserving, not on the strength of any résumé, not through *our* holiness, but through *his*, there to be welcomed by the King of glory, and to be transformed into shining brilliance not according to *our* design but according to *his*, not praising our *own* glory but reflecting *his*.

To be a Christian is to be a light-bearer. It is to reflect the light of God in Jesus Christ into every shadowed life, into every gloomy alley, into every dark corner—not a light of interrogation, not a light that blinds, but the light of hope, the light of forgiveness, the light of generosity, the light of peace that draws us to Bethlehem like a star and then streams out from a crib, from the cross, from a tomb whose cold, lifeless stone has been rolled away to reveal God's resurrection power that embraces us and lifts us to life eternal—the light that warms and illumines us and must be reflected in lives that are like mirrors, multiplying the light and directing it wherever it is needed to light up the whole world like mirrors enable a single candle to light up an entire room. We ourselves are not the light, but we are wooed into a relationship of love and repentance and obedience and mutuality so that we can *testify* to the light with every word that we speak and with every deed that we do, stewards of the grace that has shined upon us in Jesus Christ. We are the church, and that is our purpose, our mission and our trust—to show like a mirror God's revelation of the Light to all the world, faithfully, authentically, lovingly, hopefully. Our faith is not a private matter, but a gift entrusted to the church, to *us*, in the service of God's purpose of bringing all of creation into the embrace of God's saving love.

The Light of the world has come.

> Arise, shine....
> Lift up your eyes and look around;
>   they all gather together, they come to you;
> your sons shall come from far away,
>   and your daughters shall be carried on their nurses' arms.
> Then you shall see and be radiant;
>   your heart shall thrill and rejoice,
> because the abundance of the sea shall be brought to you,
>   the wealth of the nations shall come to you.
> A multitude of camels shall cover you,
>   the young camels of Midian and Ephah;
>   all those from Sheba shall come.
> They shall bring gold and frankincense,
>   and shall proclaim the praise of the Lord. (Isa 60:1a, 4–6 NRSV)

THE BAPTISM OF THE LORD

Spanish Springs Presbyterian Church, Sparks, Nevada

JANUARY 9, 2005

Isaiah 42:1–9
Acts 10:34–43
Matthew 3:13–17

"From Bath to Meal"

Something very unique happens once in the life of every Christian. In an era of faddish behavior and trendy affectation, it is as old as Christianity itself and has nothing to do with computers or electronic gadgets. In an age of people asking, "What's in it for me?" it has nothing to do with economic advantage, nothing to do with physical fitness, and, if it is entered into in a *proper* frame of mind, it has nothing to do with enhancing one's reputation or one's prestige. It is simple. It is primitive. It is, as far as a casual observer might be concerned, a strange or even senseless thing to do. It is a ritual bath, an activity of ancient origin but eternal significance. It marks our incorporation into the people of God and seals God's acceptance of us as having been chosen from all eternity. It marks our empowerment by the Holy Spirit for the purpose of being obedient servants in lowly and anonymous ministry to others. It sweeps us up in the great drama of God's love for creation, stretching across the ages from the primeval moment when God tamed the swirling waters to the future day when *all* people will witness "the river of the water of life, bright as crystal, flowing from the throne of God and of the Lamb through the middle of the street" (Rev 22:1–2a NRSV) of the new Jerusalem. It plunges us into the dark and deathly tomb with the crucified Jesus and buoys us up to new and everlasting life with the resurrected Christ. It is a splash of water on the head that launches us headlong onto the ocean of God's merciful redemption. It is the most uncomplicated of human actions, but it is so significant that the Reformers insisted it should be administered without delay to every newborn infant of every Christian parent. It is the most fateful decision any father and mother can make for a child or any unbaptized adult can make for him- or herself, and yet it has *nothing* to do with *learning* enough or *knowing* enough or being *smart* enough. It is all about our relationship with the holy God, and yet it is inextricably bound to the reality of human sinfulness. It reminds us of the gush of waters at our birth from a mother's womb, but it is not about birth from the *flesh*, but *re*-birth by the Spirit. It identifies who it is that we belong to, and yet it is not the possession of any of us as individuals, but belongs to the church as a whole. It is the sacrament of Christian baptism.

No *description*, certainly no *sermon*, can fully express the *meaning* of baptism. And in the sacramental minimalism that characterizes the modern church, including many a Presbyterian church, where there is a premium on the cognitive and a disregard of the affective, so that what people *know* and *understand* is considered to be more important than what they *do*, and *words* are considered more meaningful than *actions*, the practice of a few drops of water on the head hardly begins to express either the hazard or the renewal involved in the sacrament. Indeed, in most Protestant sanctuaries over the past four centuries or so, the sacrament is virtually unspoken of save for the occasions on which a baby is brought, dressed in frills (as I was, and as my children were) to a font, more often a finger bowl hidden in a piece of furniture, in which the water, most likely added only for that morning, is not even visible. A single drop is no *less* baptism than an entire *tubful*; it is not the *method* of baptism that is important, as even the ancient church fathers testify. But does an eye-dropper's worth of bath speak clearly about dying with Christ and being raised with Christ, or being washed of sin and made clean by God's sacrificial love? Can it visually communicate being born anew of water and the Spirit, or receiving the yoke of humble servanthood? Does it forcefully testify to what it *means* that we are being empowered to do what Christ *calls* us to do, even following him to the *cross*, even *dying* for his sake?

It may be that we who have become *comfortable* with baptism need to be reminded of *our* baptismal *vows* and *God's* baptismal *promise* on a regular basis, perhaps every time we gather in Christ's name. After all, *Jesus*' very *identity* is wrapped up in what happened when *he* came from Galilee to the Jordan to be baptized by John: "[J]ust as he came up from the water, suddenly the heavens were opened to him and he saw the Spirit of God descending like a dove and alighting on him. And a voice from heaven said, 'This is my Son, the Beloved, with whom I am well pleased'" (Matt 3:16b–17 NRSV). *Our* very *identity*, *yours* and *mine*, *ought* to be just so wrapped up in what happened when *we* came or were brought to the font in the midst of some congregation somewhere and were washed with water and, perhaps, anointed with oil, testifying that *we* have been chosen and set apart by God and that *we* belong to Jesus the Christ, the Messiah, the anointed one, and that *we* have been received into the covenant that God first made with Abraham, and so *we, too*, have been blessed to be a blessing.

So important is baptism in the life of the Christian that *baptism* was the action that finally broke down the walls of custom and prejudice, allowing faith in Jesus Christ to flow out of Israel and into the rest of the world. Matthew tells us in the very last words of his Gospel that the risen Lord Jesus Christ commissioned his disciples to make disciples of all nations, baptizing them. With that commission by Jesus so clearly set forth in Matthew, it may be difficult for us, many centuries after the fact, to understand why *Peter's* baptism of a *Roman centurion* should raise such a *furor* in the fledgling church, that is, among the church leaders back in Jerusalem. The centurion had not been circumcised, did not live according to the laws of Moses about what a person *can* eat and *can't* eat. He hadn't, in other words, been converted to the faith of Abraham and Isaac and Jacob. And the gatekeepers in Jerusalem thought that, without conversion first to *Judaism*, no *Gentile* should be baptized in the name of Jesus Christ or received into Christ's church.

In *some* churches *today*, baptism will not be administered without evidence of conversion. But the *Reformers* recognized that *conversion* is *not* an *instantaneous* event, but a life-long *process*; baptism was *not* given by Christ to mark the *culmination* of faith, but to mark the *inauguration* of faith. It is the *beginning*, not the *conclusion*; it is an *enrollment*, not a *diploma*. In the case of the baptism of *Cornelius*, if a conversion *was* involved, it was not so much the conversion of *Cornelius* the *Roman centurion*, but rather the conversion of *Peter* the *Jewish guardian* of Christianity. He had had a vision that foods *forbidden* by the law of Moses—the law observed by all good Jews—were legitimately edible. And, just moments afterward, Peter was summoned to the non-kosher house of a Gentile soldier, where, at invitation, he told the story of Jesus' baptism and ministry, Jesus' crucifixion and resurrection. And at the *conclusion* of his sermon, and rather as God's own divine affirmation of Peter's testimony, the Holy Spirit came upon Cornelius and all his household. It was *then* that *Peter* was converted—converted from someone who could never have believed that God would welcome a *Roman*, into someone who perceived that God never excludes *anyone*. It is not a matter of *our deserving*. It is a matter of *God's accepting*. " . . . Peter said, 'Can anyone withhold the water for baptizing these people who have received the Holy Spirit just as we have?' So he ordered them to be baptized in the name of Jesus Christ. Then they invited him to stay for several days" (Acts 10:47–48 NRSV). And Peter himself, the stubbornly orthodox Jew, found himself eating non-kosher food at a non-kosher table with his non-kosher hosts, under a non-kosher roof.

When the church leaders back in Jerusalem, thoroughly Jewish in outlook and thoroughly Jewish in table manners, received the news of what Peter had done, eating with uncircumcised Gentiles, they howled in objection. Peter replied how he had received with the vision about the unclean meat the command, "What God has made clean, you must not call profane" (Acts 10:15b NRSV), and how he had immediately been summoned to Cornelius's house and how he had preached there and how the Holy Spirit had fallen upon the members of the household. "And," Peter explained, "I remembered the word of the Lord, how he had said, '*John* baptized with *water*, but *you* will be baptized with the *Holy Spirit*.' If then God gave *them* the *same* gift that he gave *us* when *we* believed in the Lord Jesus Christ, who was *I* that *I* could hinder *God*" (Acts 11:16–17 NRSV)? And so Peter had baptized Cornelius and his household, and that was the explanation of how he had come to be at the *same* table eating the *same* food as people who were so un-Jewish, so vastly different in *everything*—everything, that is, except their inclusion in the body of Jesus Christ through the waters of baptism. The common experience of receiving the sacrament of baptism provided the answer to the question, "With whom shall we eat?" The shared baptism that broke down the walls of difference and exclusion paved the way immediately for all to approach the dining table together. The bath led to the meal. And the *meal* was all about celebrating the reconciliation that baptism in the name of God the Father and God the Son and God the Holy Spirit makes not only *possible*, but *inevitable*.

Something else very unique happens in the life of every Christian, but more regularly than baptism; indeed, there is every theological reason that it should happen each and every Lord's Day. In an era of faddish restaurants and trendy cuisine, it is as old as Christianity itself and has nothing to do with impressing our neighbors or counting carbs. In an age of people asking, "What's in it for me?" its very meaning depends upon its being an experience shared with others. It is simple. It is primitive. It is, as far as a casual observer might be concerned, a waste of time. It is a ritual meal, an activity of ancient origin but eternal significance. It demonstrates our unity as the people of God and reaffirms Christ's acceptance of us as friends upon whom he depends to carry out his ministry in the world. It is not reserved for the pure, but is offered even and especially to the wretched. It is food not for angels fluttering about in *heaven*, but for human beings who have work to do in *this* world. It reminds us of the blood that poured out from

Christ's side on the cross and the flesh that was broken for our salvation. It reminds us of who it is that we belong to, and yet it is not the possession of any of us as individuals, but belongs to the church as a whole. It is the sacrament of the Lord's Supper. Our frequent and repeated approach to a common table to eat from one loaf and partake of a common cup is the bodily enactment of the reconciliation Christ worked for us in his death on the cross—reconciliation with God, reconciliation with each other, as people of every background, every race, every tongue, reminded of their *shared* identity through the waters of Christian baptism, come to receive of Christ himself who is the food for the journey of faith and the refreshment for the service to which he calls us. And *our* conversion into the loving and forgiving and faithful people God *intends* for us to be is nurtured as again and again we join with others, names perhaps even unknown to us, coming to the table of grace. You have been bathed clean and set aside as Christ's own in your baptism. Now come to the Lord's table and be fed.

Second Sunday in Ordinary Time

Spanish Springs Presbyterian Church, Sparks, Nevada

January 17, 1999

Isaiah 49:1–7
1 Corinthians 1:1–9
John 1:29–42

"Witness"

The baptizer had caused quite a stir in and around Bethany. He was drawing crowds of sinners who responded to his call to repentance, and *that* drew the attention also of the guardians of religion, the protectors of God. Priests and Levites came all the way from Jerusalem to interrogate him. "Who are you?" they demanded to know. The Pharisees sent agents to inquire of him, perhaps to ensnare him. "Why are you doing this? By what authority?" Had he been so inclined, he could have declared himself to be Elijah returned to earth, or some other prophet, even the Messiah. But he always replied that he was not any of these, only a voice, an unworthy servant, a heralding forerunner of someone he himself did not fully comprehend.

His habits were peculiar. His diet was, well, *strange*. His clothing was not quite civilized, apparently. He lived apart from polite society, and spent his days out in the wilds. But word of him spread, *and* word of his message. For days, for weeks, for months—we don't know exactly how long—he was there, washing people clean of their sins in the Jordan, telling them to prepare for the coming of the Lord. Then, one day, he looked up and saw Jesus walking toward him, and he said to those who were near him,

> "Here is the Lamb of God who takes away the sin of the world! . . . I came baptizing with water for this reason, that he might be revealed to Israel. . . . And I myself have seen and have testified that this is the Son of God."

> The next day John again was standing with two of his disciples, and as he watched Jesus walk by, he exclaimed, "Look, here is the Lamb of God!" The two disciples heard him say this, and they followed Jesus. (John 1:29b, 31b, 34–37 NRSV)

It must have been a bittersweet moment for John to realize that, at a fairly young age, his life's work was over—the work of pointing toward someone who would be greater than he. Anyone who has ever spent his or her own career doing the spadework for another to take advantage of, laying the foundation for someone else to build upon, can perhaps be forgiven a few moments of wistfulness, of yearning, of envy even. I don't think that our piety requires us to deny John his humanness. He had developed a loyal following, disciples of his own. But now, *Jesus* had come, the Lamb of God, and the *old* loyalties had to be forgotten, for a *superior* truth had arrived. The flickering candle that John had been holding heroically before Israel all that time had been a significant and necessary beacon, but now its feeble glow was swallowed up in the full brilliance of the Son of God. And so John leaves the stage of salvation's drama without even a bow in order that all eyes can focus on the main character. John the baptizer was not the truth; he was a *witness* to the truth. And when the truth finally appeared on the horizon of Israel's hope, *John's* task was fulfilled.

That is the *role* of a witness. A witness is a person who testifies to what she or he has seen and heard. A witness declares the truth that that person has come to know. Something important hinges on the witness's vow to state openly and accurately, clearly and without any expectation of personal gain. The witness is there to point beyond her- or himself. John's very success at being a *faithful* witness is why *some* of his disciples left him and began to follow *Jesus*. And any later reckoning of John as a saint, any feasts and celebrations in *his* name, tend to distort the whole point of who John *was* and what he *did*. Scripture remembers him not because of any achievement of his *own*, but because he faithfully pointed other people to *Jesus*.

We have had so many "trials of the century" over the past hundred years, from the Scopes and Hauptmann trials to the ones in today's headlines, each with their star witnesses whom the media makes into instant celebrities, that the *legal function* of a witness gets confused and lost in all the publicity. What is *primarily* important becomes *obscured*. What is *chiefly* significant becomes *hidden* rather than *revealed*. It seems to me that there is an important lesson for congregations and Christian leaders in scripture's various accounts of John the baptizer. He was a window, a signpost, an invitation to look for and see and understand someone else. As churches grow and, of necessity, begin to take on the characteristics of an institution, and as ministers and other church leaders become, as human nature would have it, promoters of programs and scrutinizers of budgets and keepers of statistics and preservers of traditions, the church's role of witness to the truth of God in Jesus can be obscured, even lost. Our attention can get distracted. Our reason for being can become muddled. Our deadlines can lock us into a routine for the routine's own sake. We can lose perspective of the fundamental task of pointing beyond ourselves to the Lamb of God who takes away the sins of the world, and insist that people admire the window frame *before* looking through the window to Christ; that the signpost be so artistic that people never notice that it is pointing beyond the programs and potlucks to *Jesus*; that people respond to *our* invitation to meet the Son of God and forget to give thanks to God that people *are* responding to *someone's* invitation. It doesn't take being around a church very long to notice how we tend to fall in love with the *instruments* of proclaiming—whether they be the stained glass windows or Mrs. Adams' Bible study or the color of the sanctuary carpet. You know what I'm saying. Anything that distracts us from being transparent, unambiguous, welcoming proclaimers of Jesus Christ must be reckoned expendable, must remain secondary, must be held in check.

Pastors should always preach first of all to themselves. And as we enter the phase of our new church development when we are formalizing our congregation—holding classes to prepare people for communicant membership so that we can move toward being recognized as a self-governing and self-budgeting Presbyterian church, beginning to think about the sort of building that we want to house our worship and study and fellowship events and meetings and meetings and meetings, considering office equipment and secretarial and other staff—we, and I in particular, will be tempted to spend our energies on developing Spanish Springs Presbyterian Church as an institution. And every institution tends, over time, to focus more and more attention upon itself. Nobody knows better than *Presbyterians* do how *temporary* committees tend to become *permanent* committees, how *mission* funding always seems to require an increase in *administration* funds, how difficult it is to let go of stale, ineffective programs that were once innovative and responsive to a real need. We will each need to cultivate an attitude for ourselves, and a habit for all of us together, of being willing openly and honestly to examine our congregational budget and program and behavior to make certain that we aren't demanding too much attention on ourselves— the curtains on the window, if you will, the landscaping around the signpost, the engraving on the invitation—and either ignoring the *rest* of Reno, Sparks, and Spanish Springs, or failing to point beyond *ourselves* to *Jesus*.

We will constantly be tempted to rationalize a narrow focus and a convenient constituency. I have never yet been in a meeting of a committee dealing with both church membership and evangelism in which someone didn't say, "Why are you proposing giving so much attention to people who aren't even church members? I say we need to take care of our own before we go out and try to get more people in." Well, I've learned the hard way that evangelism and church membership need to be two separate committees. Because once a congregation becomes established, the tendency will always be for it to focus on itself—its own care, its own maintenance, perhaps its own comfort—and pointing beyond itself to Christ can be just another item down toward the bottom of the to-do list. The pastor cannot by her- or himself keep a church centered on the task of pointing beyond itself; in fact, the *pastor*, because of the expectations surrounding administration and budget and pastoral care to the *members*, may be the most tempted of all to give in to the satisfactions of having a nice building and a nice choir and a nice church school and a nice balance in the bank, and congratulate her- or himself that it's all the result of the talented pastoral leadership.

But the building and the choir and the church school and the bank balance are only *instruments* for the mission of helping people to come and see Jesus Christ. As a congregation that is faithful to our *calling, we* must be as willing as *John* was to let our individual and corporate lives be only a *lens* through which people look to see the Lamb of God beyond. And that means that every program will always and only be tentative, every budget will always and only be an estimate, every brick and piece of furniture will always and only be a *tool, never* an end in *itself.* For the *only goal* is *Jesus Christ*, and welcoming people to life eternal and abundant and free and whole in him.

We honor John the baptizer for his faithfulness to the task that God assigned to him—for the humility to live a life that must have been lonely sometimes, austere often, dangerous certainly, as his martyrdom makes clear, and for the single-minded devotion that it must have taken to step out of the spotlight and allow it to shine fully and solely on Jesus Christ, the Lamb of God. How many times he must have wondered whether *anyone* was really paying attention to the significance of what he was saying, whether *his sacrifices* were making any *difference*, whether his own disciples understood that *he* was not to be the object of their hopes, but another more *worthy* than he. The pastors and lay leaders and congregations of little struggling churches in the inner city wonder the same sorts of things, and churches with just a few remaining members out at the dusty country crossroads; also, in their more reflective moments, the suburban churches that are just holding their own in membership and attendance, and even the mega-churches about which we hear so much these days. I think as priests questioned his authority and Pharisees questioned his motives and Levites questioned his worthiness, John must have taken comfort and courage from the ancient prophets who also struggled with doubts about *their* effectiveness and strove to maintain the integrity of *their* witness, must have been refreshed in spirit and renewed in commitment when he read such testimony as this:

> And now the Lord says,
>   who formed me in the womb to be his servant,
> to bring Jacob back to him,
>   and that Israel might be gathered to him,
> for I am honored in the sight of the Lord,
>   and my God has become my strength—
> he says,
> "It is too light a thing that you should be my servant
>   to raise up the tribes of Jacob
>   and to restore the survivors of Israel;
> I will give you as a light to the nations,
>   that my salvation may reach to the end of the earth."
> Thus says the Lord,
>   the Redeemer of Israel and his Holy One,
> to one deeply despised, abhorred by the nations,
>   the slave of rulers,
> "Kings shall see and stand up,
>   princes, and they shall prostrate themselves,
> because of the Lord, who is faithful,
>   the Holy One of Israel, who has chosen you." (Isa 49:5–7 NRSV)

God has put us in this place at this time to be a window, a signpost, an invitation to live in the truth of the Son of God—to proclaim that what Jesus said and did long ago are the will of God for Sparks and for Reno and for Spanish Springs *today*, that the forgiveness that God pronounced through Jesus long ago is God's mercy for Sparks and for Reno and for Spanish Springs *today*, that the ministry to the poor and the hungry and the sick and the lonely that God offered through Jesus long ago is God's promise for the afflicted and the oppressed and the suffering and the forlorn of Sparks and of Reno and of Spanish Springs *today*, and not just for the people in this room and in the church buildings in this town, but for all, even those who have never crossed the threshold into a sanctuary. The reason we are here is to be a witness—a witness to the merciful love of Jesus Christ, the *living* Lord, *still* the Lamb of God, who takes away the sin of the world.

Third Sunday in Ordinary Time

Spanish Springs Presbyterian Church, Sparks, Nevada

January 23, 2005

Isaiah 9:1–4
1 Corinthians 1:10–18
Matthew 4:12–23

"Sine Qua Non"

When Paul had something on his mind, it did not take him long to get to the point. The customs of letter-writing in the Greek and Roman world called for a gentle and flattering introduction in written communications—it was a mark of being sophisticated and urbane—but Paul often felt an urgency about the situation in the churches he had helped establish that prompted him to forgo the flowery conventions and hasten to the heart of the matter. And, for Paul, nothing was as urgent as the health of the church, because the church was Christ's own appointed instrument for spreading the gospel, upon which human salvation depends. In Galatians, Paul's greeting was *especially* terse as he quickly confronted what he perceived to be division and false doctrine. And in his first letter to the Christians at *Corinth*, he *also* moved quickly to the problem as he saw it.

Paul had heard from "Chloe's people"—perhaps traveling agents, even slaves, of Chloe, who seems to have been a businesswoman of some means and a major benefactor of the Corinthian church—that there was quarreling and dissension in the congregation. And so he rapidly moved through the greeting and the compliments to say, "Now I appeal to you, brothers and sisters, by the name of our Lord Jesus Christ, that all of you be in agreement and that there be no divisions among you, but that you be united in the same mind and the same purpose" (1 Cor 1:10 NRSV).

Unity, in our time, has become a common theme and oft-spoken hope in political rhetoric and in our social ideals. Some people dismiss it as sappy sentiment, even arguing that if *unity* is the *goal*, then *truth* will be the *victim*. Insistence upon unity is often thought of as papering over differences that should be faced squarely rather than ignored. But *dis*unity can be disastrous and destructive. Our Old Testament reading this morning about vindication for Zebulun and Naphtali, regions of the northern kingdom of Israel, looks toward a time when Israel will rise up from under the yoke of the Assyrian empire. Had Israel and Judah not been two separate nations, had they remained united as in the days of David and Solomon, or had the stronger *Judah* come to the aid of beleaguered *Israel*, the Assyrians would not have been able to invade and defeat Israel in the *first* place. It was the *breach* between the two halves of God's covenant people that had left them *both* vulnerable to foreign predators, and, in time, the foreign predators took advantage of their respective weakness. Unity was not a sappy sentiment in that case. And *dis*unity proved to be *fatal*.

So, it would undoubtedly be with the *church* in *Paul's* time. The environment was hostile *enough* to the gospel of Jesus Christ; the Son of God *himself* had been crucified, and Christ's *followers* could expect no better treatment at the hands of the authorities than their *Master* had received. What hope was there for survival against the *outside* threats if the people of the church were busy fighting among *themselves*? What sort of testimony about Jesus Christ was the church *making* if it were to be embroiled constantly in dissension and debate? What peripheral issue could be so important that it was worth hazarding the possible wreck of the whole Christian witness? And the wreck of the whole Christian witness, as a strategic issue, was a real possibility.

But, for *Paul, unity* was not simply a *strategic* concern. It was at the very *heart* of what the church was *about*. And, more fundamentally, it was the very *essence* of what *Christ* was about. Paul had heard from Chloe's people that some Christians at Corinth claimed to belong to Paul, some claimed to belong to Apollos, some claimed to belong to Cephas, some claimed to belong to Christ. We don't know exactly what that means—whether some congregation members were championing particular points of view espoused by different apostles, or whether some were claiming somehow to be *better* than others based on who had *baptized* them. At any rate, it had led to quarrels among people who *should* behave as brothers and sisters because *Christ* was the brother of them *all*. "Has *Christ* been *divided*?" Paul asked in exasperation. "Was *Paul* crucified for you?" Of *course* not. "Or were you baptized in the name of *Paul*" (1 Cor 1:13 NRSV)? Again, of *course* not. But the very fact that Christ died on the cross for *all*, and that the faithful share a common *baptism*, meant *then* and means *now* that *any* division within the body of believers is not only *embarrassing*, not only *incapacitating*, but it is simply *unacceptable*.

What we have in the Christian church today, however, is just what Paul railed against. Not only have we divided into denominations—the very notion of denominations itself, of course, is a scandalous problem—but some of those denominations (and, for that matter, many churches that call themselves nondenominational) will not honor each other's administration of the sacrament of baptism. There are denominations that will not admit other Christians to the Lord's table (and many nondenominational churches scarcely ever *have* communion). There are even individual congregations that insist on *re*baptizing new members and refuse to allow people from other congregations of the *same denomination* to receive the sacrament of the Lord's Supper in their sanctuary. You can't get much more fundamentally *dis*united than that! And then there is a whole constellation of other issues that cause division among Christians of different traditions—from "debts" and "trespasses" and "sins" to the prohibition of ordination of whole classes of people, starting with women—as well as all of the issues that arise in the life of a particular congregation and that are allowed to take on a life of their own out of all proportion to their real significance—the color of carpet, for example. We are prompted to excuse such instances by referring to it all as simple human nature—we say it's the sort of thing we have to expect when we're dealing with *any* group of people.

Paul did not want and did not call for uniformity. Indeed, he appreciated the diversity of gifts that people had been given by the Holy Spirit, and even the diversity of perspectives and, perhaps, practices. But Paul understood that when believers in Jesus Christ, people who have been baptized into his death and baptized into his resurrection, become *jealous* and *quarrelsome*, then there is nothing at all to distinguish them from people who *aren't* believers in Jesus Christ and who *haven't* been baptized into his death and baptized into his resurrection. In First Corinthians, Paul used the Greek word *adelphoi*—"brothers," translated in our Bible as "brothers and sisters," recognizing that Paul meant people of *both* genders who are bound to Christ and, *through* Christ, are bound to *each other*—thirty-eight times, more than twice as often as in any of his other letters. He was signaling to his readers the level and depth of commitment and relationship to one another that they should be exhibiting at *all* times and in *all* circumstances. The most distinguishing feature of Christians is *supposed* to be their *unity* in *Christ*, and Paul regarded anything *less* than unity to be a sign of spiritual immaturity.

In fact, our unity in Christ already *exists*, whether believers choose to be faithful in *exhibiting* it or *not*. If we have been incorporated into Christ through baptism, our unity is a *fact*. It is not a *choice* on our part. It is a *gift* that we have received from *Christ*. But whether we *honor* Christ's gift, and whether our lives and the lives of our congregations and larger church bodies *demonstrate* the unity that is ours, *is*, of course, a matter of choice. It would be interesting to know what the differences of doctrine and practice *were* between Paul and Apollos and Cephas. The fact that Paul doesn't spell out the differences, and uses *himself* as the straw man in his arguments— "Was *Paul* crucified for you? Or were you baptized in the name of *Paul*?" (1 Cor 1:13b–c NRSV)—rather than criticizing the others, suggests that whatever differences there were (and real differences there must have been), they were not so important as to allow them to become reasons for contention or dissension. Quarreling and discord belong to the *old* way of life. *Baptism* is supposed to be a *death* to the old way of living, but, for *many* in the Corinthian church, it obviously had *not* been. And so their very understanding of *baptism* was flawed, and therefore, so was their understanding of what it was to be Christ's church.

It seems not to have been very long after Jesus began preaching the need to repent—that is, to change direction—and proclaiming the nearness of the kingdom of heaven, that he started calling on *others* to *follow* him and *learn* from him and be involved in the *same* sort of ministry that *he* was. As far as the Gospel according to Matthew is concerned, Jesus' call to Peter and Andrew and James and John was unplanned. Jesus was walking along the shore, saw them working at their trade, casting and mending nets, and invited them, or commanded them, to follow him, and immediately they did so—dropped their nets, got out of their boats, walked away from family members, even—without premeditation and without discussion. And, it would seem, without taking any sort of personality test to see if they would all get along together. And, indeed, it seems that the twelve hung together remarkably well through the months or years that they traveled in company with Jesus around Galilee and up to Jerusalem. Looking always to Jesus as their Master, relying always upon Jesus for their wisdom, listening always to Jesus for their instruction, there were disagreements, owing no doubt to personalities and interests and temperaments, but there was no falling out among them. Given all that we know about human nature, considering all of the strain of worldly uncertainty that they were experiencing, taking into account the constant hostility of the religious leaders, *that* was *remarkable*, I think. And I don't believe it was because they were exceptional people— there is not the least suggestion that they were smarter than anyone else or more skilled or more spiritual, such that Jesus had sorted them out from all the other possibilities for his inner circle of disciples. In fact, their unity had nothing to do with *them* at *all*, as individuals, other than the fact that they had been willing to drop their nets and get out of their boats and leave their families when Jesus invited them or commanded them to do so. Their unity was because of *Jesus. He* was the *only* thing that fishermen and a tax collector and some followers of John the Baptist had in common. But he was enough. And all the other things, all the other likes and *dis*likes, all the other aptitudes and interests, were put in their proper perspective as being purely and only *secondary*. Differences there were, and they proved important and useful when, after the crucifixion and resurrection, disciples became apostles and carried the church throughout Palestine and even far beyond. But they belonged to *Christ*, and in and because of *that simple fact* they possessed a remarkable and overriding unity. When the Christian church experiences *dis*unity, it is a telltale sign that Christ is not at the church's center.

Last Friday night, some people from this congregation and from a Roman Catholic and a Lutheran and a United Methodist church, and perhaps some others too, joined together in worship to give witness that Christ is the center of the whole church, and that, through him, we have received the gift of unity, even though we don't always act like it, don't always appreciate the gift Christ has given us. The occasion was the Week of Prayer for Christian Unity, to pray hopefully for the real and visible unity of Christ's church, not as sappy sentiment, but because we confess that unity in Christ is our *sine qua non*—that quality without which the church is nothing, of no importance, of no use, no genuine part of Christ. And yet, even within that group, there were those who wouldn't officially recognize another's baptism, couldn't dine together at the Lord's table. Why? "Has *Christ* been *divided*?" Paul might well ask of us. "Was *John Calvin* crucified for you? Or *John Wesley*? Or *Martin Luther*? Or *John Paul II*?" Of *course* not. "Or were you baptized in the name of *Calvin* or *Wesley* or *Luther* or . . . ?" Of *course* not. But the very fact that Christ died on the cross for *all*, and that the faithful share a common *baptism*, meant *then* and means *now* that *any* division within the body of believers is not only *embarrassing*, not only *incapacitating*, but it is simply *unacceptable*.

Fourth Sunday in Ordinary Time
Spanish Springs Presbyterian Church, Sparks, Nevada
January 31, 1999

Micah 6:1–8
1 Corinthians 1:18–31
Matthew 5:1–12

"Beatitude"

Mr. Groves looked impatiently at the gold-cased clock on his desk. He had planned to leave the office early to avoid some of the traffic on his way to the dinner, but now he felt doomed to be late. At this time of the day, his big European luxury car would be nothing more than an expensive easy chair hemmed in by all the other steel tortoises inching along the 401 freeway. He, the guest of honor, would be late. His donation to the Hospital for Sick Children was one of the largest that the institution had ever received, and had attracted media coverage from across the country. His name, and the name of his company, were being broadcast into every home from coast to coast. Tonight would be a triumph, if he ever got to the suburban hotel where the banquet was being held.

"Look" he barked into the telephone, "I don't care *what* your problems are. We both knew that this wouldn't be easy. I want results. I pay you for results. You just find a way to get the information. I want the complete design of Digitech's new model in time for *us* to beat *them* to the market."

He swiveled his leather chair around to look out on the lights of the city and the lake beyond illumined by the rising moon, listening to the person on the other end of the line. The view from his office was superb, but if anyone else had been in the room, they could have seen that it was not *appreciation* on his face, but a growing sense of *agitation*. "I *know* it's confidential. *Of course* it's confidential. That's just the *point, isn't it*? Why do you think we're *playing* this game? We're going to *beat* Digitech to the market this time, and that's going to put us on top once and for all." He listened again. "Well, just do whatever's necessary, and make sure that your tracks are covered. Call me by Friday, and I mean with the full schematic." He slammed the receiver down. "Incompetent," he muttered as he stood up and opened his briefcase, picking up a file folder from his large mahogany desk.

The intercom buzzed. "Yes," he said, absently setting the file folder down again. His secretary announced that he had another call waiting. "I'll have to call him back tomorrow," he said, and then he added, "Call down and have my car brought around."

No time, he thought. *At the top of the heap, a seven-digit salary, and never time to enjoy it.*

He had risen far and fast in the industry, and was in fact one of the most powerful and admired of the new generation of business leaders. Market analysts had almost universally acclaimed him as a wizard, and had declared that the sky was the limit for his company.

Mr. Groves reached in his pants pocket and pulled out a money clip. He quickly flipped through the bills, counting mentally, and frowned. "The ATM in the lobby," he mumbled to himself as he fastened the clasps on the briefcase and crossed his large corner office to the door. "I'm late," he said as he paused at his secretary's desk. "Call Jack Conrad in Chicago and tell him that I want his report overnight—*fax* it. And call Robert Higgins and tell him that I'll be a few minutes late for the testimonial dinner. He may still be at the hospital, or he may be en route to the hotel. Tell him I'll make it up to him by cutting the length of my speech and making an additional contribution." The secretary did not know if this was meant to be a humorous statement or not, but before she could decide whether she should laugh, Mr. Groves had disappeared into the hallway walking briskly toward the elevator.

The high-ceilinged lobby of the office tower was adorned with considerable greenery, including several potted ficus trees, that constituted an exotic contradiction to the winter drabness outside. While Mr. Groves had been on the telephone in his office high above the ground level, a team of deliverymen from an office furniture company had arrived in the lobby with their merchandise destined for a suite on the forty-third floor. One of the deliverymen had slipped on the water that had melted off of his shoe, and had fallen backwards, bumping into one of the potted trees that stood near the automatic teller machine not far from the bank of elevators. He had knocked the tree and its planter over, spilling a pile of dirt onto the polished marble floor. As the elevator doors opened and Mr. Groves stepped out, he emerged into a scene of considerable confusion—a chaos of deliverymen, an office desk and chairs and credenza, and Homer, one of the office building custodians, just arriving with a broom and a dry mop.

"What's going on?" demanded Mr. Groves of the custodian as he tried to find a path through the chaos to the automatic teller.

"Just a little accident, sir," explained Homer in a genial voice as he set down his cleaning instruments.

"Well, I'm in a hurry," said Mr. Groves as he pushed past the deliverymen, who were still flustered by the disarray they had created.

As Homer and one of the deliverymen were setting the planter and its tree upright, Mr. Groves placed his briefcase on the little ledge alongside the automatic teller machine and opened it, extracting a plastic card which he inserted in the appropriate slot, entered a code number and the amount of cash he wished to withdraw, and waited for the machine to discharge the bills. In the brief time it took for the machine to deliver the money, the furniture deliverymen had resumed their work, blocking access to the elevators in the process. Mr. Groves counted the money and lifted the lid of his briefcase to return his ATM card to the place where he always kept it, when he noticed that something was missing from his leather case. He flipped through the various documents that he was taking out of the office with him, but did not find what he was looking for. "My speech. Where's my speech?" he said to himself, softly, but loud enough for Homer and the others nearby to hear. He replaced his papers as he searched his memory. "My desk. Must've left it on the desk when Sheila buzzed me."

Just then, Mr. Groves looked toward the elevator and saw the continuing chaos caused by the delivery of the office furniture, then quickly glanced at his watch. "Great!" he muttered. He quickly pushed his way past the deliverymen again toward the elevator panel. "Get out of the way!" he said at one point, shoving against a uniformed deliveryman whose colleague had stopped one of the elevators. Mr. Groves leaned on the button which had an arrow pointing "up." Under the circumstances, the twenty seconds it took for a pair of elevator doors to open for him seemed like twenty *minutes*, and when they *did* open, a crowd of people emerged, taking up more precious time.

"Back so soo—," his secretary began, rising up from her chair as he brushed past her desk.

"Forgot something," he said brusquely, opening the paneled door of his office.

"I made your calls," she said as her boss emerged again, drawing a perfunctory "Thanks" as he disappeared again into the hallway. She sat down with a sigh, looking at the pile of work that would keep her once again past quitting time into the early hours of the evening, long after her children's dinnertime.

The elevator became crowded as it descended from the uppermost floors of the office tower. The office furniture deliverymen were squeezing their chairs into another elevator car when Mr. Groves passed them, locked in the middle of the crowd that had spilled out toward the lobby. Two other elevators had arrived on the ground floor at the same time, so that there was now a tide of humanity surging toward the glass doors and out into the darkness of a late winter afternoon.

Mr. Groves reached in his pocket to tip the attendant who had driven his car to the front door from its heated parking space, and realized that the money from the ATM was not there. Instantly, he realized that he had left the money—several hundred dollars' worth—and his briefcase, sitting alongside the automatic teller machine. A sense of disaster came over him, not because he couldn't afford to *lose* the money—in fact, he was worth many millions of dollars—but because it was an indication of an unaccustomed stupidity. He cursed softly under his breath as he closed the driver's door of his car and hustled back into the lobby of the office building. It would take a *miracle* for the money still to be there, and *another* miracle for the briefcase to be where he left it, and he did not believe in miracles.

His fears were quickly confirmed—or one of them was. His briefcase was still in its place, now with the lid closed, but the money was gone. A few feet away, Homer was dry-mopping the floor. Mr. Groves grasped the handle of the briefcase, and then noticed that the clasps were still unfastened. He cast a suspicious glance at Homer.

"Oh, there you are," said the custodian as he turned and saw the business tycoon.

"Yes, here I am," the businessman said, with deliberate slowness. He knew that Homer was only one of a hundred people who could have taken the money in the time that it took him to go back up to his office to retrieve the file folder containing his speech for the testimonial dinner.

"I noticed that you forgot your briefcase," the custodian said, matter-of-factly.

"Clumsy of me," the businessman said. "I was distracted."

"That happens to all of us, I guess. I hope you don't mind, but I closed it for you," the custodian continued.

"Thank you," said Mr. Groves. He paused, then added, "Did you notice anything else?"

"Yes, I did. I put it inside. I thought that it shouldn't be left out in full view. And then I've been kind of watching it while I've been cleaning up here. Quite a little mess. But accidents happen. That's what I'm here for."

"I'm much obliged," said Mr. Groves, but there was no warmth in his voice. He needed to be on his way to the dinner, but he was intrigued by the little drama that had just taken place. "How much do you earn each week?" he finally asked.

"Oh, well, now, Mr. Groves, I don't like to boast."

Was he serious? Mr. Groves wondered. He stifled the impulse to laugh. "Well, then, just an approximate figure. I'd really like to know."

"It's quite enough to provide a roof and place food on the table," said Homer. "The Lord knows what I need. And the Lord provides," he added, patting his stomach and grinning good-naturedly. In fact, Homer was of slender build, a man in middle-age, a quiet worker who possessed a certain native dignity. "I'm even able to help my sister and her children a little bit after giving to the Lord."

"Five hundred, six hundred a week?" Mr. Groves persisted, rather rudely, actually.

"Oh, not quite so much as that," said Homer, blushing slightly. "I don't know what I'd do with all that." He tried to resume mopping the floor.

"Do you know what *I* make a year?" Mr. Groves asked.

"No, sir," replied Homer, looking at the perfectly clean floor that he was still mopping in embarrassment. "No, sir, I never really thought about it."

"My salary this year is $1,200,000. And I receive an annual bonus half again that much. And stock options—"

"My goodness," Homer said, still refusing to lift his eyes from the floor. "You must work awfully hard, Mr. Groves. But then, I know you do. And I know that you do some real good with your money, too. I've seen in the newspaper about your gift to Sick Children's." He finally looked up. "God bless you, Mr. Groves. That's a wonderful thing. Anytime I think of a child being real sick, it breaks my heart. My niece and nephew were both born with a serious condition. They've been in and out of Sick Children's."

Mr. Groves opened his briefcase and looked at the stack of bills placed neatly in one corner. He made a sound somewhere between a snort and a chuckle. "Did you count the money that you put in here?"

"Oh, no sir, it's not my business."

"Let's count it together," said Mr. Groves, taking the bills in his hand. "I'll set them down and you count them aloud."

Homer was clearly uneasy. "Yes, sir," he said slowly, "if I can be of help."

Mr. Groves began laying them down on top of his briefcase one by one. Homer stammered his words. "One hundred, two hundred, three hundred, four, five, six, seven, eight, nine, ten, eleven, twelve, thirteen, fourteen, fifteen. That would be one thousand five hundred dollars."

"That's right," said Mr. Groves. "You had fifteen hundred dollars in your hands. Have you ever had that much money in your hands before, Homer?"

"No, sir, I don't suppose that I have."

"How many people do you think passed by this pile of money before you saw it and put it in my briefcase?"

"Oh, I wouldn't know," said Homer, who could only guess at the point that the businessman was making with his excruciating questions. "This time of day, several dozen, I suppose."

"And any one of them—any person in this lobby—could have taken this money without my ever knowing it. And if I questioned any of them about it, including the person who took it, they could say that someone else must have taken it. Don't you think that's so?"

"That's why I thought I should put it in your briefcase. So nobody *would* take it. I hope I didn't do anything wrong."

"As much as you could make in a month."

Homer stared at Mr. Groves blankly, totally oblivious to the implications of what the businessperson was saying. Then suddenly, he understood what Mr. Groves had been hinting at.

"Why, I'd never—My Lord would be awfully disappointed in me."

"Homer," said Mr. Groves, fastening the clasps on his briefcase, "you're a fool." He turned toward the entrance and went out to his car.

An hour later, Homer was walking through the dark cold from the subway station to his rooming house. The snow along the sidewalk left over from the big blizzard a couple of weeks earlier looked tired and hard and dirty under the feeble light from the street lamps. When he arrived at his little apartment, he made himself a supper of some canned meat, vegetables, and bread, asking God's blessing at the beginning of his meal and reading a Psalm of thanksgiving at the end. Then he called his sister as he did every night to see how her day at work had been, how the children were, and whether she needed anything. He opened the mail—a bill and an advertisement—and then read from the Gospels for a while, and then a chapter from Sir Walter Scott—he loved Luke and he loved Sir Walter Scott. Tomorrow night would be choir, but tonight was a night for reading. Finally, he changed into his night clothes and turned on the little black and white television that sometimes worked and sometimes didn't work. Tonight, it was working. And as the news came on, the first report was about the lavish dinner that had been held earlier that evening to honor Mr. Groves, the famous business wizard, for his large donation to the Hospital for Sick Children.

Fifth Sunday in Ordinary Time

Spanish Springs Presbyterian Church, Sparks, Nevada

February 6, 2011

Isaiah 58:1–12
1 Corinthians 2:1–16
Matthew 5:13–20

"No Double Standard"

One of the features of medieval Christianity to which the Protestant Reformers strongly objected was the practice of monasticism. The common person could well resent the wealth that many monasteries and convents had accumulated; some of them had become great landowners over the centuries, and had become part and parcel of the feudalistic economy. True, some of them were great institutions of learning, and quite a few offered welcome hospitality to travelers in a time when journeying from place to place was a dangerous undertaking. A few had even earned reputations as centers of reform. But, fundamentally, and from the very beginning, the monastic life had been based on the premise that ordinary people could not really follow all the ethical standards laid down by Christ, and that only a few men and women could truly fulfill the role of being a Christian as thoroughly as the scriptures envisioned. Only the spiritually elite could actually emulate Christ—and even *they* had to be insulated from the cares of family and livelihood. The double standard meant that nobody really expected the masses to strive for righteousness—not even to be all that familiar with the Bible, which, of course, was available only in a language unknown to most people and, until the invention of the printing press, was much too expensive for the average peasant to be able to afford even if he or she *could* read Latin.

Eventually, a growing number of church leaders like Martin Luther and John Calvin rejected the proposition that the average Christian was either excused or exempt from living according to the teachings and example of Jesus Christ. According to their reading of scripture, the call to discipleship was just as urgent and complete for *one* person as for *another*. And the vocation of a *farmer* or a *tradesman* was just as holy as living the *cloistered* life. When the teachings of the Reformers became the law of their respective communities, monasteries and convents were closed and their lands were confiscated. Some Protestant leaders went so far as to force monks and nuns to marry.

Acceptance of a double standard of responsibility and behavior was not new with medieval Christianity. Many centuries before, in the time of Jesus, Judaism was much the same way. The Pharisees, for all of their scrutiny of Jesus and his disciples, criticizing the Nazarene for desecrating the sabbath in this regard or that and for allowing his disciples to violate sabbath rules or neglect standards of purity, really did not expect everyone to obey all of the laws laid down by Moses, much less the additional rules the Pharisees advocated in order to protect the Torah as they interpreted it. They enjoyed their status of being popularly regarded as holier than the average person, based largely on their punctilious and very public display of piety. And, rather predictably, they tended to look down upon those who did not satisfy every detail of religious observance.

But even the Pharisees were only a later example of an ancient phenomenon among the people of God. During the exile in Babylon, observing the sabbath and participating in fasts had been encouraged as ways to maintain Jewish identity in a land of pagan idolatry. Fasting had long been a common practice of the Day of Atonement, but now four additional days of the year came to be identified as regular occasions for fasting. Fasting was an age-old practice. At first, it was associated with rituals of mourning. But, over time, it had come to be a normal part of petitioning God for favors and calling on God to intercede at times of illness or other trouble. In times of national crisis, the leaders of the people called for fasting as a way to get God's attention. But when it came to be institutionalized as a regular event on the calendar, the door was opened for it to become more spectacle than penitence, a way of asserting the superiority of one's holiness over his fellows rather than genuinely humbling oneself before God. The upper classes were more likely to fast than the working class; they had the leisure and, frankly, the means to compete for divine attention and human praise.

Doubtless, the destruction of their nation and their captivity in Babylon had a leveling effect among the exiles. But as soon as the Israelites were permitted to leave Babylon and return to Judah, many of the old class distinctions reappeared. For the lower classes, rigorous sabbath-keeping was a burden. For those already suffering from malnutrition, the requirement of fasting was a cruelty layered upon a hardship. Meanwhile, for all of their display of religiosity, including fasting, the people of Judah still were disappointed in their efforts to rebuild their nation. The country never again achieved the degree of prestige and prosperity it had known before Nebuchadnezzar's army had besieged Jerusalem and destroyed the temple and abducted its leading citizens. It seemed as if God was turning a deaf ear to their plight. And the national malaise only fostered a reappearance of the old social stratification, reinforced by religious claims.

At least one prophet, conscious of the wide gulf between pious ritual and true righteousness, tried to expose the hypocrisy that prompted God's stony silence. A preacher known as Isaiah, probably someone who shared the same spiritual outlook as the first Isaiah a couple of generations before, voiced God's complaint against the people: "[D]ay after day they seek me and delight to know my ways, as if they were a nation that practiced righteousness and did not forsake the ordinance of their God; they ask of me righteous judgments, they delight to draw near to God" (Isa 58:2 NRSV). Meanwhile, the people were complaining, "'Why do we fast, but you do not see? Why humble ourselves, but you do not notice'" (Isa 58:3a–b NRSV)? The answer was that the religious practices of the people—their fasting and putting on sackcloth and ashes and whatever other rituals they were performing to try to get God's attention to their plight—were making no difference in their actual behavior toward *one another*—the same sort of behavior that had led God to allow the Babylonians to conquer Judah in the first place. "Look, you serve your own interest on your fast day, and oppress all your workers" (Isa 58:3c–d NRSV). According to the law, fasts meant not only refraining from eating, but ceasing labor as well. But while the upper class—the captains of Israel's economy—were making a public display of their own devoutness, they apparently were insisting that their working-class employees keep laboring, perhaps without a lunch break.

Just so, during Jesus' time, no one really expected the working class to keep the Torah—or to benefit from it—but only their wealthy employers. Speaking through the prophet, God had said, "Look, you fast only to quarrel and to fight and to strike with a wicked fist" (Isa 58:4a NRSV). Had fasts become occasions for falling into contention, trying to outdo one another in the ritual, or, perhaps, had businessmen decided not to permit *their* fasts to interfere with the normal competitive rough and tumble of their business dealings? Whatever the case, as far as the prophet was concerned, their fasting resulted in no difference in their behavior toward one another, which was far from honoring God. "Such fasting as you do today will not make your voice heard on high. Is such the fast that I choose, a *day* to humble oneself" (Isa 58:4b–5a NRSV)—and then leave it at that? "Is it to bow down the head like a bulrush, and to lie in sackcloth and ashes" (Isa 58:5b–c NRSV)—but then resume business as usual on the morrow? "Will you call this a fast, a day acceptable to the LORD" (Isa 58:5d NRSV)—that produces not genuine repentance, but only empty ceremony?

They knew the mechanics of fasting. They had the rituals down pat. But, content with the double standard that had developed, they were missing the entire point and were even *compounding* their sin. "Is not *this* the fast that I choose: to loose the bonds of injustice, to undo the thongs of the yoke, to let the oppressed go free, and to break every yoke" (Isa 58:6 NRSV)? Did they think that the goal was simply to refrain from eating for a day now and then and abstain from a few of their luxuries? "Is it not to share your bread with the hungry, and bring the homeless poor into your house; when you see the naked, to cover them, and not to hide yourself from your own kin" (Isa 58:7 NRSV)? If they would do *these* things, the whole purpose of God forming a people for himself would be fulfilled—to show all nations what God desires, and encourage them, with their behavior toward each other as well as their offerings in the temple, to honor the Creator of all:

> Then your light shall break forth like the dawn,
>   and your healing shall spring up quickly;
> your vindicator shall go before you,
>   the glory of the LORD shall be your rear guard.
> Then you shall call, and the LORD will answer;
>   you shall cry for help, and he will say, Here I am.
> If you remove the yoke from among you,
>   the pointing of the finger, the speaking of evil,
> if you offer your food to the hungry
>   and satisfy the needs of the afflicted,
> then your light shall rise in the darkness
>   and your gloom be like the noonday . . .
> Your ancient ruins shall be rebuilt;
>   you shall raise up the foundations of many generations;
> you shall be called the repairer of the breach,
>   the restorer of streets to live in. (Isa 58:8–10, 12 NRSV)

They would, in truth, be the salt of the earth, the light of the world, all as God had hoped and intended.

But, in fact, in Jesus' time, the disregard of the wealthy for the poor was every bit as evident as it had been during the time of Isaiah. Judah had been successively under the thumb of many heathen nations, and the chosen people, never willing fundamentally to change their ways of living with each other, had never again achieved greatness. God had done everything necessary to equip the people to fulfill their part in the redemption of the world. But greed and pride and jealousy, love of self and protection of one's own affluence, concern for one's own prestige rather than love for neighbor and attention to the needs of the poor and the powerless, crippled Israel's ability to be a beacon from which could stream the light of salvation.

And then came a teacher and healer from Nazareth in Galilee, a region despised by those who considered themselves to be ritually pure and spiritually superior, proclaiming to a crowd gathered on a mountainside one day:

> "You are the salt of the earth; but if salt has lost its taste, how can its saltiness be restored? It is no longer good for anything, but is thrown out and trampled underfoot.
>
> "You are the light of the world. A city built on a hill cannot be hid. No one after lighting a lamp puts it under the bushel basket, but on the lampstand, and it gives light to all in the house. In the same way, let your light shine before others, so that they may see your good works and give glory to your Father in heaven." (Matt 5:13–16 NRSV)

The people of Israel prayed to God. They looked to God for favor. They talked about God all the time. But were they acting as God *wanted* them to act? Did their lamps shed any *light*? Did their salt have any *flavor*?

> "Do not think that I have come to abolish the law or the prophets; I have come not to abolish but to fulfill. For truly I tell you, until heaven and earth pass away, not one *letter*, not one *stroke* of a letter, will pass from the law until all is accomplished. . . . [U]nless your righteousness exceeds that of the scribes and Pharisees, you will never enter the kingdom of heaven." (Matt 5:17–18, 20 NRSV)

God wants the same obedience from all people. There must be no double standard. But the *point* of the *law*, and certainly the point of such rituals as *fasting*, is to bend *our* will to match *God's* will, which means to set one's own desires aside in favor of serving others, and especially those who *already* have too little to eat, those whose shelter is uncertain, those whose clothing is thin, those whose rights are easily ignored—not to take food *away*, not to have yet *another* occasion for foreclosing and evicting and forcing out into the cold, not to use the courtroom to work what is *in*justice in the eyes of God. Worship and its rituals cannot be distinct from the life of justice and compassion. Did they want their nation to be blessed? The answer was not to observe the rituals but then to live by the standards of the world, not to fast and pray but then to adopt the habits of greed, but to practice in each and every interaction, on each and every day, what God intended for them—a righteousness that begins in ritual, but extends throughout life, and life together. So, what we do here today, gathered for prayer, gathered for praise, gathered to hear God's word, gathered to share God's goodness, should mold our lives in the ways of God and equip us for discipleship in home, in workplace, in school, in government, in courtroom, in marketplace. There must be no double standard.

Sixth Sunday in Ordinary Time

First Presbyterian Church, Dodge City, Kansas

February 11, 1996

Deuteronomy 30:15–20
1 Corinthians 3:1–9
Matthew 5:21–37

"The Point of the Game"

It's almost spring—or at least it feels like it, compared with a couple of weeks ago. For the Taylor family, that means that it is almost baseball season. The attorneys and agents are already in spring training, I understand. Shortly, the players will be making their appearance or will announce that they are holding out, and owners will decide whether America will have its pastime this year. Jesse and I will soon again be spending some time playing ball in the vacant lot next door to our house, I hope, if the wind stays down enough that our trash-cart backstop doesn't blow away. Jesse and I went to the Baseball Hall of Fame last year, and he is already talking about going to see it again this year, since, as he says, the only part of it that he remembers is the bathroom. Before that, of course, we will be checking the television schedules to try to see our favorite teams; if we do go back to the Hall of Fame someday, we will plan the trip in order to see a game or two on the way and back.

A new feature of our baseball routine this year will be a Major League Baseball rulebook, which my wife got for Jesse and me at Christmas. There have been occasions, from time to time, when I wished that I had had the rules handy, and to read for *myself* the rationale for certain calls by the umpire. So far, I have only leafed through the book a few times, but, already, something about the official rulebook impresses me. The game of baseball obviously has a lot of rules, but the rules do not make the game. The game is played on real grass (some of the time) in real weather conditions (most of the time) by unpredictable people who have a variety of personalities and physical abilities (all of the time). The rules speak about the scoring effect of certain situations encountered during the play of baseball, but the rules do not really describe *how* to play baseball, and the rules do not *begin* to convey why people enjoy playing it and why people enjoy watching it and what makes a good game and what makes a poor game. They say nothing about whether a runner should try to stretch a single into a double. They say nothing about whether a fielder should decline an easy out at first in order to try to save a run at home. They say nothing about whether the manager should leave in a shaky rookie pitcher in order to try to build his confidence by getting one more out. They say nothing about whether the manager should allow an aging veteran one more time at the plate to show that he can still work some magic with a bat. The rules do not tell you how to play baseball. The rules are not what the game is about.

Now, a lot of preachers at this point would be tempted to say, "Life is like baseball." (It is.) But what our Gospel reading today concerns is the relationship between the rulebook and the game. Not only in baseball, but in every sport, and not only in sport, but in the way we live each day, the rulebook is not the point of the game. The matter is nowhere more dramatically expressed than in Jesus' teaching to the crowd gathered one day on the side of a mountain when the *living* Word of God commented on the *written* word of God in these terms: "You have heard that it was said . . . . But *I* say to you . . ." (Matt 5:21a, 22a NRSV). Had Jesus been preaching to fans gathered in a baseball park among the smells and tastes of peanuts and hot dogs, he might have said, "You know what the rulebook says. But I want to tell you what the game is all about." And he went on to speak about situations in life in terms that applied the rules—the laws found in the Old Testament—more broadly than any teacher had ever done before him, and so *radicalized* the commandments of God—so got to the *root* of God's commandments as not to allow anyone to escape the sweep of God's purpose for creation.

The Pharisees and the scribes and others prided themselves on observing the letter of the law in all respects, and yet it is certainly clear in the Gospels that, in the very scrupulousness of these legalists, they never understood God's intent that lay at the root of the law. They did not make mercy and generosity their guiding standards. Compassionate love was not their motive in dealing with other people. Putting the *needs* of others ahead of their own *desires* was *not* how *they* lived. Ultimately, in what they regarded as defense of the *written* word of God, they even destroyed Jesus, the *living* Word of God. They supported the death penalty. They denounced women caught in adultery. They observed the legal niceties about divorce.

They were certainly careful not to break any promise given under oath. They knew the rulebook from cover to cover, and yet they missed the entire point of the game. "Do not think that I have come to abolish the law or the prophets. . . . For I tell you, unless your righteousness *exceeds* that of the scribes and Pharisees, you will never enter the kingdom of heaven" (Matt 5:17a, 20 NRSV). "I have not come to abolish," said Jesus, "but to fulfill" (Matt 5:17b NRSV). Righteousness is the key to entering the kingdom of heaven, Jesus says here, but it is a righteousness that goes far beyond simply abiding by the *rules* of the game. Indeed, if we understand Jesus to have been issuing a new and better set of *rules* when he talked about anger and lust and divorce and oaths, we face the very same danger that the scribes and Pharisees faced with the laws of the *Old* Testament—the danger of supposing that a life of following the *rules* is the same thing as a life of *faith*.

Jesus didn't add to the rules or subtract from the rules or replace the rules. Jesus shifted the focus to the point of the game:

> "You have heard that it was said to those of ancient times, 'You shall not murder'; and 'whoever murders shall be liable to judgment.' But I say to you that if you are *angry* with a brother or sister, you will be liable to judgment; and if you insult a brother or sister, you will be liable to the council; and if you say, 'You fool,' you will be liable to the hell of fire. . . .
>
> "You have heard that it was said, 'You shall not commit adultery.' But I say to you that everyone who looks at a woman with lust has already committed adultery with her in his heart. . . .
>
> "It was also said, 'Whoever divorces his wife, let him give her a certificate of divorce.' But I say to you that anyone who divorces his wife, except on the ground of unchastity, causes her to commit adultery. . . .
>
> "Again, you have heard that it was said to those of ancient times, 'You shall not swear falsely, but carry out the vows you have made to the Lord.' But I say to you, do not swear at all."
> (Matt 5:21-22, 27-28, 31-32b, 33-34b NRSV)

The rules are there in black and white, but they only hint at what a life faithful to God is all about. The law is what one follows to avoid punishment for one's own actions, but life in fellowship with God as a faithful follower of Jesus Christ is life that springs from the much higher motive of living for the benefit of others.

Jesus shifts our attention away from ourselves, and our little strivings to be safe from reproach, and puts it upon the other person in each of our relationships—on whether that person's life is being whittled away by our thoughts and our conduct. It is no longer a question of our claiming our rights, but one of our offering our love. Far less can we ever justify allowing *our desires* to stand in the way of *someone else's needs*. At best, the rules—the law—dictate the *minimum* behavior for *earthly* society to function. Jesus told the crowd, and *Matthew* is telling *us*, that a life worthy of the kingdom of God is one that envisions a much broader horizon of responsibility *to* others and *for* others. All anger and hostility are outside the bounds of the kingdom. All gifts from God are to be used according to *God's* purpose and intention—including the gift of sex; the gifts of God are not our private possession, but must be treated as a stewardship. All people are entitled to the inherent dignity with which God created them—female as well as male; no one should be regarded as another person's property—that is why the custom of "giving away the bride" is disappearing from marriage services in favor of affirmations of support for the marriage by family and friends, for "giving away the bride" is a vestige of transferring the woman as an item of property from her father to her husband. All oath-taking and oath-making should be *superfluous* for a *Christian*, whose word must *always* be truthful and who must *never* even *entertain* the possibility of saying something *un*truthful, or as gossip.

Fulfilling such a standard of attitude and behavior may seem impossible among imperfect people in a fallen world. It is the reason that we so often resort to sets of rules that are more conducive to measuring performance, less subject to the uncertainties of human motive, less dependent upon our reading of the human heart. But whenever legalism takes over, we, like the scribes and Pharisees, invariably *miss* the *point* of the game. Then we mistake the rules for the object, and consider the effect upon *us* and *our salvation* to be more important than the effect upon *other people* and *their welfare*. Only *love* can fulfill the commands of God—love for God and love for others, love which does not seek to gain anything for itself but only to pour itself out in words and deeds of kindness and generosity and self-sacrifice, love which does not count the cost, but counts only the need. And our model for that kind of love is Jesus Christ. His life, death, and resurrection are the entrance for his followers into the kingdom of God, where that kind of love is the common currency.

No set of laws can cover all of the cases. Our response of genuine love in a particular situation might well push us into waters as yet uncharted by codes and formulas and best left without hard and fast rules. God's commands cannot be fulfilled by an exhaustive research of case law to make certain that we are safe from error. Jesus came to free us from trying to justify ourselves. Jesus came to liberate us from constant introspection and from dwelling on our own imperfection. Jesus came to enable us to live a life that is totally devoted to our neighbors. Jesus came to prompt us to get our noses out of the rulebook and get ourselves out on the field to play ball. The point of the game is to live every moment genuinely, to respond to every person lovingly, to give everything we have for the sake of others faithfully. The point of the game is to be the people God intended us to be, as he has shown us in Jesus Christ.

Seventh Sunday in Ordinary Time

First Presbyterian Church, Ponca City, Oklahoma

February 23, 2014

Leviticus 19:1–2, 9–18
1 Corinthians 3:10–11, 16–23
Matthew 5:38–48

"Holiness"

I don't know exactly how it happened, but somewhere back in the early centuries of Christianity, a large number of preachers and other theologians, and then the people who *heard* what they *said* and *read* what they *wrote*, came to assume that the language of the Bible is only and always to be taken in a spiritual sense. That is, a lot of folks came to believe and teach that whenever the Bible uses concrete words and images, they are really only allegories. The words of scripture, they assumed, were not to be taken literally, but stand for some spiritual truth. According to that approach to interpreting the Bible, when Jesus commands this or that, he is to be understood only figuratively.

Fortunately, many later theologians and biblical scholars ultimately realized that the Bible frequently means exactly what it says. Sometimes, rather obviously, Jesus intended a spiritual meaning. Sometimes, rather obviously, Jesus exaggerated in order to set forth a spiritual truth. But, when a *literal* meaning requires us to do something that is inconvenient or uncomfortable, many people even today still take refuge in the possibility, hope, that the Bible is really only interested in *spiritual* matters. We know that when Jesus described himself as the bread of life that has come down from heaven, he wasn't suggesting that we can find him packaged in a Wonder Bread wrapper and sitting on the grocery shelf—not even a Roman Meal wrapper. But some people think, then, that they can excuse their failure to follow his teaching, "[F]or I was hungry and you gave me food.... Truly I tell you, just as you did it to one of the least of these who are members of my family, you did it to me" (Matt 25:35a, 40 NRSV), on the grounds that Jesus must really have been talking about sharing the *gospel*, not literally giving from our table to feed the poor. Some find it easy to overlook the beatitude in *Luke* which says quite plainly, "*Blessed* are you who are *hungry* now, for you will be *filled*.... *Woe* to you who are *full* now, for you will be *hungry*" (Luke 6:21a, 25a NRSV), in favor of *Matthew's* seemingly more *spiritual* "Blessed are those who hunger and thirst for *righteousness*, for they will be filled" (Matt 5:6 NRSV). So they ignore the *woe* that Jesus pronounced upon those who have grasped not only their *own* share of food, but the *hungry* person's share as well. And when Jesus fed the multitude who were hungry—an event reported in each of the Gospels—our hasty speculation about how Jesus *worked* the miracle causes us to ignore the most obvious point of the story: that Jesus, whom we are supposed to *imitate* and whose ministry we are supposed to *continue* and *expand, fed the hungry*!

Several years ago, I discovered in a Bible study session that the verse that stands at the very middle of the Pentateuch, the Torah, the first five books of the Bible that all through history have been recognized as being a special collection of writings that somehow all belong together and are read all the way through every year in each Jewish synagogue, is astonishingly concrete in its subject matter. By itself, it doesn't appear to represent high *spiritual* truth. Instead, it's a commandment that is about as mundane as we can get, concerns a matter that some people wonder is even *in* a book as holy as the Bible: "You shall not defraud your neighbor; you shall not steal; and you shall not keep for yourself the wages of a laborer until morning" (Lev 19:13 NRSV). God commands that the worker is to be paid at the end of each day's work.

Were you aware that there was even such a law *in* the Bible? Did you know that it has the prominence of being at the exact *center* of the five books of the law? Have you ever heard a *sermon* about paying employees daily at the end of their shift? Did you think that the *New* Testament makes all such antique requirements irrelevant? "Do not think that I have come to abolish the law or the prophets," Jesus said;

> "I have come not to *abolish* but to *fulfill*. For truly I tell you, until heaven and earth pass away, not one letter, not one stroke of a letter, will pass from the law until all is accomplished. Therefore, whoever breaks one of the least of these commandments, and teaches others to do the same, will be called *least* in the kingdom of heaven; but whoever does them and teaches them will

be called *great* in the kingdom of heaven. For I tell you, unless your righteousness *exceeds* that of the scribes and Pharisees, you will never enter the kingdom of heaven." (Matt 5:17b–20 NRSV)

Now, there are a lot of peculiar rules and statutes in the law of Moses. Many of them we have become accustomed to dismissing as quaint relics of an unenlightened age that was overly concerned with meaningless details, and not just us *Christians*, but *Jews* as *well*. But Jesus' words in the Sermon on the Mount are a caution against our easy disregard and habit of spiritualizing into virtual irrelevance much that is remarkably specific about daily life and interpersonal relations. And no matter how we may rationalize, for instance, not going to the inconvenience of paying workers at the end of each work day for the work they have performed, the importance of their employees being able to buy food each day and secure shelter each night surely requires of employers *more* than just spiritual reflection. This law exposes the unfairness not only of *employers*, but also of *banks* and even *governments* that make interest off *of* or take investment risks *with* money that *really belongs* and should already have been *paid* or *refunded* to the worker, the depositor, the taxpayer. And the fact that such practices have become routine and accepted doesn't mean that God has rescinded the commandment.

And what about this one, just a few verses previous to the very center of the Torah: "When you reap the harvest of your land, you shall not reap to the very edges of your field, or gather the gleanings of your harvest. You shall not strip your vineyard bare, or gather the fallen grapes of your vineyard; you shall leave them for the poor and the alien: I am the Lord your God" (Lev 19:9–10 NRSV). In wheat country, we sometimes see a combination harvester and thresher made of unpainted galvanized metal and bearing the name "Gleaner." The very name is an advertisement that *this* brand of combine will harvest the entire crop, and leave very little if any grain behind in the field. The subliminal message is that the farmer who buys a *Gleaner* combine will maximize his efficiency, and therefore will maximize his profit. But the farmer for whom maximizing efficiency is the principal goal, for whom maximizing profit is the prime concern, has not taken to heart the law about making sure that he leaves enough behind in the field for the poor to gather and live on. No matter what the *deed says*, the field *ultimately belongs* to *God*. God's interest in planting and watering is that *everyone* will have enough to eat.

The fact that less than 2 percent of Americans are engaged in raising food does not make this commandment irrelevant for the rest of us. God's concern that the poor be cared for is just as strong in an *industrial* or *service* economy as in an *agricultural* one. *Everybody* needs to *eat*. What does the commandment mean for the shareholders and managers of the modern high-tech corporation that looks for every conceivable way to eliminate jobs by mechanization or computerization, or by paying for overtime rather than hiring an additional employee? Has some *other* allegiance or rule or maxim taken precedence in our society that makes it convenient to spiritualize or to ignore altogether what seem to be pretty concrete and straightforward statutes of God? Their location in the books of the law suggests rather strikingly that God takes seriously *especially* those laws designed to protect the poor and the working class and others who are vulnerable to abuse and unfair treatment, those who are easily pushed to the sidelines of society.

These laws, important as they must be to be put at the center of the Torah, are but a few that are listed in a section of Leviticus that is concerned with holy behavior. The chapter *begins* with God's instruction to Moses that he declare to God's people, "You shall be holy, for I the Lord your God am holy" (Lev 19:2b NRSV). Some of the laws are essentially restatements of the Ten Commandments. Some are expansions or interpretations; in a way, the commandment to leave enough in the field and the vineyard for the poor derives from the commandment, "You shall not steal," because harvesting *everything* means taking away from the poor the gleanings that they need to survive, the part of the harvest—all of which ultimately belongs to God—that God destined for the *hungry poor*. The holiness of God has to do with loving fully and indiscriminately. And *we* are to be holy as *God* is holy. Did you hear the final words in our Old Testament reading this morning, and how they follow upon each other? "[Y]ou shall love your neighbor as yourself: I am the Lord" (Lev 19:18b NRSV). Those two things—our obligation to love neighbor as self and the true identity of God—are related to each other. We, *God's people*, are to be holy because *God* is holy. In concrete terms, holiness means that we are to love our neighbor as ourselves, because *God's* holiness is all about how God loves *us*. All the individual laws, all of the details of behavior, are not just quaint relics of the bygone era of a primitive religion designed for simple-minded people living in a pre-industrial age. They are the nuts and bolts of how we are to behave toward each other, what it means to love our neighbor.

The word "holiness" has *itself* been over-spiritualized through the centuries, made to imply something different from how the Bible actually describes it. While, at root, holiness means to be *set apart*, it doesn't mean to be *untouchable*. While, at root, holiness means to be *distinct* from, it doesn't mean to be *aloof* from or *unresponsive* to the physical needs of human beings, or of *other* creatures, or of the earth itself. It is not what is *popularly* thought of as spiritual, all halos and harps and mapping the geography of heaven. God's holiness is the central characteristic of God that compels God to be profoundly involved in providing for everything and everyone that God has created. And the holiness to which Leviticus *summons us*, holiness as *Jesus* understood it, has to do first and foremost with the way people who *answer* God's injunction to holiness treat one another, and not just the neighbor next door, or the neighbor whom we see at church, or the neighbor whom we meet at our polling place, but the neighbor who lives half way around the world and speaks a different language and sleeps in the gutter—the neighbor who has never had an opportunity to save up, and therefore who needs *tonight* what he or she has earned *today*, the neighbor who could easily be cheated because he or she is not as *sophisticated* or not as *educated* or not as *experienced* as *we*, the neighbor who receives *too little* when *we* take *too much*.

If we are holy, as God is holy, our behavior will not be motivated by that to which *we* are *entitled*, but by that which our *neighbor needs* from us. "Be perfect, therefore, as your heavenly Father is perfect" (Matt 5:48 NRSV), Jesus said in the Sermon on the Mount, summing up his teaching to offer the other cheek, to give up the last garment, to carry the burden an additional mile, to love one's enemies, and to pray for one's persecutors. Indeed, that is what it *really* means to be concerned with *spiritual* matters. That is what it *really* means to be *holy*. And when Jesus, the holy one, finished his great sermon, he came down from the mountain, and immediately began to heal people's sickness, to cast out the demons plaguing their lives, and to feed those who were hungry.

Eighth Sunday in Ordinary Time

Spanish Springs Presbyterian Church, Sparks, Nevada

February 27, 2011

Isaiah 49:8–16a
1 Corinthians 4:1–5
Matthew 6:24–34

"To Believe and to Trust"

If Matthew is at all accurate in his reporting of the Sermon on the Mount, a speech three chapters long that Jesus delivered somewhere in the Galilean hinterland, the Savior's audience must have been people who did not have much in the way of pressing obligations, people whose lives were not tied to the clock, so to speak. They must not have been the people who were the Israelite equivalent of captains of industry and commerce. They were more likely people of modest means, living rather humble lives, some of them getting employment as they could for a day or a week at a time, perhaps as laborers in the fields and vineyards, maybe some fisherfolk, maybe some tradesmen, maybe even some children and youth among the crowd. It probably was not a very close mirror of the typical modern suburban congregation. We today tend to have many pressing obligations, do indeed live by the clock, most of us, are owners and managers of businesses, live, some of us, in houses many times the square footage of the typical Galilean cottage, could likely ill afford to be out on the mountainside listening to an itinerant preacher on what was probably a workday, not the sabbath.

But some of what Jesus taught that day sounds, to *our* ears, more appropriate for the *powerful* and the *affluent* than for poor *peasants*. "No one can serve two masters; for a slave will either hate the one and love the other, or be devoted to the one and despise the other. You cannot serve God and wealth" (Matt 6:24 NRSV). Logically, Jesus' audience that day was not in danger of serving wealth, certainly not in the amount of money and possessions that *we* would all consider enough to constitute wealth: "Therefore I tell you, do not worry about your life, what you will eat or what you will drink, or about your body, what you will wear" (Matt 6:25a NRSV). And yet, while Jesus was preaching this to the poor who might have been able to come out to hear him that day, we imagine that worrying about the future and providing for it was *exactly* what would have been on the minds of the people whose responsibilities meant that they *couldn't* spend the day on a mountainside in Galilee—merchants, industrialists, professionals. So, in fact, wasn't Jesus being rather *cruel* when he was preaching that day, probably to the poor who didn't have much money to their name, the humble who would have had very little in the way of possessions, that they shouldn't fritter their lives away worrying about making money and more money, dressing smartly and better than their neighbor, eating well and far more than was absolutely necessary to be healthy? Surely this was a teaching more appropriate for those whose very homes and dining tables and closets showed how concerned they *were* about wealth! Surely *those* were the people who needed to be warned about not serving two masters, and who gave every indication that they were more interested in serving *greed* than *God*!

The teachings of Jesus on this and every occasion were appropriate for the affluent and the powerful. But the poor and the humble are in the position of having to be concerned *not* just with the things that pose spiritual dangers to the *rich* and the *influential*—gluttony, greed, injustice, indifference—but the *additional* danger of *envy*, and the *very* real danger of *anxiety*—much more than the rich and the influential for whom a day's drop in income does not forebode homelessness or nakedness or starvation, but merely a delay in gratification, or at most a scaling back of what will still be good living. "Is not life more than food, and the body more than clothing" (Matt 6:25b NRSV)? Well, for the wealthy and the powerful, life can mean yachts and villas and holidays in exotic places. For those who most likely were *listening* to Jesus on the mountainside that day, life pretty much *was* food and clothing and shelter, all very basic, all very necessary. The rich and well-connected in fact had such resources that they could pretty much care for *themselves*. But the people of the Galilean hill country were on a scale of dependence rather closer to the birds of the air and the lilies of the field. It was for *them* that Jesus had an important reminder, good news that they needed to grasp and hold on to:

> "Look at the birds of the air; they neither sow nor reap nor gather into barns, and yet your heavenly Father feeds them. Are you

not of more value than they? And can any of you by worrying add a single hour to your span of life? And why do you worry about clothing? Consider the lilies of the field, how they grow; they neither toil nor spin, yet I tell you, even Solomon in all his glory was not clothed like one of these. But if God so clothes the grass of the field, which is alive today and tomorrow is thrown into the oven, will he not much more clothe you—you of little faith?" (Matt 6:26–30 NRSV)

It has long been the habit of biblical interpreters and others who are generally well fed and adequately housed to *romanticize* the poor. Blessed are the poor, many of us think, for they are closer to God. And we don't mean by that the slightest sarcasm or paternalism, but really suppose it is so. Still, we don't covet such a close relationship with God that we would be willing to exchange social positions with them. One of the reasons is, we are fearful that such a life would *indeed* cause us to "worry, saying, 'What will we eat?' or 'What will we drink?' or 'What will we wear'" (Matt 6:31 NRSV)? For it isn't, in fact, *only* the *Gentiles*, or shall we say the *non*believers, the *non*tithers, the *non*church members, who strive for all these things.

The most important point that Jesus was making here is one that can easily be read over, lost in the sentimental imagery of birds of the air and lilies of the field. "[I]ndeed," Jesus said, "your heavenly Father knows that you need all these things" (Matt 6:32b NRSV)—referring to food and clothing and life's other necessities. "[D]o not worry," Jesus had said. You have no reason to, if you *believe*, and if you *trust*—if you believe that God *created* you, as God created birds and flowers, for which God cares enough to provide, and if you trust that you, too, are *important* to God. And here, again, the message was especially pertinent for the poor and the humble, those who seem habitually to be at the bottom of the ladder in life, those who are most likely, because of the way that *society* treats and regards them, to think that *God, too,* holds them in little regard.

For Jesus even to have to have preached such a message to the crowd that day was a judgment upon the people who weren't there to hear it. The poor and the humble probably had good reason to suspect that God might have little regard for them—they had heard it so often from the people who stood on a higher rung on the social ladder, they had experienced it so often in the way they were treated by people of means and authority; even their religious leaders sometimes implied that their station in life was a punishment for sin, the sin of laziness, the sin of having been born into the wrong family, some hidden sin that would continue to plague them until proper atonement was made. And it raises for *us* the question, what attitudes do *we* display, what words do *we* speak, what deeds do *we* do or *refrain* from doing, that might lead the poor and humble of our *own* day to suspect that God doesn't really care about them? Jesus assured his listeners that they were children of God, and that God, like a good parent, cares and will provide.

The fact that birds neither reap nor gather into barns, the fact that flowers neither toil nor spin, isn't offered for us to imitate, but rather as a powerful example and assurance of God's providential love. Jesus was not instructing his listeners to be passive, certainly not excusing them from seeking employment or doing their best at their job. He *was* calling them to believe *implicitly*, and to trust *completely*. Jesus was issuing a summons not to spend life worrying. That is not what God created us for. And *anxiety* shows that we in fact *doubt* God's creation, *doubt* God's love, *doubt* God's power, *doubt* God's promise. God did not give us life in order to abandon us. The God who made our bodies and endowed us with a soul will certainly attend to the things that are of lesser value than these—of lesser value, but important just the same.

A few chapters later, *after* the Sermon on the Mount, Matthew says that Jesus summoned his twelve disciples and gave them authority to go out and minister, and there Matthew gives us the disciples' names. Already, though, *before* the Sermon on the Mount, Matthew tells us that Jesus called various disciples, and they stopped what they were doing and immediately followed him. Not many, if any of them, were well-schooled professionals, but they did all have livelihoods and other responsibilities. Now they were venturing radical reliance on the goodness of God. Now they were leaving behind the occupations by which they had attempted to provide for themselves. Now they were like the poor and the powerless, whom society usually disregarded and sometimes despised, these followers to whom Jesus was giving *authority* over *demons* and *diseases*, these followers to whom Jesus would entrust *forgiveness* of *sins* and *entrance* into the kingdom of *heaven*. Theirs would not be a life of ease and plenty, but their experience, as they traveled with Jesus through Galilee and down to Jerusalem, and after the resurrection carried the gospel to faraway corners of the world, was that God was dependable indeed, that what was needful for their vocation was always supplied. They learned in the most basic way the truth of what Jesus had said: "[S]trive first for the kingdom of God and his righteousness, and all these things will be given to you as well" (Matt 6:33 NRSV). And so anyone who would follow Jesus Christ is assured of the same thing, despite the privations, despite the persecution, even. God is greater than our needs. The kingdom of God is of greater worth than worldly fortune and comfort. And each of us—rich and poor alike, the powerful and the humble—was *created* by God, is *known* by God, is *valued* by God, will be *cared for* by God. Contrary to the heretical promises of those who preach the health-and-wealth gospel, trusting in God is not a strategy for being free from disease or gaining earthly treasure—none of the apostles died wealthy, and they *did* all *die*. But trusting God to provide *does* allow us to be free from anxiety about the things that are *secondary* in life—the *means*—so that we may concentrate on what is *primary*—the *purpose*. Without such trust, the disciples of old could never have done what Jesus commissioned them to do. Nor, without such trust, can *we*. And among the things that Jesus has commissioned *us* to do is to care for the poor and the powerless.

The first disciples, and the apostles after them, received hospitality from people who had wealth and influence but were free enough from anxiety that they were able to put them at the service of the gospel. The way that God met the needs of the *disciples* is the *same* way that God meets the needs of the *poor* and the *powerless*—through the generous and merciful love of people who *have*, but for whom *having* is not the *goal*. Jesus assured his hearers that, in God's sight, the poor are of more value than birds and flowers, whose life demonstrates God's continuing care. But God's care no longer drops out of the sky like manna, but through human instruments, people who are so trusting of God's promises, of God's power, of God's goodness and love, that they can freely part with what the poor need, can freely share food and clothing, even authority and prestige.

The original audience for Jesus' words might well have been the poor and humble, but Jesus summons those of us who read and hear them today who are affluent and influential, who have no need ourselves to be concerned about life's basic needs, to identify with and have compassion for people who have every logical reason to be anxious about such things, and to turn our efforts toward embodying God's loving concern for the world's have-nots. Unbelievers, Jesus said, both rich and poor, set their sights on amassing their own security. "[I]t is the Gentiles who strive for all these things" (Matt 6:32a NRSV). But people who believe they are God's own creation, people who trust God's promises of providential care, are not to be *like* the Gentiles. Instead, they will know that life does not consist of reaping and spinning, but will be grateful for daily bread and simple shelter, and confidently share in trust that God, our loving Father who knows what we need, will provide again *tomorrow* what God has provided *today*. As a prophet put it in another context, speaking of God's trustworthy care for all of God's people: "Can a woman forget her nursing child, or show no compassion for the child of her womb? Even these may forget, yet I will never forget you. See, I have inscribed you on the palms of my hands" (Isa 49:15–16a NRSV).

We can spend a lifetime fretting over how we shall live, and come to the end of life having never lived it. That isn't why God gave us the gift of life.

In fact, that attitude rather shows a lack of gratitude for the gifts that God does provide, including the gift of life itself. Very little of Jesus' teachings, very few of his deeds, will make any sense to us if we don't accept the invitation to believe and to trust. "Therefore I tell you," said Jesus, "do not worry about your life" (Matt 6:25a NRSV).

Transfiguration of the Lord

Spanish Springs Presbyterian Church, Sparks, Nevada

February 3, 2008

Exodus 24:12–18
2 Peter 1:16–21
Matthew 17:1–9

"The Light that Shines Brightest in All the Dark Places"

"As they were coming down the mountain, Jesus ordered them, 'Tell no one about the vision until *after* the Son of Man has been raised from the dead'" (Matt 17:9 NRSV). Presumably, the three disciples who were with Jesus on the mountain *followed* Jesus' instruction. Presumably, they didn't tell *anyone* about the amazing spectacle of Jesus' face shining like the sun and his clothes becoming dazzling white, nor of the miraculous appearance of Moses and Elijah talking with him, nor even of the voice speaking from the cloud overshadowing them, "This is my Son, the Beloved; with him I am well pleased; listen to him" (Matt 17:5b NRSV)! Good thing, because they undoubtedly would have *misinterpreted* what they had seen.

In fact, they *did* misinterpret it—*Peter* did, anyway, when he suggested that the final age had arrived, and that he and the others could live eternally in its light. The *Transfiguration* was not the great day *itself*—only an assurance and foretaste. Shrines, booths, dwellings were not appropriate; there were many miles to traverse before the final day, many needs to fill, and as it turned out, many sufferings to be endured. Much later, Peter could refer back to the extraordinary privilege of having been present for the event at Jesus' invitation: "[H]e received honor and glory from God the Father when that voice was conveyed to him by the Majestic Glory, saying, 'This is my Son, my Beloved, with whom I am well pleased.' We ourselves heard this

"The Light that Shines Brightest in All the Dark Places"

voice come from heaven, while we were with him on the holy mountain" (2 Pet 1:17–18 NRSV). And Peter understood now the *meaning* of the event: "So we have the prophetic message more fully confirmed" (2 Pet 1:19a NRSV).

"Why didn't people believe?" I am often asked. "They saw the miracles, they heard the words. They should have understood that the prophecies were being fulfilled." Faith cannot be forced, not even by God. And, in fact, it seems from the Bible that God doesn't *want* to force belief upon anyone. So two people can be present at the same healing, or at the same extraordinary catch of fish, or at the same pouring of exceptional wine from jars known to hold nothing more uncommon than water, and they can be in the same crowd and hear the same words spoken, the same teachings, the same parables, and yet *one* will *understand* and the *other won't*. That is the nature of revelation. The bright cloud that suddenly appeared and overshadowed the company at the top of the mountain at the same instant both *revealed* God and *concealed* God—indicated God's presence, and yet shrouded God in mystery. And even the disciples—Jesus' most constant companions and his closest observers—while being mightily impressed that this event revealed the unique importance of Jesus, still didn't understand what that importance *was*. They *wouldn't* understand, and apparently they *couldn't* understand, until the story was *complete*—until Jesus had been to Jerusalem, had suffered at the hands of his enemies, had died even, and had been raised from the tomb. And between the Mount of Transfiguration and the hill called Golgotha, there were a lot of dark places of sorrow and frustration and misery and despair where the light of God in Jesus first had to shine.

The fact is that neither *you*, nor *I*, nor *anybody* can know the *truth* about Jesus Christ unless we take the time to *listen* to him, as the voice from heaven said, and make the voluntary decision to *follow* him. "This is my Son, the Beloved; with him I am well pleased; listen to him" (Matt 17:5b NRSV)! commanded the voice from the cloud. And after the wondrous vision was over, "Jesus came and touched them" (Matt 17:7a NRSV)—Peter, James, and John—and they followed him back down the mountain, and they came to a crowd where Jesus cured a boy who was possessed by a demon. We don't know, we can't know, Jesus in a vacuum, separate and apart from his teachings and ministry. We don't know, we can't know, Jesus as the Son of God and the Savior of the world, unless we are actively following him and doing the same sorts of things that *Jesus* did and commanded his *disciples* to do.

I was first exposed to the writings of Albert Schweitzer through the words of an anthem that I sang with the high school choir of my home church—words from his very noteworthy book, *The Quest of the Historical Jesus*:

> He comes to us as One unknown, without a name, as of old, by the lake-side, He came to those men who knew him not. He speaks to us the same word: 'Follow thou me!' and sets us to the tasks which he has to fulfil for our time. He commands. *And to those who obey Him*, whether they be wise or simple, He will reveal Himself in the toils, the conflicts, the sufferings which they shall pass through in His fellowship, and, as an ineffable mystery, they shall learn in their own experience Who He is.[1]

Schweitzer's observation from more than a century ago is not only a condemnation of the fluff that is being passed off as Christianity today in too many places and by too many preachers and composers. It seems to me that it is also an astute commentary on the truth about Jesus Christ that is shown in the Transfiguration episode. And it is a truth that Schweitzer himself lived.

Most people today know of Albert Schweitzer as a medical missionary in Africa. But before that, he was a pastor in Strasbourg, a lecturer at Strasbourg University, and the principal of a theological college. He was also an accomplished musician and interpreter of Johann Sebastian Bach; his organ recitals were popular, and his edition is still considered the definitive version of Bach's compositions for the organ. It was not until after writing three of the most important theological books of his time that Albert Schweitzer received his medical degree, and in 1913, he turned away from the academic life. His conscience stricken by the white man's responsibility for the Dark Continent, Schweitzer abandoned promising European careers in music, medicine, and theology to devote himself at Lambaréné in French Equatorial Africa to the care of the sick and to missionary activities. He was interned in France during World War I, but after returning to Strasbourg for a few years following his release, he went again to Lambaréné and restored the hospital, which remained his principal work during the rest of his life. There, he encountered terrible diseases and wretched living conditions, but focused upon them the brightness of the gospel—Christlike *deeds* as well as Jesus' *words*—which shined that much brighter in the overwhelming darkness. In 1953, he was awarded the Nobel Peace Prize.

Matthew begins his telling of the Transfiguration with the words, "Six days later . . . " (Matt 17:1a NRSV). Like all of the Gospel writers, Matthew was an artist and a theologian. He wrote nothing that was without meaning for him. "Six days later," Jesus took three of his disciples up a mountain. Immediately, as people familiar with the Old Testament, we are reminded of *Moses* taking three of his assistants with him up on the mountain where

---

1. Schweitzer, *Quest of the Historical Jesus*, 403 (emphasis added).

he encountered God, and "[t]he glory of the LORD settled on Mount Sinai, and the cloud covered it for six days" (Ex 24:16a NRSV) before, on the *seventh* day, the glory of the Lord spoke to Moses from the cloud, bright as a fire. Matthew wanted his readers to associate Jesus' climb up the Mount of Transfiguration with Moses' trip up Mount Sinai. But the words "six days later" *also* tie the Transfiguration to whatever Jesus was doing six days before it *happened*—what Matthew reported just before this incident. And *that* was Peter's declaring in the Gentile region of Caesarea Philippi that Jesus was "the Messiah, the Son of the living God" (Matt 16:16 NRSV), *and* Jesus declaring to his disciples that he must undergo great suffering at the hands of the elders and chief priests and scribes and be killed, and on the third day be raised, and his pronouncement that those who want to become his followers have to deny themselves and take up their cross and follow him, being prepared and willing to lose their lives for his sake.

Why was it so important for Matthew to tie the Transfiguration—this exceptional but short-lived revelation of Jesus' glory—to all *that*, and then to show Jesus immediately coming down the mountain to the crowd and curing a boy of his epilepsy? For much the same reason, I think, that Jesus told his disciples they mustn't tell anyone about the vision until after the crucifixion and resurrection. They, like so many Christians today, would be tempted to seize on the spectacular moment and make much of the glory of Christ without in the least bit understanding what his glory consists of— that it has no substance apart from Jesus' servanthood, has no point apart from Jesus' ministry, has no correct interpretation apart from his death on the cross and God's raising him from the tomb, just like singing today about Jesus' shining glory has no substance apart from his unglamorous work of healing the afflicted and curing the diseased (all of whom were suspected of being sinners), just like waving arms in the air today has no point apart from obedience to his teachings about ministering to the poor and the outcast and forgiving the unpopular and the notorious, just like praising his sacrifice has no truth to it unless it prompts us likewise to pour out ourselves for the sake of Christ Jesus and those he loves. It is like going up *another* mountain—Mount Zion, the place of the temple, and, by extension, the place where Christ is worshiped *today*, the *church*—and being mightily impressed by a glimpse of Christ's glory, wanting to enshrine it, perpetuate it, bottle it up, if you will, but then going back out into the world unfazed by the scandal of hunger and the tragedy of disease and the obscenity of war, heedless of Christ's call to follow him as cross-bearers through all the dark places heavy with death and shining upon them the light of the resurrection. By weaving together these scenes here, Matthew is attempting to grab the church by the lapels and shake it and say, "Don't you understand who Jesus Christ *is*, and what that demands of *us*?" Much more than a self-satisfying shout of "Yes, Jesus!" it requires a rolling up of sleeves, a touching of festering wounds, a willingness to wade through the toxic muck of real human distress, and affirming, "I have heard Jesus, the Son of God, and I am here to bear witness to his shining brightness, to testify with my deeds as with my words, with my treasure as with my prayers, with my life as with my church membership, that even here, even now, Christ fulfills all the law and all the prophets. He is the Son whose every utterance, whose every gesture, pleased God his Father. In the name of Jesus Christ, be *released* from your demons, be *healed* of your disease, be *freed* from your prison, be *forgiven* of your sins!"

We come to worship, to the mountaintop, to glimpse Christ's glory and to give praise to God. But we can't stay here, swathed in prayers and anthems. Communion is not a sit-down feast, but food for the journey back down the mountain, following Christ, who calls us to give testimony to what we have seen by shining the light of his love into every dark recess where sin and disease and oppression and death seem to be having their way, whether it be in the depths of Africa or in a penthouse office high above Wall Street or anyplace in between. "[S]uddenly a bright cloud overshadowed them, and from the cloud a voice said, 'This is my Son, the Beloved; with him I am well pleased; listen to him!' When the disciples heard this, they fell to the ground and were overcome by fear. But Jesus came and touched them, saying, 'Get up and do not be afraid'" (Matt 17:5–7 NRSV). And then they came down from the mountain and continued on toward Jerusalem, and the cross, and the empty tomb, healing, and forgiving, and blessing along the way.

Ash Wednesday

First Presbyterian Church, Ponca City, Oklahoma
March 5, 2014

Joel 2:1–2, 12–17a
2 Corinthians 5:20b—6:10
Matthew 6:1–6, 16–21

"Why Lent?"

The years were 1515 and 1516. The place was the University of Wittenberg, in Germany. A young monk was lecturing on Paul's letter to the Romans. He later reminisced that it was in the tower of the monastery at Wittenberg that he arrived at his illuminating interpretation of Romans 1:17 (NRSV): "For in it the righteousness of God is revealed through faith for faith; as it is written, 'The one who is righteous will live by *faith.*'" He clarified this passage in his exposition of Romans 3:24 (NRSV): "They are now justified by [God's] grace as a *gift,* through the redemption that is in Christ Jesus." He made a highly significant discovery, which grew out of his own religious experience and theological study and which he found confirmed in the writings of Augustine. It marked the turning point of his life. He called it his entry into the "gates of paradise,"[1] and it started him down a path that revolutionized Christianity. The young monk was Martin Luther, and the theological interpretations which grew out of his reading of Romans, more than any other single event, mark the *beginning* of the Protestant Reformation.

Luther developed an understanding of God's grace much different from that of medieval Roman Catholicism. Luther declared, on the basis of scripture, that grace is not a magical and mechanical result of sacramental ritual, but a constant, dynamic, ethical force in the believer, enabling him or

---

1. See Luther, *Career of the Reformer IV,* 337.

her to combat sin and to fulfill the law. All of this, God has made possible by sacrificing Christ on the cross.

"*Sola fidei!*"—"By faith alone!"—became the battle cry of the Reformation. In the Middle Ages, the church of Rome had become encrusted with so many traditions and rituals that the simplicity of the gospel had been lost. God's grace had been hidden behind a formula of salvation that depended upon calculated *human* activity. The believer could reduce the debt owed to God on account of sin by making regular deposits of certain good works to his or her spiritual account—pilgrimages, fasts, masses, and the like. In the *early* church, public contrition was considered a way of being washed anew from the effects of sin. But by the twelfth century, penance was a sacrament, like baptism and the Lord's Supper, and for several centuries after that became more and more elaborate.

By the sixteenth century, penance was no longer a *spiritual discipline*. It had developed into a *lucrative business*. Finally, when the pope sent representatives to Germany to finance the construction of St. Peter's by selling indulgences—exemptions from punishment for sins—Luther could no longer hold his peace. "By faith alone!"—not by outward sign, not by fasts or pilgrimages, not by buying one's way out of purgatory. Not by confessing to a priest, not by participating in the mass, not by venerating relics, but "By faith alone!" are we made right in God's eyes, through the sacrifice of his Son on the cross.

Much of church history is action and reaction, a struggle to find the middle ground between two extremes, each of which is truth but not the *complete* truth. In some Protestant circles, Christians who reacted against the Catholic sacrament of penance went to the opposite extreme of rejecting *all* penitential behavior as unnecessary, papist, and the work of the devil. The *spiritual* discipline that the *Roman* practice, at its *best*, provided, was replaced by a completely *intellectual* approach, rejecting centuries of Jewish and Christian witness to the importance of uniting *word* with *act* in matters of faith.

As ecumenical dialogue has increased in recent years, Protestants have come to understand that the Catholic *teachers* never *said* that faith is unnecessary; their theology *agrees* that it is *absurd* to suppose that anyone could receive forgiveness, or experience salvation, simply by doing certain *acts*. And Protestants have recently been more willing to *admit* that *activity* can *reinforce* faith, and even provide a discipline through which faith is strengthened and made effective.

Two of the casualties in the Protestant reaction to medieval Catholic abuses were the penitential seasons of Advent and, more especially, Lent. The idea of forty days of spiritual discipline strikes some champions of the

Protestant creed "By faith alone!" as being exactly what the Reformers protested against.

We know that thought and behavior are related. Actions reinforce attitudes. That is one important reason that Christians have always met weekly to worship together—the act of physically gathering in each other's presence to give testimony to our need of salvation and the grace by which God has met that need, to confess our sinfulness, to hear of our forgiveness, to respond by making an offering that symbolizes—*symbolizes*—our dedication of all that we are to being instruments of God's will in the world. Worship is a *physical* activity, or *should* be.

We affirm that God has already accepted each of us in his grace and that no sacrament is necessary for salvation, yet we still recognize the importance of *baptism*, and call upon parents to have their children receive the physical application of water that symbolizes an anointing in spirit. We could simply read the Bible to learn the significance of the Last Supper. Yet we gather around the communion table to celebrate the *Lord's* Supper. We take bread and share the cup not because it is a magical meal, but because we believe that it is a way of inviting the Holy Spirit to enter into our lives and into our life together.

Behavior, action, *doing*, is important in the life of the faithful. The Jews realized that soul and body are inseparable—that God is worshiped with movement and activity as well as with the emotions and the intellect. The Christian church has recognized that from the beginning. So Protestants in the *Reformed* tradition should *affirm* that we belong, *body and soul*, to God, who did not count it unnecessary that he should come to live among us in the *flesh*. And our *worship* should move us to *action* as well as *thought*, should involve our *bodies* as well as our *minds*, so that it might fully engage our *spirits*.

The Old Testament prophets interpreted national calamities as the result of God's wrath, occasions for repentance. Military defeat, the failure of the harvest, or, as in our Joel passage, an infestation of locusts, were interpreted as signs that the people had turned away from God, and that the day of wrath was approaching. The ritual of rending one's clothes, of fasting, wearing sackcloth, and sitting on ashes, was a discipline to prompt the people to repent—to turn back to God. The point was not sackcloth and ashes, but a broken and contrite heart. But sackcloth and ashes in the face of a plague of locusts surely would bring forcefully to mind the immediate need to repent! Joel did not ask the people merely to go through an *external* ritual of returning to God, but for a fundamental change in behavior.

When the Protestant Reformers closed the monasteries, it was not so much because they believed that the *spiritual discipline* of the monks and nuns was *bad*, but that *all* Christians should practice genuine spiritual discipline. Some of you have perhaps read Richard Foster's book, *Celebration of Discipline*. Foster writes that "the Spiritual Disciplines are intended for good. They are meant to bring the abundance of God into our lives. It is possible, however, to turn them into another set of soul-killing laws. Law-bound Disciplines breathe death."[2] *This* is what Luther and the other Reformers were reacting against—a new set of *rules* which had become an end in themselves, unrelated to faith and to the marvelous grace of God. Foster admits, "It is easy in our *zeal* for the Spiritual Disciplines to turn them into the *external* righteousness of the scribes and the Pharisees."[3] But, if we observe them properly, *spiritual disciplines* can be a door to great spiritual *freedom*, and *penitential discipline* can be one of the most *freeing* activities of *all*.

But what about our Matthew passage? Did not Jesus himself protest against Jewish ritual? In Jesus' day, righteousness was thought to be a matter of almsgiving, prayer, and fasting. So ritualized had these acts of piety become that many people performed them without experiencing any change of heart, without ever really *repenting*. Almsgiving, prayer, and fasting had become ends in themselves, and even opportunities for competition, rather than helping people to approach God with a broken and contrite heart. They were merely a parade of self-righteousness. Jesus regarded deeds of conspicuous piety as hypocrisy. He objected by saying that such behavior was incongruous; they *preached righteousness* and *did injustice*. They *prayed* for *forgiveness*, but *begrudged* their *neighbors*. They fasted and gave alms only in order to be praised by those around them. Jesus taught, "Do not let your left hand know what your right hand is doing" (Matt 6:3 NRSV). He was saying, do not even let your closest friend know of your pious acts, for if you seek the reward of *human* recognition for your piety, that is all you will get—a human reward.

Some people, who wished for their piety to be seen, commonly arranged to be in very *public* places at prayer times, and would make hours-long devotions. Jesus did not condemn public prayer, but insisted that prayer must be sincere and simple and single-minded. Many Pharisees kept two fasts each week, going around with faces unwashed and feet bare and ashes on their heads. Jesus did not reject fasting, but told his disciples to reject *public displays* of their fasting as mere show. The person who fasts, he taught, should wash and even anoint him- or herself, as if preparing for a *feast*, not a *fast*. Otherwise, fasting becomes another parade of righteousness. Jesus did not reject the disciplines associated with penitence—prayer

---

2. Foster, *Celebration of Discipline*, 9.

3. Foster, *Celebration of Discipline*, 9.

and fasting—but he took issue with the way in which the *rituals* had become ends in themselves. Penitential discipline that becomes mere *form* is an enemy of the soul. *Properly* practiced, though, such discipline can help us to master the flesh, fit our minds for devotion, instruct us in the simplicity of life, and deepen the sincerity of our praise and understanding of our faith.

That is what Lent is about, and that is why we have gathered here this evening to acknowledge our need for forgiveness and the costly price paid for our salvation. We remember how Jesus was rejected, how he was tried, mocked, and hung on a tree, and how he died. We remember, too, how he loved to the end. But if it all remains *only* a memory from the *past*, and does not become *present* reality for us, there is little likelihood that the sacrifice made for our salvation will really *change our lives*. If it remains *only* a memory from the *past*, and does not become *present* reality for us, it has little possibility of confronting us with our own sin, and the fact that a sinless man—innocent and good—had to be offered up to death in *our* place. If it remains *only* a memory from the *past*, and does not become *present* reality for us, there is little chance that we can understand Christ's death as the supreme loving act of the living God.

Christians should contemplate these things at all seasons, yet the discipline of Lent can help us remember our year-around need, and to respond to it fully. Fasting is a discipline that can enrich one's spiritual journey at any time of year, yet in *Lent*, it reinforces our attention to Jesus' sacrificial journey to Calvary. Prayer is important at all times, yet regular prayer in *Lent* especially helps us center our lives in Christ and to recall that we, too, are called to sacrifice for others. Confession is needed throughout life, yet it becomes especially appropriate as we are moved by the approach of Good Friday to acknowledge that it was for the sake of *our* sins that the Son of God was nailed to the cross.

By observing the special penitential disciplines of Lent, we stand in a long line of Christians stretching back to the early days of the church, and we make the gospel story our own present reality. We do these things not that *others* may see, but that we may open *ourselves* to God—the God who called us into being, who provides for our needs, who invites us to live life in joy, who loves us so much that no price was too great for our redemption—not even the death of his own Son.

You are invited tonight, if you so desire, to come forward to receive the imposition of ashes—a biblical sign of mourning, grief, humiliation, and penitence, but also a sign of sacrifice and purification—not to take the place of a broken or contrite heart, but as a *tangible recognition* of our need for forgiveness and our rededication to seek God's righteousness. We need not wear them beyond the church door; they can be removed as we leave the chapel, for we know that the God who calls us to repentance is the God who has already *done* all that is necessary for our salvation—a God not of condemnation, but of forgiveness. A God not of defeat, but of joy. A God not of death, but of life.

First Sunday in Lent
First Presbyterian Church, Ponca City, Oklahoma
March 9, 2014

Genesis 2:4b–9, 15–17, 25—3:7
Romans 5:12–19
Matthew 4:1–11

"Skiing Within Bounds"

There is something invigorating about being the first person off the chairlift at the top of a mountain following a fresh snowfall. The glistening blanket of white beckons the skier to exhilarate in the clear, brisk air as you plunge down the slope, raising powdery billows along your path. What a feeling! For a few minutes, the entire mountain is yours to leave your personal prints upon—to subdue with your skis and your skill and to rejoice in the intimate partnership that you have formed with gravity. You reach the bottom of the slope and ride the chairlift back to the top and decide to take the same run, but, while it is still enjoyable, it just isn't the same experience, for now there are many tracks where there were none before—your own tracks, as the pioneer on the slope earlier in the morning, but also the tracks of others who followed where you led. You are tempted to recapture the thrill of that earlier experience, but your panorama view of the mountain discloses that all of the runs that are *open* have now already been skied on by somebody.

But you see nearby one slope whose snow is yet unbroken by ski tracks, so quietly beautiful, over beyond the barricade of orange flags that marks the boundary of safe skiing, off limits, over where the ski patrol has declared the snow to be unstable, subject to avalanche. But surely the conditions over there cannot be so very much different from the conditions where you have been skiing, except that it is still pristine, untouched. Curiosity mounts—what would it be like? Thrilling, surely. Just like the first run of the day; maybe better. A quick glance over the shoulder—no one in sight, no hint of the ski patrol, and so no one need ever know about this breach of rules. What right has the *ski patrol* to deny you such joy, anyway? *You* paid for your ticket, and you're up here to *ski*! *They* don't own the mountain! At *best*, they're being over-cautious in order to protect skiers less experienced and less skilled than you are. At *worst*, they're just making a point of their authority.

You ski over to the plastic rope and flags and take another furtive glance behind you. Still no one in sight. You lift the rope over your head and glide across the boundary. There, you've done it, you're on forbidden ground, and nothing has happened to you. Better ski ahead a ways, to avoid being seen, although you know that your ski tracks tell the tale. Maybe they will think that yours were the tracks of a ski patrol member checking the slope. Who are you trying to fool? Oh well, now you're committed, and you won't be the first person ever to ski on a closed slope, nor the last. Just look at it! How great this is going to be! And if they catch you and revoke your lift ticket?—you still will have had a great experience that no one else that day will have had, right? It is a steep run that you have chosen—you can understand why it might be considered subject to avalanche, but still, it doesn't seem any more hazardous than the others. The powder is deep, but you sail through it without effort. A hundred yards or so down the mountain, you stop at a point out of sight from any authorities in order to catch your breath and enjoy the scene. What a great day, the thrill of freedom joining the thrill of the virgin slope! But suddenly, behind you, there is a low, rumbling sound . . .

Every year, in Colorado, where I grew up, avalanches claim the lives of several skiers who have been foolish enough to ski into areas said by the authorities to be dangerous, and among them are usually some who have knowingly skied out of bounds at the established ski areas. A few of these are *frustrated* with slopes on which the snow has become packed hard or icy. A few have become impatient with the *crowds* on the runs that are *open*. Most people who ski out of bounds, though, are simply curious and, constrained by rules and regulations in the rest of their life, feel the urge when they escape home and office and shop to do something that is forbidden, a snub of authority and convention that seems to risk no lasting consequences. They become their *own* authorities. They decide to make their *own* rules. With all the slopes available that have been inspected and pronounced *safe* for skiing, there are some who chafe at *any* restriction on their enjoyment of God's creation; if even a *single* run is closed at a large ski area, or if only a small *section* of the mountain country has been declared to be unsafe, *that* is where they must ski. And, inevitably, that is where tragedy strikes.

The creation story in chapters 2 and 3 of the book of Genesis declares that "[t]he Lord God took the man and put him in the garden of Eden to till it and keep it. And the Lord God commanded the man, 'You may freely eat of every tree of the garden; but of the tree of the knowledge of good and evil you shall not eat, for in the day that you eat of *it* you shall *die*'" (Gen 2:15–17 NRSV). We are not told why the one tree was out of bounds to the man and the woman—whether God was being arbitrary with this command or whether God knew the harm that could befall the creatures if they ate of it. The *reason* is not really important to the story; the point *is* that God had *spoken*, and *God's* word should have been *obeyed*. Commissioned to labor as stewards over God's creation, granted permission to have access to all of creation, and prohibited from only one activity—eating from a single tree—the woman and the man found themselves easily tempted to make their freedom absolute, to have no restraints and no restrictions, to be as boundless as God.

"Did God say, 'You shall not eat from any tree in the garden?'" (Gen 3:1b NRSV) "Did God say. . .?" In his little book, *Creation and Fall*, Dietrich Bonhoeffer wrote,

> This is the question that appears innocuous but through it evil wins power in us, through it we become disobedient to God. . . . What is the *real* evil in this question? It is not that it is asked at all. It is that the *false answer* is contained within it, that within it is attacked the basic attitude of the creature towards the Creator. [The question implies that the *human creature*] is expected to be *judge* of God's word instead of simply *hearing* and *doing* it.[1]

When they transgressed the command of God, when they denied the limits placed upon them by God, when they disregarded the boundaries that God had set down for them in their creatureliness, man and woman did, as the serpent had said they would, become *like* God. Now, man and woman had taken upon *themselves* to live on their *own* resources, like God. Now they had no need for the Creator, but had become creators themselves, to the extent that they had created their own lives without God. Now they were no longer as *creatures* of God, but had *denied* their creatureliness. But in fact they were *not* God. They could *not* be self-sufficient, but were still dependent, even if they refused to acknowledge it. They did *not* have *all* knowledge, even if they thought that they had *enough*. And—a new experience and a new feeling for them—they were alone, for the first time estranged from God and from God's other creatures and from each other—and they

---

1. Bonhoeffer, *Creation and Fall*, 67 (emphasis added).

were afraid and they were ashamed. And the fruits of the earth were no longer theirs by right, but would have to be wrested from the ground. And death—returning to the dust from which we were made—would no longer be accepted as a natural part of life as a trustworthy God designed it, but would be humankind's greatest cause of dread and foreboding.

Real temptation, the most dangerous temptation, comes upon us in the way it came upon the woman and the man—not to do something *clearly* wicked or perverse, but to go *behind* the word of God, to rationalize the doing of something that seems to fulfill plausible principles, but in fact contradicts God's explicit command. This was the sort of temptation that Jesus faced in the wilderness. In the *first* case, that of turning stones into loaves of bread, it is said that the devil suggested that Jesus use his divine powers to guarantee a part of his ministry, as by fiat; in the *second* case, that of defying physical danger, that Jesus use his divine relationship to amaze the crowds and win them to a worthy cause; in the *third* case, the most transparent of the three, that of worshiping the devil in exchange for winning a kingly rule on *earth*, that Jesus give to the *devil* that which is due *only* to God. But Jesus, fully *obedient* where Adam had *failed*, determined that he would *not* try to choose his *own* way, but would instead live *this* life and fulfill *his* ministry and achieve *God's* purpose by waiting upon God and trusting in God and depending upon God alone. Jesus determined that he would live *his* life in *faith* and *obedience*. Jesus knew himself to be under *God's* direction, not vice versa; *he* was not the lord over *God*; he did not seek to *use* God for his *own* purpose. Jesus had the sort of faith that remained intact even if miracles were not his to command, even if his obedience put him on a *cross*. Jesus had the sort of faith that did not demand any *visible* guarantee of God's trustworthy love. How far is such faith from the sort of cheap grace being advertised in some quarters these days that promises *material* rewards for being a Christian and that never seems to acknowledge that being faithful and obedient may necessitate hanging on a cross! If Jesus, the *Son* of God, was unwilling to choose for *himself* what would help or hinder him, and even what would help or hinder his *mission*, then how can the *rest* of humankind presume to make its *own* rules for living? For even the *attempt* is faithlessness toward God. "It is written, 'One does not live by bread alone, but by every word that comes from the mouth of God.' . . . Again it is written, 'Do not put the Lord your God to the test.' . . . Away with you, Satan! for it is written, 'Worship the Lord your God, and serve *only* him'" (Matt 4:4, 7, 10 NRSV).

This is a word for the church, even more than for those who seem uninterested in matters of faith. For temptation is not a sign of weakness, but a sign of strength, and the greater the strength, the greater the temptation—ironically, the stronger a person's faith in God's will and purpose, the greater the temptation for the person to become *like* God in order to *achieve* God's will and purpose, even if it contradicts God's very command. Like the man and woman in the garden, those who know God most *intimately* may be the *most* inclined to attempt living on their *own* resources, *like* God. They may begin to think and behave as if they had no *need* for the Creator, but had become creators themselves, to the extent that they are creating their own lives without God. They become no longer as *creatures* of God, but tear themselves *away* from their creatureliness.

But, in fact, no human being *is* God, and by *refusing* to usurp *God's* role, Jesus himself showed his very solidarity with *created* humanity, you and me. We are *not* self-sufficient, but we *are* still dependent, even if we refuse to acknowledge it. We do *not* have all knowledge, even if we think that we have *enough*. And disobedience can only result in our being alone, estranged from God and from God's other creatures and from each other—and leave us afraid and ashamed. True life and true freedom can be found and enjoyed *only* by observing the *limits* that God, in God's own wisdom and for God's own purpose, has set for humankind.

In my nearly fifty years of the sport, I have never gone skiing without seeing evidence of someone having been brazen enough to ski out of bounds, in an area declared to be off limits. Even concerns for safety from avalanche are not enough to convince *some* skiers to abide by the rules. As in many other human endeavors and pastimes, humility is too little in evidence among those who ski. And that is amazing. For what should be more easily inspired within someone who pauses at the top of a mountain, viewing the full majesty of earth and sky and seeing how small he or she stands alongside it all, than humility? But, then, what should be more easily inspired within *any* of us who acknowledge that we did not create ourselves or anything else in the world, but God alone, who bids us to trust God for every good thing and to obey God with absolute faith in God's wisdom and God's power and God's love and God's care?

> In the day that the Lord God made the earth and the heavens, when no plant of the field was yet in the earth and no herb of the field had yet sprung up . . . then the Lord God formed man from the dust of the ground, and breathed into his nostrils the breath of life; and the man became a living being. And the Lord God planted a garden in Eden. . . .
>
> The Lord God took the man and put him in the garden of Eden to till it and keep it. And the Lord God commanded the man, "You may freely eat of every tree of the garden; but of the tree of the knowledge of good and evil you shall not eat, for

in the day that you eat of it you shall die." (Gen 2:4b–5a, 7–8a, 15–17 NRSV)

God has *not* given us—even those of us in the church—a world without limits nor a freedom without boundaries. And when we ignore or rationalize *breach* of God's clear command, when we deny our creatureliness but choose to become like God, we declare our rebellion of unfaithfulness and we subject ourselves to the tyranny of our own desires. In that day we have lost our freedom, indeed, and have tasted the bitterness of death. True freedom—freedom to live and be who we were *created* to be—lies only in fulfilling the will of God.

Second Sunday in Lent

First Presbyterian Church, Dodge City, Kansas

March 3, 1996

Genesis 12:1–4a
Romans 4:1–5, 13–17
John 3:1–17

"The Word in the Wind"

"Do not be astonished that I said to you, 'You must be born from above.' The wind blows where it chooses, and you hear the sound of it, but you do not know where it comes from or where it goes. So it is with everyone who is born of the Spirit" (John 3:7–8 NRSV). Thus Jesus addressed Nicodemus the Pharisee. With his highly ordered mind, Nicodemus could not comprehend the fresh word that Jesus was speaking, nor conceive of the freedom with which God visits the Spirit upon the chosen. "How can anyone be born after having grown old?" Nicodemus had asked. "Can one enter a second time into the mother's womb and be born" (John 3:4 NRSV)? As one who had learned to feel with every fiber of his being the importance of keeping the law in all of its strict detail, Nicodemus believed in absolutes, and was uncomfortable with ambiguity. Having studied over and over God's revelation to the great personalities of Israel's distant past, Nicodemus found it difficult to suppose that there could be any new disclosures "from above." All that God had done, all that God proposed to do, had been set down precisely in the sacred books of old. Human destiny was writ with a steady and practiced hand in hallowed words—words which must be interpreted according to established principles, words which must be applied according to strict norms of religious behavior.

But then comes a new teacher from the hinterland, doing signs as one having authority, but heedless of convention and seemingly careless of the law. And he spoke of being born of the Spirit, comparing the action of God upon the human heart and those whom God has so acted upon and within, to "the wind"—fleeting and free and invisible, whose presence can only be detected in the rustling of leaves in the trees and the movement of clouds across the sky, real beyond question, possessing a power and direction that can be neither predicted nor tamed—the wind that, as quickly as it comes, is gone: "The wind blows where it chooses, and you hear the sound of it, but you do not know where it comes from or where it goes. So it is with everyone who is born of the Spirit (John 3:8 NRSV)."

John says that Nicodemus came to Jesus "by night." Does that mean that Nicodemus was speaking out of the darkness of spiritual ignorance, or does it suggest that he came furtively, reluctant to be seen with Jesus because he feared the other members of the Sanhedrin? Perhaps it is something of both. It seems too strong to say, as one commentator does, that Nicodemus was "spineless." Circumspect, yes, cautious, not only in his seeking out Jesus, but in his understanding of life. He knew about being born from a mother's womb, but he could not stretch his imagination to understand about being born from above. He was unable or unwilling to view life out of any perspective but the rigid, the familiar, the established. He could not comprehend Jesus' words that the Holy Spirit acts freely, unfettered by human judgment or even by accepted religious standards, and that those who are *born* of the *Spirit* possess the *same* freedom—freedom from the past, freedom from the customary, freedom from what the *world* calls wise and proper, freedom to respond to the call of God whenever it comes and wherever it sends them. Nicodemus thought that the word of God was black and white. It was tangible—he could hold the scrolls in his hands. How could it be likened to anything as fleeting as the wind?

It may be that his caution *dissolved* over the next several months as he watched Jesus and listened to him, and found himself more and more impressed with this young rabbi. Later in John's Gospel, Nicodemus ventured to speak out in the Sanhedrin on Jesus' behalf, and eventually, when Judas had betrayed Christ and Peter had denied him and the other ten had scattered, it was Nicodemus who helped Joseph of Arimathea bury the crucified body of Jesus. Perhaps he had finally come to understand what Jesus meant by being born from above. We cannot say whether he had in fact become a disciple of Jesus, but clearly, in speaking *up* for Jesus in the Sanhedrin at great personal risk, Nicodemus had been emboldened to hazard a departure, however slight, from his customary caution, and had felt the fresh wind of God blowing through his soul.

Aside from Jesus, the biblical character who offers the greatest contrast to the cautious Nicodemus, and to such an ordered view of life, is Abraham.

By human standards, Abraham was a very ordinary man, unremarkable in any respect. He had neither the sophistication of the learned nor the self-assurance of the great. Indeed, he appeared to be a rather discouraging case, summarized by the biblical description of his wife: "Now Sarai, Abram's wife, bore him no children" (Gen 16:1a NRSV). In biblical terms, to be barren was to be quite without hope. But God's history of salvation begins with this very unremarkable person, when the word of God came to him without warning, as the wind comes without warning, and God singled out Abram and said to him, "Go from your country and your kindred and your father's house to the land that I will show you. I will make of you a great nation, and I will bless you, and make your name great, so that you will be a blessing" (Gen 12:1–2 NRSV). And Abram went, as the Lord had told him. No questions. No negotiation. No hesitation. No doubts. At the age of seventy-five, Abram took Sarai, his wife, and Lot, his brother's son, and all their possessions and the servants they had gotten in Haran, and set forth on a long journey to the land of Canaan.

It might seem to us that Abram had little to lose and everything to gain by leaving his home and setting out for Canaan. But loyalty to family, and the place of the family, were very important to ancient peoples. To break the ancestral bonds was unthinkable. To leave country and kindred and home and set out on a lonely road to a place he had never been before, responsible for the welfare not only of himself but the others with him, all on faith, was remarkable. Leave your accustomed routine, says God; renounce all laziness and complacency of spirit. Abandon the familiar and the friendly, forsake every security you have ever known and every expectation that the world has of you, answer my call to the adventure of living solely in trust upon me. Then I will make you a great nation, and make your name great. To stay in the safety of the familiar and the customary and the known is to remain barren; to leave your security behind and risk answering my call, wherever it takes you, is to have hope. It is to move, for perhaps the first time, into genuine life. And so Abram went, without any evidence other than God's word! He obeyed. He set out willingly upon a journey, not knowing where he was going, but entrusting himself to God's guidance. He acted in faith. The word of God had come, who knows how, and, in an instant, Abram surrendered his will and his estate, and embraced the uncertain and the unfamiliar, and he became God's instrument for beginning the salvation of the world.

We Presbyterians are probably more sympathetic to Nicodemus than to Abram. When we examine Abram's radical sort of abandon, it strikes us as quite irresponsible, really. Rather than saving for his retirement, rather than staying close to home to be there if needed, rather than being a man who knows where he's going in a well-planned life, Abram set out on a reckless journey to who-knew-where. We pride ourselves in doing things decently and in order. Surely God's call will only come through recognized channels—it must have precedent in scripture, it must be verified with objective facts, it must not disturb established categories of reality and accepted notions about what is and what isn't religious. We can recite the Ten Commandments and name the books of the Bible (in fact, we sometimes come dangerously close to worshiping the Bible), but absolute trust in a God we cannot see is difficult for us. We acknowledge the miracles of God in the *past*, but we really don't detect any in the *present*, and we tend not to expect any in the *future*. We can tell the story of the *exodus*, but we have trouble believing that God calls *us* to liberate the politically and economically oppressed in our own day. We are nervous unless we know whence we are coming and whither we are going, so we like to establish goals for the future and evaluate our performance in the past, and sometimes we miss the importance of living *faithfully* in between. Having reformed once, nearly five hundred years ago, we may feel that that was enough adventure for one millennium.

So the wind swirls in the trees around us and maybe we don't even recognize the word of God coaxing us to let go of the caution and customs that bind us, bidding us to quit trying to control our own lives and resisting God's direction, summoning us to follow the lead of the Holy Spirit into regions unknown, beckoning us to journey where we will be forced to trust not in our bank accounts and our family and our own skills and efforts, but in God. The calling of God disputes the dominant ideologies of our time and challenges the age-old human yearning for settlement and security. After all, to respond to the call means to be *despised* as well as *displaced*, to be at odds with the world, and frequently to be misunderstood. For the values of the *Christian* are not the *world's* values; *our* frame of reference should be completely different. We must repudiate the cumbersome baggage of a life which is dedicated to comfort and status and predictability. We must be people on call, always ready for the journey to an unknown destination.

Nicodemus was surely familiar with the story of Abraham. Nevertheless, Nicodemus was a person of caution, a person of convention, a person of narrow vision. He could clearly trace the movement of God through Israel's sedimented *past*. But he had no notion of the Spirit freely active in the *present*, prompting people to abandon the securities that weigh them down and keep them from fulfilling God's will. He could read the word from a safe distance, in the ancient scrolls. But he could not discern the word in the wind.

Speaking of the life of obedient discipleship, Dietrich Bonhoeffer wrote in his book, *The Cost of Discipleship,* with regard to the call of Matthew:

"The Word in the Wind"

> At the call, Levi leaves all that he has—but not because he thinks that he might be doing something worth while, but simply for the sake of the call. Otherwise he cannot follow in the steps of Jesus ... The old life is left behind, and completely surrendered. The disciple is dragged out of his relative security into a life of absolute *in*security ..., *from* a life which is observable and calculable ... *into* a life where everything is *un*observable and fortuitous ..., *out* of the realm of finite ... *into* the realm of *in*finite possibilities ... If we would follow Jesus we must take certain definite steps. The first step, which follows the call, cuts the disciple off from his previous existence ... To stay in the old situation makes discipleship impossible. Levi must leave the receipt of custom and Peter his nets in order to follow Jesus ... The call to follow implies that there is only one way of believing on Jesus Christ, and that is by leaving all and going with the incarnate Son of God ... For faith is only real when there is obedience, never without it, and faith only *becomes* faith in the act of obedience[1]

—obedience to God's call, response to the prompting of the Spirit, which *comes* from we know not where and *goes* we know not where, but which blows through our souls like wind through the trees, which visits us at home, at work, at school, at our fishing nets, at our tax office, in the church pew, and beckons us to be born from above, unconcerned with worldly judgment and worldly ties, prepared to move at the impulse of the divine will—the Spirit, which, if *un*answered, passes *by* us as quickly as it came.

How about you? Are you free enough from trying to justify yourself through fortune and fame and the law, free enough from the values of the world, that *you* are willing to be Christ's disciple no matter what the cost to your comfort and pride? Are you free enough from fretting that God might not adequately provide for you, free enough from the love of money and possessions that you are ready to leave all your old securities to answer Christ's call to spend yourself for others? Are you free enough from self-will, free enough from the worship of doctrines and the cultivation of prejudices to be a humble instrument of the living God to be used when and where God wills in the cause of redeeming the beloved creation? Are you free enough from fear of human judgment, free enough from the whispers of caution, to read and follow the word in the wind?

This is what it means to be born from above—a new and radically different existence from having been born of the flesh. It means absolute trust, it means total commitment, it means abandoning all caution, it means

---

1. Bonhoeffer, *Cost of Discipleship*, 56, 62–63, 66–67 (emphasis added).

forsaking your own program for life. It means being willing for the Spirit of God to blow through you as freely as the wind.

Third Sunday in Lent

Spanish Springs Presbyterian Church, Sparks, Nevada

March 7, 1999

Exodus 17:1–7
Romans 5:1–11
John 4:5–42

"Wherever Jesus Is"

In her novel, *Small Ceremonies*, Canadian writer Carol Shields tells of two women having lunch out together one day—the narrator of the novel and her friend Nancy. "We ordered beef curry," the narrator says,

> and while we waited we discussed the alternating vibrations which regulate female psychology.
>
> "Up and down," Nancy complained. "A perpetual see-saw ride..."
>
> I agreed; it did seem that the electricity of life consisted mainly of meaningless fluctuations in mood so that to enter an era of happiness was to anticipate the next interlude of depression.
>
> "Of course," Nancy said, "there are those occasional little surprises which make it all worthwhile."
>
> "Such as?" I asked.
>
> "The peach," she said. "Did I ever tell you the peach story?"
>
> "No," I said, "never."
>
> So she told me how, last summer, she and Paul and their children, all six of them, had been stalled in heavy traffic. It was Friday evening and they were working their way out of the city to get to the cottage sixty miles away. The children were quarrelsome and the weather was murderously humid. In another car stalled next to them, a fat man sat alone at the steering wheel,

and on the back seat, plainly visible, was a bushel of peaches. He smiled at the children, and they must have smiled back, for he turned suddenly and reached a fat hand into his basket, carefully selected a peach, and handed it out the window to Nancy.

She took it, she said, instinctively, uttering a confused mew of thanks. Ahead of them a traffic light turned green, and the fat man's car moved away, leaving Nancy with the large and beautiful peach in her hand. It was, she said, the largest peach she had ever seen, almost the size of a grapefruit, and its skin was perfect seamless velvet without a single blemish. Paul shouted at her over the noise of the traffic to look out for razor blades, so she turned it over carefully, inspecting it. But the skin was unbroken. And the exact shade of ripeness for eating.

"What did you do with it?" I asked.

"We ate it," Nancy said. "We passed it around. Gently. Like a holy object almost, and we each took big bites of it. Until it was gone. One of the children said something about how strange it was for someone to do that, give us a peach through a car window like that, but the rest of us just sat there thinking about it. All the way to the cottage. A strange sort of peace stuck to us. It was so—so completely unasked for. And so undeserved. And the whole thing had been so quick, just a few seconds really. I was—I don't know why—I was thrilled."[1]

One hot day, stalled in the traffic of her repeatedly up-and-down life, an endless routine of duties and chores and relationships born and broken, a Samaritan woman trudged toward the village well. According to tradition, Jacob the grandson of Abraham had dug the well long ago, and the people of the village took a sort of community pride in being so connected to history, their only fame, the result of something that had happened centuries before *they* ever came along. But it was still a well; it required a long walk to get to it and it seemed like an even longer walk to get back home from it, carrying a jar made much heavier by having been filled with water, regardless that the water was precious. And in between, there was the pulling on the rope to lift the laden jar back up to the top of the well. It was a journey that the woman had probably made hundreds, perhaps thousands of times.

That day must have seemed like all the others. She surely would not have been expecting anything extraordinary to happen to her—no benefit from the habitual journey except the cool water itself, which seemed less like a *gift* the farther she had to carry it back toward her house. But it so happened that as she drew near the well, she noticed a man, a traveler from

---

1. Shields, *Small Ceremonies*, *The Box Garden*, 116–17.

Judea, sitting there. It was noon—perhaps the only time she could visit the well without being ensnared in the village gossip—and the man appeared tired and parched. She may have noticed from his clothing that he was a Jew—a member of that society that looked down its nose on Samaritans as virtual heathens, because the Samaritans did not regard the writings of the prophets as scripture, and they did not make pilgrimage to the *temple* in *Jerusalem* as their place of worship, but to *Mount Gerizim*, just a few miles from the well. How remarkable, then, that the man spoke to *her*, asking her for a drink of water. For he had no jar, or rope with which to lower it. Stunned, she asked him, "How is that *you* a *Jew*, ask a drink of *me*, a *woman of Samaria*" (John 4:9 NRSV)? Jews and Samaritans simply did not keep company with each other, and it was even more a breach of etiquette for a man to engage in conversation with a woman who was not his wife. "Jesus answered her, 'If you knew the gift of God, and who it is that is saying to you, 'Give me a drink,' *you* would have asked *him,* and *he* would have given you *living water*'" (John 4:10 NRSV).

The woman obviously did not catch Jesus' true meaning—she was thinking simply on the level of the refreshing, life-sustaining liquid, and how much easier her life would be without the chore of having to walk to the well every day and toting the heavy jar back home. As *Nicodemus* had misunderstood what Jesus meant by being born "anew," meaning "from above," by the Spirit, so the *Samaritan woman* misunderstood what Jesus meant by giving her "living water."

If the woman had just recognized who it was who was speaking to her, she would have asked *him* for *living* water—water that gives life in a much more profound and thorough way than the cool liquid. Wondrous and abundant and welcome as Jacob's gift of the well was—providing what was necessary to physical life in a place that was dry and hot—it could not satisfy thirst permanently. You drank of it, but in a few hours, its refreshment was over, and you needed more. So every day, you had to make a trip to the well. But Jesus' gift of living water *does* satisfy, and *permanently*. Jesus offers the water that gives life full and complete, and those who drink of *Jesus'* water—those who draw deeply from *him*—"will never thirst," will never be parched of spirit, will never want for another Savior.

But even though the woman had missed the point, she had in fact responded appropriately. She was still thinking in terms of overcoming the need to make the daily trip to the *miraculous well* to fill her jar, and so she did not recognize the *miracle standing* in her *midst*. She supposed that Jesus was a *miracle worker* who could meet her immediate physical needs, and failed to perceive that Jesus *himself* was God's *truest* miracle. Still, she had recognized the *graciousness* of Jesus who ignored boundaries of prejudice and judgmentalism—that he was someone who, in some way, offered a gift that, at some level, *could* meet her need. He had no bucket, but she *believed* him when he said that he had water to give her. So she made the *right request*, even though it was for the *wrong reason*—"Sir, give me this water, so that I may never be thirsty or have to keep coming here to draw water" (John 4:15 NRSV). She wanted to take a big bite of whatever it was that Jesus was holding out to her.

At this point in the conversation, it seems to me that the woman at the well was in the situation of Nancy in the automobile, the windows down, and a perfect stranger holding out a peach to her from a passing car. It was an act of pure grace—completely unasked for, so undeserved, as Nancy said. What would she do? Would she gratefully take hold of it, luscious and refreshing, accepting it as a pure gift? Or would she let the hundred questions in her mind about "Why?" and "How?" prevent her from receiving the blessing? Her husband's first instinct had been to reject it as something unwholesome—hiding a razor blade, if you will—because he assumed that no one did such a simple thing as a pure act of kind, unexpected generosity—handing a perfect stranger a perfect peach.

> "What did you do with it?" I asked.
> "We ate it," Nancy said. "We passed it around. Gently. Like a holy object almost, and we each took big bites of it. Until it was gone. One of the children said something about how strange it was for someone to do that, give us a peach through a car window like that, but the rest of us just sat there thinking about it. All the way to the cottage. A strange sort of peace stuck to us. It was so—so completely unasked for. And so undeserved. And the whole thing had been so quick, just a few seconds really. I was—I don't know why—I was thrilled."[2]

In a few moments, despite the impropriety of speaking with a *man*, despite the awkwardness of keeping company with a *Jew*, the Samaritan woman held out her hand and received the peach.

Then, abruptly, Jesus seemed to change the subject. "Go, call your husband, and come back" (John 4:16 NRSV). She responded to him that she had no husband, and he proceeded to tell her her own life story—that she had had *five* husbands, and that the one she was now with was *not* her husband. And she was amazed, and recognized that this traveler at the well was no ordinary man—not even an ordinary miracle worker—but a prophet. (Notice, by the way, that Jesus did not judge her in any way, in contrast to a lot of modern interpreters of this passage, and neither should *we* make any

---

2. Shields, *Small Ceremonies, The Box Garden*, 117.

judgments or assumptions. There could be many reasons other than moral failure that she had been married several times, though probably none of the reasons was particularly happy.)

Jesus' insight into her life and words finally led her to recognize him and declare him as a prophet, and then she *acted* on her conclusion by posing to him the question that for so long had divided Jew and Samaritan: Was God to be worshiped at the shrine on Mount Gerizim in Samaria or in the temple on Mount Zion in Jerusalem? And Jesus responded that the time was coming when it would no longer be a matter of *place*—not a question of worshiping in *Jewish* territory or in *Samaritan* territory—but of recognizing that God is present with us, and of worshiping God according to God's own character of spirit and truth. For God is not bound to any one place or any single people, and God is not restricted to any tradition or assumption. The woman understood that Jesus was talking about something she knew of—the coming of the Messiah. "When he comes, he will proclaim all things to us," she said. And then Jesus told her that the time was fulfilled—the era of limits and boundaries and convention and prejudice was past. "I am he," Jesus said, "the one who is speaking to you" (John 4:25b, 26 NRSV).

Wherever Jesus is, God is present. What Jesus does, what Jesus says, what Jesus prays, is the work, the promise, the will of God. Wherever Jesus is, life abundant is possible and available. The old boundaries fall. The old wisdom is irrelevant. The old customs are passé. Wherever Jesus is, the new day has dawned. The kingdom has arrived. The promises of God are fulfilled. The hour is not only *coming*. It is now *here*.

The Word has become flesh, as John testified back at the beginning of his Gospel, and he is living among us. A surprising offer of grace meets us in our daily routine, opens up our discouraging past to the light of the truth of God's unchanging purpose, invites us into a future pregnant with God's faithful promise, redeems our toilsome present with God's boundless hope. But we have to be open and anxious to receive the gift of Jesus in our midst, before the signal changes and the flow of daily traffic pulls us from any chance of epiphany at the well, back to grumbling about being stuck thirsty in life's dry and dusty desert. It cannot have been *coincidence* that brought Jesus and the woman together at the well the one noontime that Jesus was passing by that way and paused to rest. And through her excited testimony to the townspeople about "the man who told her everything that she had ever" done, the Samaritans flocked out to meet him, a mass of people not reckoned by any disciple as being among the chosen, but welcomed by Jesus as a field ripe for harvesting. What a shame it would have been if she had declined the gift, had let convention and custom and propriety and prejudice convince her that she shouldn't accept the big, beautiful, ripe peach being held out to her by the stranger, and went on about her routine as normal, dipping her jar in the well and totally missing out on the living water available wherever Jesus is!

Perhaps there are some people here this morning who aren't quite sure whether Jesus is the Messiah they have been looking for. The Samaritan woman, it seems, was not quite sure, even when she dropped her jar and hurried back to the city to tell the others. "He cannot be the Messiah, can he" (John 4:29b NRSV)? For he didn't fit the Samaritan expectations of the Messiah, just as, in fact, he did not fit the *Jewish* expectations of the Messiah. Would someone as pure and holy as the Messiah, for instance, ever be seen talking to a *woman*? And yet, she recognized that Jesus offered her what she needed, even if she had at first *misdiagnosed* what she needed. To be treated respectfully as a full human being, a worthy recipient of the unexpected gift he held out to her, regardless of what society says, regardless even of what people who consider themselves as religious experts say! Jesus himself is the judge of what is clean and holy, and he rejects no one. When Jesus is present, wherever Jesus is, there *is* and there *must* be a *new* reality—a reality of forgiveness and acceptance and hope and life. God's salvation is available now to anyone who thirsts for it—to anyone who will roll down the window and stick out their hand and receive the grace of Jesus Christ and take a big bite or a deep swallow. He will not reject. He will not ridicule. He will not condemn. He will not abandon. Wherever Jesus is, there is living water, and those who drink of the water that Jesus gives them will never be thirsty. Wherever Jesus is, there is living water, a spring gushing up to eternal life.

Jesus promised all who hunger and thirst to be present with them in this sacrament. He is here now, not remote and far away, but present with us, happily receiving all who worship in spirit and truth, offering living water to all who recognize their need. Is this the day that, even in something as routine as coming to a table to eat and drink, you perceive Jesus graciously holding out his gift to you?

Fourth Sunday in Lent

Spanish Springs Presbyterian Church, Sparks, Nevada

April 3, 2011

1 Samuel 16:1–13
Ephesians 5:8–14
John 9:1–41

"To See or Not to See"

My grandmother—my mother's mother—lost her eyesight long before I was born. I never knew the details, except that, once when I was with her in a doctor's office, I heard her answer his question about her scarred and clouded eyes by saying that it began in childbirth—whether that of my mother or one of my mother's older brothers, I don't know. But for most of her life, nearly all of her adult life, and despite numerous surgeries, my grandmother did not have the use of her eyes.

    I remember being fascinated by my grandmother's ability to navigate through her house—the same one in which my mother grew up—and her ability to function so well in her kitchen that had become so familiar over the years, until her final illness, and by her ability to read braille. She kept up with world events through the several braille magazines to which she subscribed, as well as talking books. When I visited her, she would sometimes read to me. Her aged fingers were still quite delicate, sensitive to the raised dots on the page. In fact, over the years, she taught braille to many others in and around Manhattan, Kansas who were losing or had lost their eyesight. She also told me stories from memory—*Peter Rabbit* was a favorite, but only one of many. Her situation hindered her ability to understand *some* things about the world that kept changing following her loss of eyesight, of course. But her curiosity and interest remained. I remember her asking me one time what a cloverleaf was—that is, the type of freeway interchange. She could not comprehend my poor verbal explanation, until I thought of taking her fingers in mine and tracing the different roadways in the air with them, as if we were driving straight, or turning this way or that onto the other highway. Suddenly, understanding dawned on her face in the form of a broad, satisfied smile.

Over the years that I knew her, my grandmother's hearing became more acute as she relied more upon it, until it, too, began to fail, and she sometimes commented that it constituted a greater loss than the disappearance of her eyesight had been. Still, even without eyesight, she perceived much. She always expected, I think, to be able to see again someday, and perhaps she did. The first thing she always did in the morning, out of habit, or out of hope, was to put on her glasses. My cousin, a nurse, who was at her bedside in the hospital, tells that, just before my grandmother died, she opened her eyes quite wide as if she were looking at something very compelling.

Sometimes, eyesight can actually be a handicap. We come to rely too much on physical appearances, and are blinded to a deeper reality. Many of us, probably most of us, have had experiences in friendship and romance that demonstrate that truth—the quicker we learn the lesson from an unwise choice based on the book's cover, so to speak, the better off we are later in life. But, as in other things, some of us are slow learners. Samuel the prophet should have learned a lesson from having been so impressed with the handsome and athletic appearance of Saul, when he chose him to be king of Israel. Well, to be fair, even *God* was a bit dazzled by Saul's appearance. Both God *and* Samuel were disappointed when things didn't work out as expected. Then God sent Samuel to Bethlehem to select the *next* king from among the sons of Jesse.

By then, *God* had learned *his* lesson, even if *Samuel* had *not*. One after another, God rejected each of the good-looking lads that Samuel thought surely must be the appropriate candidate, until, coming to the end of the line that Jesse had assembled for review, Samuel asked the Bethlehemite in perplexity, "'Are all your sons here?' And [Jesse] said, 'There remains yet the *youngest*, but he is keeping the sheep'" (1 Sam 16:11 NRSV). At Samuel's insistence, Jesse sent for his youngest son, David, who also happened to be handsome, with beautiful eyes. "The LORD said [to Samuel], 'Rise and anoint him; for this is the one'" (1 Sam 16:12b NRSV). The Lord had explained to Samuel earlier in the process, when the prophet was impressed with the very first of Jesse's sons, "'Do not look on his appearance or on the height of his stature, because I have rejected him; for the LORD does not see as mortals see; they look on the outward appearance, but the LORD looks on the heart'" (1 Sam 16:7 NRSV). And "Samuel took the horn of oil, and anointed [David] in the presence of his brothers; and the spirit of the LORD came mightily upon David from that day forward" (1 Sam 16:13a–b NRSV).

The Pharisees of Jesus' day could see remarkably well, as far as eyesight was concerned. They were very attentive to appearances, and swift to judge the rightness or wrongness of what they witnessed. Laymen who had come to assume, and by popular consent were granted, the role of policing enforcement of the laws of Moses, seem, many of them, to have busied themselves with investigating all sorts of infractions of a rather detailed set of rules of behavior which admitted no concern for the motive or intention behind whatever *they* considered to be *mis*behavior. Like most religious people of the time, they interpreted any physical impairment to be a sign of God's punishment; the afflicted person *must* be a *sinner*, *must* have violated the *rules*. Until the offender made atonement for the particular sin, he or she could neither *expect*, nor did that person *deserve*, to be *healed*. And even Jesus' disciples seem to have assumed that someone who, for instance, was *blind*, was being *penalized* for some *misdeed*. And so it was that, one day, a few minutes after Jesus had said to his disciples, "'I am the light of the world. Whoever follows me will never walk in darkness but will have the light of life'" (John 8:12 NRSV), and after some Pharisees who had overheard Jesus and had picked an argument with him in the temple had tried to stone him, he happened to see a man who had been blind from birth, and "[h]is disciples asked him, 'Rabbi, who sinned, this man or his parents, that he was born blind'" (John 9:2 NRSV)?

The other Gospels tell of Jesus *restoring* sight to people—surely a miracle—but only in the Gospel of *John* do we have the report of Jesus giving sight to a man who had *never* been able to see *before*. I think this is important to our understanding of what John wanted his readers, 1,900 years ago, and *today*, to know about Jesus. He was not just giving sight *back* to someone who had *lost* it; he was giving sight for the *first* time to someone who had never *had* it. And so, the sight that Jesus was imparting was something that the man had never *had* prior to encountering Jesus. It was not just *physical* sight, which can be lost by accident or illness, or, as some might suppose, as punishment for some sinful act. So the disciples' question was, at least in part, nonsensical—it wasn't because the *man* had *sinned* that he was *born* blind. And Jesus' response to the disciples showed that the reason for the man's blindness wasn't important anyway, so far as Jesus or his followers were concerned. "[H]e was born blind," Jesus replied, "so that God's works might be revealed in him. We"—notice the plural, which some ancient scribes thought they were correcting by substituting the word "I," supposing that Jesus could only have been referring to himself and not to his followers, including themselves—"*We* must work the works of him who sent me" (John 9:3b–4a NRSV).

For anyone who would be a follower of Jesus, the proper response to blindness is not to assess *blame*, surely not to leave someone *in* their blindness as if not presuming to take it upon *themselves* to commute a *sentence* that *God* had handed down for the other person's *crimes*. For anyone who would be a follower of Jesus, the proper response to blindness is to help the person *see*. "As long as *I* am in the world, I am the *light* of the world," Jesus said (John 9:5 NRSV). And then he spat on the ground and made mud and slathered it on the man's eyes and told him to go wash in the waters of the pool of Siloam, which means "Sent"—and surely John meant for us to have an "Aha!" reaction that the man was to bathe in the pool called "Sent," directed to do so by the person whom, John says over and over in his Gospel, was sent by God—"We must work the works of him who *sent* me while it is day; night is coming"—a prediction of the crucifixion?—"when no one can work" (John 9:4 NRSV). Then the man went and washed in the waters of the pool called "Sent," and when he had done so, he came back able to "see." Do *we* know of a pool of water where *washing* sets us on a path toward *seeing*?

I once heard a pastor declare that he was not a sacramentalist, by which I took him to mean, in the context of his comment, that he didn't think that baptism and the Lord's Supper really had anything to do with salvation, despite the fact that he had been ordained as a "minister of Word and Sacrament." I thought that was an astounding statement, if for no other reason than the Gospel of John is a twenty-one chapter interpretation of the sacraments—baptism and the Lord's Supper—which certainly argues forcefully for their tremendous importance in the life of the believer. In the case of the man born blind, his baptism, if we may call it that, was the beginning of his growing comprehension of who Jesus, his healer, *was*. His neighbors, who had known this person only as a blind beggar, weren't even certain that it was the *same man* after he gained his eyesight. That is understandable. Later, the man himself said, in response to the interrogation of the Pharisees, "'Never since the world began has it been heard that anyone opened the eyes of a person born blind'" (John 9:32 NRSV). It was totally unprecedented, beyond the ability of anyone who had come along before. When the *neighbors* asked him how he received his sight, "[h]e answered, 'The man called Jesus made mud, spread it on my eyes, and said to me, "Go to Siloam and wash." Then I went and washed and received my sight.' They said to him, 'Where is he?' He said, 'I do not know'" (John 9:11–12 NRSV).

The *next* time he was asked about Jesus, this time by the *Pharisees*, "'What do you say about him? It was your eyes he opened,'" the man said, "'He is a prophet'" (John 9:17 NRSV). When he was interrogated yet *again* by the Pharisees, he said, "'We know that God does not listen to sinners, but he does listen to one who worships him and obeys his will. . . . If this man were not from God, he could do nothing'" (John 9:31, 33 NRSV). And finally, when Jesus found him after hearing that the Pharisees had driven the man out—presumably, out of the temple or out of the synagogue—and Jesus asked him, "'Do you believe in the Son of Man?'" and he answered, "'And who is he, sir? Tell me, so that I may believe in him,'" and Jesus said to him, "'You have *seen* him, and the one speaking with you is he,'" the man came to the fullness of faith and declared, "'Lord, I believe.'" "And," John says, "he worshiped him" (John 9:35b, 36, 37, 38 NRSV). Then Jesus said, explaining that all that had just happened was to demonstrate exactly why he had been *sent* into the world: "'I came into this world for judgment so that those who do *not* see may *see*, and those who *do* see may become *blind*'" (John 9:39 NRSV).

Jesus had told the disciples that the man's blindness from birth was *not* a judgment, so it must be, mustn't it, that Jesus' giving *sight* to the *sightless*, and the objection of those who thought that they already saw quite *well*, is what the true and accurate judgment of *Jesus* is all *about*? "Some of the Pharisees," who had heard what Jesus had said, demanded of him, "'Surely *we* are not blind, are we?' Jesus said to them, 'If you were *blind*'"—that is, if they had been *without* eyesight, and thus had some *excuse* for not recognizing who Jesus was, the one who has compassion, the one sent by God to give *true* sight,—"'you would not have sin. But now that you say, "We *see*," your sin *remains*'" (John 9:40-41 NRSV).

Kneading mud, like kneading bread, was a violation of the rules about the sabbath. Almost in a whisper, rather as a footnote, John tells us, "Now it was a sabbath day when Jesus made the mud and opened [the man's] eyes" (John 9:14 NRSV). In the eyes of the *Pharisees*, in *their* sight, in *their* view, not only was the blind *beggar* a sinner, but so was *Jesus* who healed him on the *sabbath*—Jesus, whom the Samaritan woman at the well discovered to be the living water gushing up to eternal life, the one whom God sent into the world and who now had directed a man born blind to go wash in the pool called "Sent" and he was able to see and confess, "Lord, I believe," and worship him, the one who would soon, on the night before his execution, direct his followers to *wash one another*, the one out of whose pierced side flowed not just blood, as expected, but also water—the water of life?—this one, those whose *eyesight* was just *fine* but whose *understanding* was *blind*, judged to be a *sinner*. Ever since their birth, there had never been a day, an hour, a minute when their eyes didn't work. But, still, they didn't see. They didn't believe, they didn't have faith, that Jesus was the one sent from God. And, Jesus concludes this episode, *that* made *them* sinners. As for the man born blind, whom everyone assumed was a sinner because of his affliction, whose condition everyone judged to be the result of breaking some rule or other, all of that faded into insignificance alongside his bath in the waters of Siloam that led him, ultimately, to confess, "Lord, I believe."

And so it was the man born *blind* who could actually *see*. "Do you believe in the Son of Man?" Jesus had asked him. "Do you believe in the one whose coming, according to scripture, whose being sent, will mark the beginning of God's final judgment? A judgment based not on whether people have kept the rules about not laboring on the sabbath, for instance even for the purpose of healing or teaching or feeding or forgiving, nor any of the other myriad rules by which the Pharisees like to judge people 'in' or 'out,' 'saved' or 'not saved,' but judgment based upon whether one believes that I, Jesus, am everything that God is?" "Lord," the man said to Jesus—the man who had all his life, until that very day, never been able to see *anything* with his *eyes*, had never been able to name colors or distinguish faces, had never even been able to read the law and the prophets,—"I believe."

Ironically, the one who, through all this story, came to perceive the truth in its fullness, to see *perfectly*, was driven out by the people whose refusal to believe that Jesus was the person sent by God rendered them *unable* to see the truth about Jesus, and therefore, despite all their flaunted adherence to the rules, identified themselves as *sinners*. Ironically, too, when he heard that the man had been excluded from the place where God was customarily worshiped, the one who was *sent* became the seeker of the one who had been *discarded*. *Both* of them had been rejected as *sinners* by the people who considered themselves *sinless*. It may well be that the believers in John's own congregation, years later, had *themselves* been excluded from the synagogue, rejected as sinners by Pharisees or some other group who judged people on the very same basis that the Pharisees had judged the man born blind. But those people in John's congregation had been baptized in the waters of him whom they believed to have been sent by God, and had come to acknowledge him as Lord.

The Gospel of John teaches that to have our eyes opened by bathing in the water that leads to belief in Jesus, to come to faith that he is the perfect expression of God, the light that has been sent into the world to allow it to see, is salvation from sin. *Not* to *believe* is *not* to *see*, and thus to *remain* in sin. To alter a phrase from Shakespeare, "To see or not to see." *That* really *is* the question.

Fifth Sunday in Lent
Spanish Springs Presbyterian Church, Sparks, Nevada
March 17, 2002

Ezekiel 37:1–14
Romans 8:6–11
John 11:1–45

"Faith Debunking Futility"

As we marked earlier this week the passing of six months since the terrible day when thousands of people, our countrymen and women and people of other nationalities, too, were killed in the largest loss of life to terrorism in American history, and hundreds of others were injured, some horribly, and hundreds or thousands of spouses were widowed, children orphaned, and parents made childless, the images of the attack were played once more on our television screens and printed again in our newspapers and etched anew in our minds and thrust afresh upon our hearts. The eruption of flames as hundreds of tons of aluminum were hurtled at thousands of tons of steel, with the human destruction on both sides of that equation; the screams of fear and grief and rage; the sense of sudden vulnerability and disorientation from unknown forces and unidentified foes—all these things came back to us afresh, as they will continue to do until the end of our lives, those of us who were old enough to know the terror of September 11, 2001. And some new pictures, for me anyway, of the amazing suddenness with which great billows of ghostly-gray ash and dust engulfed all of lower Manhattan, surging up the avenues and blanketing everything and everyone in sight, then hanging over New York like a pall as, in Washington, rescue workers were responding to the carnage at the headquarters of our Department of Defense, defenseless, in truth, against an insane hatred that regards even *self*-destruction a virtue. Six months on, news of a dozen more bodies recovered last Tuesday, and still the majority of those entombed in an instant at the World Trade Center yet to be uncovered, doubtless unrecognizable even to those to whom they were most dear. We have gone through a tumult of emotions. Just when we think we have felt it all, a picture, a story, a last word captured on tape at an emergency response center, finds in us a fresh reservoir of tears and pain.

Then there are the stories that somehow got lost in the first enormity of fear and rage and grief, like the woman on one of the morning news programs this week who, that horrible day, was struck by a wall of fire as flaming jet fuel spewed out of an elevator shaft, burning her over 80 percent of her body, but she is alive, in rehabilitation therapy, after countless skin grafts and countless prayers, no longer, perhaps, a cover girl for magazines that fawn over shallower beauty, but qualified without question for the cover of new "life." We can only hope that the history books will one day make *her* name, and the names of many more *like* her, as well known as the names Mohamed Atta and Osama bin Laden.

I've not spoken personally with anyone who has been to Ground Zero, but from all of the reports in the press, it is a grimly sobering experience, one that must affect visitors as deeply as the Allied soldiers who came upon the ovens at Auschwitz, or those who discovered the killing fields of Cambodia, or those who walked through the ruined streets of Dresden, or those who surveyed the skeletal remains of Hiroshima. Or, to draw from the Bible, a prophet whom the Lord set down in the middle of a valley full of human bones—the relics of a battle that spelled despair for the nation of Israel and that plunged anyone who saw it into utter hopelessness. Of the bones that mutely marked the scene of slaughter, by then several months in the past, Ezekiel says that "there were very many lying in the valley, and they were very dry" (Ezek 37:2b NRSV). There was no possibility that any of these soldiers was just wounded and could be revived with medical treatment or even prayers for healing. They were dead beyond decay, as it seems Israel's hopes of prosperous nationhood were dead beyond resuscitation, with the added grief of sensing that it was all somehow the result of being disobedient to the God who had covenanted to be their protection—a covenant that *they* had broken with their idolatry and their disloyalty, their abuse of the poor and their trust in their weapons.

Here is what it had come to. And the Lord asked Ezekiel a surprising question: "Mortal, can these bones live" (Ezek 37:3a NRSV)? It was not only a *surprising* question. It must have seemed like a *stupid* question. And yet, Ezekiel knew that it was even *more* stupid to suppose that *anything* was impossible, if *God* were in the thing. "O Lord God, you know" (Ezek 37:3b NRSV), Ezekiel responded. And there and then the Lord commanded

Ezekiel the prophet to prophesy—to preach the truth of God's will and God's purpose and God's ways—what seemed to all human sense a silly, pointless exhibition of lunacy. *Or,* the faithful sign of trust in the same God who brought the world into living, fruitful being out of the void of nothingness.

> "Prophesy to these bones, and say to them: O dry bones, hear the word of the Lord. Thus says the Lord God to these bones: I will cause breath to enter you, and you shall live. I will lay sinews on you, and will cause flesh to come upon you, and cover you with skin, and put breath in you, and you shall live; and you shall know that I am the Lord." (Ezek 37:4–6 NRSV)

And Ezekiel did so. And God *undid* the process of decomposition and decay and corruption. But when bone had been joined to bone, and sinews connected them, and flesh appeared on them, and skin covered the flesh, still there was no *life* in them, until God breathed into them as God had breathed into the first human being in Genesis, and *gave* life. "Wind," "breath," "spirit"—it's all the same word in Hebrew. The spirit that had moved over the waters at the creation moved over the battlefield in the valley. The wind that blew upon the cadavers and brought them to life was the breath of God without which *none* of us has *life*, only *existence*. Then the Lord said to Ezekiel,

> "Mortal, these bones are the whole house of Israel. They say, 'Our bones are dried up, and our hope is lost; we are cut off completely.' Therefore prophesy, and say to them, Thus says the Lord God: . . . I will put my spirit within you, and you shall live, and I will place you on your own soil; then you shall know that I, the Lord, have spoken and will act." (Ezek 37:11–12a, 14 NRSV)

Once, at a presbytery meeting I was attending, a retired minister who was serving as the interim pastor of a church in a small town in south-central Kansas got up to tell about something that had occurred in the little congregation. The church had seemed to be dying even faster than the town. Everyone assumed that the future of the congregation was limited; its days were numbered, as one by one, funerals marked the steady decline in the church rolls. It seems that the minister had noticed, when he first came to the church, that it had no nursery for young children. When he remarked upon that situation, he was told by the gray-haired Session, "We have no *need* for a nursery, because we don't have any *babies* in the congregation." The minister began a steady drumbeat of preaching that the church needed a nursery—depending upon the attitude of the listener, "prophecy" sometimes sounded a lot like "harangue" to the point that some people were getting pretty tired of it. But when they finally got the message that the minister wasn't going to stop *talking* about it, and that he didn't intend to *leave* the church anytime soon, the Session finally relented, borrowed a modest amount of funds, and built a nursery, grumbling all the way that it was a silly waste of time and a grievous waste of money. And, indeed, they felt confirmed in their opinion when, after the construction was completed and a nursery attendant had been secured, the nursery sat empty. What had the minister expected—a *miracle*? But, the minister, when he stood up at the presbytery meeting to report on what had been happening at his church, said that, a few weeks earlier, lo and behold, there was a young family in worship who used the nursery for their baby, and then a second family visited, and a third. And he testified that *faith* had *debunked futility*—the same silliness as Ezekiel prophesying to a valley of dry bones. And, he was happy to report, the Session was starting to make plans for remodeling its decrepit old Sunday school classrooms, which had been unused for almost a generation.

"Take away the stone," Jesus told those who were gathered at the house of Lazarus to mourn with Mary and Martha, Lazarus's sisters. "Lord," Martha warned him, "already there is a stench because he has been dead four days" (John 11:39 NRSV). He couldn't just be healed as Jesus had healed many others; the body of their brother was already decayed and decomposing. "Jesus said to her, 'Did I not tell you that if you believed, you would see the glory of God?' So," with a shrug and an exchange of glances, probably, "they took away the stone. And Jesus looked upward" and said a prayer, and then "he cried with a loud voice, 'Lazarus, come out'" (John 11:40–41a, 43 NRSV)! We can imagine the people looking now at Jesus, now at the entrance to the tomb, now again at Jesus, wondering which was the sorrier case. But then, after seconds, after minutes, we don't know, "[t]he dead man came out, his hands and feet bound with strips of cloth, and his face wrapped in a cloth. Jesus said to them, 'Unbind him, and let him go'" (John 11:44 NRSV). And many of the people who had come to mourn with Mary and Martha, as was the custom, *saw* what Jesus did, and *believed* in him.

You and I might not have the same results if *we* were to go to the cemetery and command the dead to rise up from their graves. But *we* haven't been directed by God to do so. Jesus was authorized by God to call forth Lazarus from the dead in order to produce *faith* in Jesus among those who witnessed this extraordinary sign—the culminating event that led directly to Jesus' death on the cross and his being raised by God for the salvation of us all. By bringing Lazarus back to *life*, Jesus had signed his own *death* warrant as far as the priests and the scribes and the Pharisees were concerned—people who were used to dictating to everyone around them what was futile, pronouncing what *could* be done and what *couldn't* be done, *claiming* to represent *God* and *denying* the *authority* of God's own *Son*, dry bones in a valley of self-serving skepticism and comfortable convention and dim expectation, dousing the fire of God's spirit and fanning the ashes and billowing the dust that choked off the people's hope of renewal to salvation. "Mortal, can these bones live?" *They* would have answered in an instant, "Of course not!" And when they heard tell of a man dead for four days who walked out of the stench of death into the sunlight of God's promise, *they* didn't *glorify* God. *They* plotted to *destroy God's Son*.

How can anyone *not* have faith in God's ability to make all things new, to give life to anyone who wants it, to raise up the dead from their tombs and to raise up the living from their despair, in a world that has seen devastated nations rise up from the wreckage of war, that has seen civilization demand an accounting from those who do the despicable and vow that such atrocities shall not happen again even if we must sacrifice our own lives to stop it, that has seen a young mother rise up from the flames and ashes of the World Trade Center and once again embrace her husband and her child, whom all conventional medical wisdom wrote off six months ago as beyond the physiological boundary back across which *no one* can return—the same sort of sophisticated wisdom that will scarcely notice a dying little church in a declining little town building a nursery and smiling now through tears of joy that a *whole new* generation of children will learn about the love of Jesus and the power of God and all the things for which they will grow to give thanks and pass on faithfully to *their* children? Faith is not a silly refusal to accept a hopeless reality. Faith is trust that *God*, the *source* of *all life*, is faithful to God's saving purpose. So faith debunks futility.

Palm/Passion Sunday

Spanish Springs Presbyterian Church, Sparks, Nevada

March 12, 2008

Isaiah 50:4–9a
Philippians 2:5–11
Matthew 21:1–11

"Through the Gates and into the Valley"

As a young child in Sunday school, few Bible stories captured my imagination quite like the story of Jesus riding a donkey into Jerusalem. Each spring, I heard again about Jesus being hailed by followers and well-wishers who waved branches that they had cut from the trees, and then laid them down in his path. Our children's hymns echoed the scripture's song of triumph, "Look, your king is coming to you" (Matt 21:5b NRSV)! Everybody loves a parade. Why didn't *everyone* come out to meet Jesus, come out to greet Jesus, come out to give Jesus the homage he deserved? I wondered. It seems so clear that they should have put Jesus on a throne, then and there. The story seems to start out that way—a donkey-ride up the mountain and into Jerusalem. A prancing white steed might have been more impressive, might have turned more heads. What *should* have happened next was a royal welcome, everybody falling to their knees, and the world made right. But, of course, events took a very dramatic turn.

    A child's mind did not quite grasp the leap from Palm Sunday to Good Friday. Perhaps it's hard for an adult mind, too, to see how things went so quickly from joyful to tragic, from acclaim to condemnation, from palms to passion, from the city gates to the cross on Calvary. Here came Jesus, into the great holy city where God's temple was, given a hero's welcome by friends and well-wishers. Here came Jesus, right into the headquarters of the Pharisees and scribes and priests—into the very hands of the enemy. It was almost as if he had made a blundering miscalculation, riding right into a trap.

It reminds us of the story of another famous ride into death that many schoolchildren over the past century and a half have memorized here, and especially in England and other nations of the British Commonwealth.

> Half a league, half a league
>   Half a league onward,
> All in the valley of Death
>   Rode the six hundred.
> 'Forward, the Light Brigade!
> Charge for the guns!' he said:
> Into the valley of Death
>   Rode the six hundred.
>
> 'Forward, the Light Brigade!'
> Was there a man dismay'd?
> Not tho' the soldier knew,
>   Some one had blunder'd:
> Their's not to make reply,
> Their's not to reason why,
> Their's but to do and die:
> Into the valley of Death
>   Rode the six hundred.[1]

Alfred, Lord Tennyson went on to say, "Boldly they rode and well, / Into the jaws of Death, / Into the mouth of Hell / Rode the six hundred."[2] The poem memorializes not only the *death* of hundreds of British soldiers, but also the disciplined obedience to *duty* that *led* hundreds of British soldiers to follow orders in the face of great danger. An otherwise unremarkable and undistinguished place became a valley of death during the Crimean War, a spot sacred now by their blood and immortalized by Tennyson's words.

Duty. Obedience. Faithfulness to one's calling, which no abuse or threat could negate. Long ago, a prophet heard God's summons to the duty of witnessing to the truth of God's promise and God's purpose to a people who seem not to have wanted to hear it. As the nation of Israel had been abused and despised by its neighbors, so now Isaiah the prophet apparently was being abused and despised by his own countrymen living in exile in Babylon. The nations had invaded Israel and ruined its farms and destroyed its cities and plundered its wealth and carried off its people. The prolonged strain of the Babylonian exile had left the captive Israelites fatigued and

---

1. Tennyson, "Charge of the Light Brigade," lines 1–17.
2. Tennyson, "Charge of the Light Brigade," lines 23–26.

distrustful. They were suspicious of God and skeptical of anyone who would preach that God still *cared* for Israel, that God would *restore* Israel, that God would *use* Israel as the instrument through which all the nations of the earth would come to know and honor God. They had *turned* on the prophet—disfiguring him and insulting him by plucking out his hair and his beard, striking him and beating him, no doubt slandering him and making him an object of contempt.

Some messengers would have *abandoned* the task they had been assigned, would have turned *away* from their mission when it became so full of peril, would have *complained* against the one who sent them on such a *humiliating* errand, would have *rebelled* when they found the way difficult and dangerous. But Isaiah did *not* complain, because he was sure of his message and the one who commanded him to proclaim it. And so he *faced* the abuse, faced even the possibility of *death*, not a *victim* of God's *miscalculation*, but a *servant* of God's *redemption*, obedient even though it might mean his own destruction, even though it meant, so to speak, riding into the valley of Death. Would anyone contend with him? Let them know that whatever *they* might inflict upon him would not be the punishment of God! Whether *they* recognized it or not, Isaiah the servant was God's own response to Israel's predicament of hopelessness. And he wasn't just spinning ideas and spouting dogmas. *He* was one *with* them in their struggle against despair and degradation. *He* was suffering, *too*, there with them in the very trenches of their affliction, sharing the pain, submitting to the oppression, but giving testimony with his own life to the trustworthiness of God's promise and the certainty of God's forgiveness. God had opened Isaiah's ears to hear God's own call to sustain the weary, to give hope, to summon faith. And, so certain was he of God's purpose and *his role* in the *fulfillment of God's promise*, he didn't try to escape to someplace *beyond* danger and *beyond* the misery of his people. Quite to the contrary, he dutifully became God's instrument for their salvation, *his* life of obedient servanthood offered for *others*.

Since the time of Christ's crucifixion, Christians have recognized that the obedient servanthood spoken of in Isaiah was lived out perfectly by Jesus. All the honors of heaven were his by right—God's own Son from before the world was created, *his* proper *inheritance* is the *majesty of heaven*, not the *agony of the cross*. He deserves to be *served* by all, not to be the *servant* of all. But he was given a commission by God to work the salvation of humankind, to overcome the deadly effects of human sin by dying for the sake of sinners. He came into the world fully human in the powerlessness of a baby. All the forces of nature were at his command, but he voluntarily gave up the power even to turn a stone into a loaf of bread to feed his own hunger, refused to suspend the laws of gravity to prove his own prestige, rejected the thought of becoming the world's ruler by the crafts of Satan. Instead, he took the role of a slave, serving others, and the proud and the privileged and the pompous and even many people who were politely *proper* came to despise him for it, came to hate him for it, came finally to kill him for it. And not just kill, but kill by crucifixion—the cruel and barbarous form of execution that the Romans reserved specially for rebels against the government and slaves who had disobeyed their masters or who had run away from their duties.

The people who *first* heard the story of Good Friday would have been shocked and horrified by the scandal of the cross. Some would have been put off by it; they would have *scoffed* at the suggestion of worshiping one who had been *crucified*! But those people would have missed the profound truth of *God* that towers over *human* prejudice and *human* logic and *human* etiquette. What an irony! The Lord of all creation tried and condemned for treason because of his unwavering loyalty to God. What an injustice! The only true and perfect servant of all people executed as if he were a slave who had tried to *escape* his obligations. In fact, it was his single-minded devotion to doing the will of God by serving others, even the outcast and the unclean and the despised and the rejected, that made his date with the cross an absolute certainty. It was confirmed on a mountaintop in a conversation with Moses and Elijah—yes, the way of obedience to God, the way of faithfulness to the law and the prophets, the way of salvation, was the road through the gates of Jerusalem that would take him into the valley of Death. And far from turning *away* from the valley of Death, he set his face toward it and rode straight into it, on the back of a lowly little animal recognized by all as a symbol of humility and peace, as befits a servant, half a league, half a league, half a league onward, because he *was* the perfect servant, because he knew what was required of him, and he would not turn away from his obedience to God, to whose purpose of your salvation and mine he had submitted his whole being.

In some quarters today, Christianity is advertised—and "advertised" is the word—as the road to privilege, the road to health, the road to wealth, the road to power, the road to superiority over our fellow men and women. Christ Jesus, the Savior of the world who lived the life of a servant and died the death of a slave, did not find his glory in *raising* himself *above* others, but in *pouring* himself out *for* others. The cross was not a seat of *prestige*. It was an instrument of *death*. Paul found it important to *remind* Christians of that—Christians who were making claims to privilege and quarreling among themselves who was most worthy of honor in the kingdom of God. He was reminding them that when Jesus himself was riding through the gates of Jerusalem, no waving of palm branches or shouts of "Hosanna!," appropriate as they were, should make us forget that Jesus was knowingly and purposefully riding into the valley of Death. His concern was only one thing—to be obedient to God, fulfilling God's commission, doing precisely what was necessary to achieve God's purpose of salvation.

During the days of Nazi control of Germany, and the Nazi control of the state church, many pastors and congregations heroically *resisted* Hitler's designs, honoring *instead* the will of *God* and the Lordship of *Christ*. Refusing to bend to hatred's dominion, they knowingly put themselves at peril to hide Jews and befriend the other groups that were on Hitler's list for extermination. Some were tempted to flee their country and carry on their campaign as refugees, but the slowness of the Allies to neutralize Hitler taught them that resistance from *outside* of Germany would be futile to achieve the purpose of saving the German people from Hitler and saving the world from the German army. Many of the resisters believed that, in any case, it was not the *world's* business to restore order, justice, and decency to Germany, but rather the obligation of the Germans *themselves*. Dietrich Bonhoeffer, a German Lutheran pastor who was active in the resistance against the Nazi movement, was invited by friends in America to come teach theology at Union Seminary in New York, safe from the Nazi threat, safe from the possibility of imprisonment and execution for his beliefs and for *acting* on his beliefs. Shortly after he arrived in New York, though, he decided that his coming to America was not the *faithful* thing to do. He could have had a long and distinguished career, doing much good and advancing the cause of bringing the gospel to bear on the moral issues of modern society—something that personally appealed to him greatly. But obedience to God's call required living *not* in the safety of the seminary classroom, but rather in the peril of thrusting a spoke in the wheel of Hitler's march toward world domination and the extinction of the Jews and other despised peoples and the corruption of the Christian gospel. He wrote a letter to his friend and colleague at Union Seminary, Reinhold Niebuhr, explaining his decision to return to Germany:

> "I shall have no right to participate in the reconstruction of Christian life in Germany after the war if I do not share the trials of this time with my people.... Christians in Germany will face the terrible alternative of either willing the *defeat* of their nation in order that Christian civilization may *survive*, or willing the *victory* of their nation and thereby *destroying* our civilization. I know which of these alternatives I must choose; but I cannot make this choice in security."[3]

---

3. Leibholz, "Memoir," 16 (emphasis added).

He would not turn away from his duty to obey God and serve others. A modern-day prophet who neither cursed God for his *fate* nor turned from the *commission* God had set before him, Bonhoeffer followed Jesus into the valley of Death, and was hanged, ignobly, at Flossenburg concentration camp on April 9th, 1945. Just days later, the concentration camp was liberated by the Allies.

It is easy for us to imagine ourselves in the parade honoring Jesus as he rode through the gates of Jerusalem. It would have been a natural time to think how good life was, more pleasant, by far, than where obedience to God was leading him—a slave's death, a rebel's death, a criminal's death, death on a cross. But it was Christ's total obedience to *God* that *won* our salvation. And it is *our* obedience to God as Christ's *followers* that gives *us* a *share* in the *glory* of the *cross*. "Let the same mind be in you that was in Christ Jesus, who, though he was in the form of God, did not regard equality with God as something to be exploited, but emptied himself, taking the form of a slave" (Phil 2:5–7a NRSV).

Maundy Thursday

Spanish Springs Presbyterian Church, Sparks, Nevada

March 24, 2005

Exodus 12:1–4, 11–14
1 Corinthians 11:23–26
John 13:1–17, 31b–35

"The Meal of Anticipation"

If your family is like mine, you mark birthdays and anniversaries not just with cards and gifts and cake, but with a special meal. In *our* family, each of our children annually gets to *choose* the meal with which we celebrate his or her birthday on, or at least very near, the anniversary of the date on which he or she entered this world several years ago. And on *my* birthday, the meal is always the *same*—it is a ritual that has been carried forward from birthday celebrations in the home in which I grew up into the home that I have established with my wife and children—seasoned brisket, green beans with onion and bacon, stuffed baked potatoes with *chili con queso* whipped into them, and, in my adult years, Boston cream pie.

It is natural to celebrate the anniversary of important events in a person's life, or in a *people's* life, as Americans do on Independence Day, which has its own culinary traditions. With the most important annual celebration in the Old Testament, however—Passover—there is a subtle, but very important difference. According to the book of Exodus, the *original* Passover, the occasion on which the Hebrews *first* ate the roasted lamb and the bitter herbs and the unleavened bread, celebrated *not* something that had happened in the *past*, but something that God was promising to do in the *future*—to pass over the houses of the Hebrews with the deathly punishment that was going to befall their Egyptian taskmasters and to bring them up out of bondage in Egypt through the divided waters of the Red Sea. God commanded that every year all of Israel was to celebrate the exodus with a meal prepared just so, and to do it in specific attire and posture. "This is how you shall eat it," God told Moses and Aaron in the land of Egypt:

> your loins girded, your sandals on your feet, and your staff in your hand; and you shall eat it hurriedly. It is the passover of the LORD. For I *will* pass through the land of Egypt that night, and I *will* strike down every firstborn in the land of Egypt, both human beings and animals; on all the gods of Egypt I *will* execute judgments: I am the LORD. The blood shall be a sign for you on the houses where you live: when I see the blood, I *will* pass over you, and no plague shall destroy you when I strike the land of Egypt. (Exod 12:11–13 NRSV)

The original Passover meal, to be repeated annually thereafter, was a meal of *anticipation*—a meal that was eaten in faith that God *would* act to save God's people. The annual *repetition* of the meal would be done in *remembrance*. "This day shall be a day of remembrance for you. You shall celebrate it as a festival to the LORD; throughout your generations you shall observe it as a perpetual ordinance" (Exod 12:14 NRSV). But the meal *itself* was an act of *hope*, an act looking *forward* to God's *fulfillment* of God's *promises*. And ever since, the meal has been a reminder to God's people that God's faithfulness to the promise of salvation many hundreds of years *ago* is a sign and seal of God's faithfulness to the promise of salvation *yet to come*.

By reenacting the original Passover, participants today incorporate themselves into God's history of salvation. It both makes them a part of the story they *relate* to, and projects them into the future for which they *hope*. For the people of God are *always*, today every bit as much as in ancient Egypt, to be ready for the march out of the oppressiveness of Pharaoh's empire and into the blessedness of the promised land. The very *expectation of* God's kingdom and *hope for* God's kingdom is an act of defiance against the imperial claims of earthly governments, earthly economies, earthly values, earthly satisfactions.

Likewise, the *Lord's Supper* has its roots in a meal that *anticipated* what had *not yet happened*. For during the *Last* Supper, on the night before Jesus was put to death on the cross, the night on which he was betrayed by one of his own, Jesus "took a loaf of bread, and when he had given thanks, he broke it and said, 'This is my body that is for you. Do this in remembrance of me.' In the same way he took the cup also, after supper, saying, 'This cup is the new covenant in my blood. Do this, as often as you drink it, in remembrance of me'" (1 Cor 11:23b–25 NRSV). On the night before the crucifixion, Jesus gave his disciples bread broken, as his *body* was to be broken, and wine poured out, as his *blood* was to be poured out, the next day. And he commanded them to repeat the meal in *remembrance* of what had *not yet happened.*

But also like the Passover meal of the Jews, the Lord's Supper was *not* to be simply a *commemoration,* but a *participation,* not just an anniversary of a *past event,* but a *present engagement* in a continuing reality that gives hope of a *future fulfillment.* "For as often as you eat this bread and drink the cup, you proclaim the Lord's death until he comes" (1 Cor 11:26 NRSV). It was to be a ritual that looked *forward* as much as it looked *backward,* and to offer living hope even in the midst of oppression and injustice, disappointment and discouragement. And the young church quickly and eagerly, after the resurrection, made the meal a part of the weekly gathering for its worship in the name of its risen Lord. Indeed, it became the most distinctive feature of Christian worship and the most characteristic activity of Christian life, the geographical center of Christian fellowship and the enacted witness to the Christian hope, the meal of anticipation of the saving miracle God promised to do next.

As often as we Christians, years after the crucifixion, take part in the Lord's Supper, come to the table and eat the bread and drink of the cup, as members of Christ's body, the church, we are giving testimony not only to the sacrifice Christ made for us long ago, but giving testimony too to the belief that Christ will return in glory to bring a close to history and inaugurate the age of the new heaven and the new earth—to bring an end to cruelty and disease, to sin and death, and to reign visibly over all creation, acknowledged by everyone as Lord. Although we annually receive the meal on Maundy Thursday, the liturgical anniversary of the last supper Jesus shared with his disciples *before* the *crucifixion,* we remember the scriptures' witness that he dined with his disciples on many occasions *after* the *resurrection,* physically, until the Ascension. And very soon, the early Christians began to sense his real presence with them in the power of the Spirit *whenever* they gathered and took bread and blessed it and broke it and shared it, began to sense a truth greater than the proclamations of emperors and governors and the threats of disease and poverty and the hurts of loneliness and neglect.

The Lord's Supper was not restricted to an annual commemoration, as the Passover meal had been; Christians shared it frequently, every time they came together, for they were eager not only to proclaim the Lord's saving death but also his glorious return, and to be in Christ's presence as often as possible. They *remembered,* but it was not a memorial *only;* weekly they recalled the events surrounding Jesus' death because in the *cross* was the prerequisite to the *empty tomb* and *everlasting life.*

This most fundamental and central act of Christian worship is also *our* participation in Christ's saving life and death, and *our* testimony that Christ's life and death mark God's decisive entry into human history in a way that gives us hope that the promises of salvation are for *us* and that the renewing of all things is certain. And it is the very participation of the community of faith, coming to the table together, that proclaims the meaning of the bread broken and the wine poured out for us; it enacts a great parable about Jesus' life and death being for *us*. The Lord's Supper isn't something just to know *about*; we don't proclaim the Lord's death and anticipate his coming just by hearing a *sermon* about the Last Supper, however excellent it might be. We proclaim the Lord's death and anticipate his coming by having a *part* in it, *doing* it *with Christ, dying* with him and continually *rising* with him. So, when the *Corinthians* started becoming very *subjective* about the Lord's Supper, each coming to the table at his or her own *leisure* and for his or her own *benefit* and *grabbing* rather than *sharing*, Paul objected sternly and gave them a *reminder* of what the supper was *about*—a reminder that provides us our best insight into what it means *today* to eat and drink together the bread broken and the wine poured, remembering Christ's sacrifice on the cross, testifying to his coming, living in anticipation of that promised *future* day by the way that we live *today*, including abiding in Christ's presence and feasting at his invitation at the table where *all* are fed, just like it will be when the kingdom is finally established, and there will be no more tears and no more pain and no more war, no more hunger and no more disease and no more sorrow, and there will be no rationing of blessing, and there will be no exhaustion of hope.

As God commanded that the Passover be a day for Israel to remember God's delivering them from the dehumanizing bondage of slavery, so Jesus commanded that the Lord's Supper be an occasion for the church to remember God's delivering us from the deadly bondage of sin. As the Passover meal anticipated the great act of salvation that God was about to accomplish in the houses of the Egyptians and at the Red Sea, so the Last Supper anticipated the great act of salvation that God was about to accomplish on Calvary and in the garden. And as the Passover meal incorporates the Jew, even today, in the ongoing miracle of the exodus, so the Lord's Supper incorporates the Christian, even today, in the even greater ongoing miracle of the death and resurrection of Christ—the miracle that brings us, dying and rising with him, to eternal life already now in the precincts of the kingdom which is yet to be.

Come, then, eagerly and often, to this table—it is the meal not just of bread and wine, but of Christ himself broken and poured out for us, a meal not just to reflect upon, but to participate in, a meal not just of introspection, but of proclamation, the meal not just of remembrance, but of anticipation.

Good Friday

Spanish Springs Presbyterian Church, Sparks, Nevada
March 21, 2008

Isaiah 52:13—53:12
Hebrews 4:14-16; 5:7-9
John 18:1—19:42

After Jesus had spoken these words, he went out with his disciples across the Kidron Valley to a place where there was a garden, which he and his disciples entered. Now Judas, who betrayed him, also knew the place, because Jesus often met there with his disciples. So Judas brought a detachment of soldiers together with police from the chief priests and the Pharisees, and they came there with lanterns and torches and weapons. Then Jesus, knowing all that was to happen to him, came forward and asked them, "Whom are you looking for?" They answered, "Jesus of Nazareth." Jesus replied, "I am he." Judas, who betrayed him, was standing with them. When Jesus said to them, "I am he," they stepped back and fell to the ground. Again he asked them, "Whom are you looking for?" And they said, "Jesus of Nazareth." Jesus answered, "I told you that I am he. So if you are looking for me, let these men go." This was to fulfill the word that he had spoken, "I did not lose a single one of those whom you gave me." (John 18:1-9 NRSV)

Judas, that rat. Curse him! His name sticks in my throat. I never liked him. I never trusted him. From the very beginning, you could tell that he was scheming. I didn't understand why Jesus wanted him to come with us. We should have known he was plotting something like this—when he got up and left the dinner. It was obvious that Jesus had something important on his mind, things that he wanted to tell us. But before he had gotten very far into it, Judas up and left. Just like that! And after Jesus had washed his feet, and the rest of us, too! At the time, I just thought he was being rude. Little did I know that he had an appointment with the police, those Roman dogs. We should never have come up to Jerusalem. It was too dangerous. And we should have warned Jesus about Judas. I suppose he got paid for his treason. I swear, if I ever see him again alive . . .

> Then Simon Peter, who had a sword, drew it, struck the high priest's slave, and cut off his right ear. The slave's name was Malchus. Jesus said to Peter, "Put your sword back into its sheath. Am I not to drink the cup that the Father has given me?" (John 18:10–11 NRSV)

Only Peter had any guts last night. Why didn't the rest of us put up a fight? Why didn't the rest of us try to defend Jesus? Yeah, we were scared. We were surprised. We were confused. But that didn't stop Peter. And Jesus told him to put his sword away. At least Peter tried. So what if we couldn't win a fight against the police and the soldiers? At least now I wouldn't feel like such a contemptible coward. Why Jesus didn't want Peter to defend him, I don't know. Something he said made me think that he didn't want any of us to get hurt. It was almost like Jesus was resigned to what was happening—thought that it had to be. He used to talk sometimes about dying . . .

> So the soldiers, their officer, and the Jewish police arrested Jesus and bound him. First they took him to Annas, who was the father-in-law of Caiaphas, the high priest that year. Caiaphas was the one who had advised the Jews that it was better to have one person die for the people.
> Simon Peter and another disciple followed Jesus. Since that disciple was known to the high priest, he went with Jesus into the courtyard of the high priest, but Peter was standing outside the gate. So the other disciple, who was known to the high priest, went out, spoke to the woman who guarded the gate, and brought Peter in. The woman said to Peter, "You are not also one of this man's disciples, are you?" He said, "I am not." Now the slaves and the police had made a charcoal fire because it was cold, and they were standing around it and warming themselves. Peter also was standing with them and warming himself. (John 18:12–18 NRSV)

You'd think people would have some rights. They didn't even say why they were arresting Jesus. But they dragged him off to Annas's house. Peter and another of our number followed along, at a distance, staying in the shadows. We all should have gone to complain about what had happened, to demand justice. But we were stunned. It had happened so quickly. And we were scared. If they'd arrested Jesus, wouldn't they arrest us, too? And we didn't know why he had been taken, so we couldn't know that they wouldn't accuse us of the same thing, whatever it was. But we should have gone. I should have gone.

But maybe we would have buckled when we got there. Peter did, I gather from rumors. Some of the others have criticized him severely. But I can't. Peter, at least, had the courage to go *there, to be* close *to Jesus and see what they were doing to him. The* rest *of us were just looking out for* ourselves.

> Then the high priest questioned Jesus about his disciples and about his teaching. Jesus answered, "I have spoken openly to the world; I have always taught in the synagogues and in the temple, where all the Jews come together. I have said nothing in secret. Why do you ask me? Ask those who heard what I said to them; they know what I said." When he had said this, one of the police standing nearby struck Jesus on the face, saying, "Is that how you answer the high priest?" Jesus answered, "If I have spoken wrongly, testify to the wrong. But if I have spoken rightly, why do you strike me?" Then Annas sent him bound to Caiaphas the high priest. (John 18:19–24 NRSV)

I think they don't even know themselves why they arrested Jesus—I mean, what his real crime was. They just didn't like *him. They didn't want people to* listen *to him, to hear what he had to* say. *They were* jealous. *They love their power, the priests do, and* Jesus *was becoming more popular than* they are. *I mean, think of the crowd when we came into the city! His reputation had preceded him all the way up from Galilee! They were the ones who should have been* afraid. *And I guess they were.*

> Now Simon Peter was standing and warming himself. They asked him, "You are not also one of his disciples, are you?" He denied it and said, "I am not." One of the slaves of the high priest, a relative of the man whose ear Peter had cut off, asked, "Did I not see you in the garden with him?" Again Peter denied it, and at that moment the cock crowed.
>
> Then they took Jesus from Caiaphas to Pilate's headquarters. It was early in the morning. They themselves did not enter the headquarters, so as to avoid ritual defilement and to be able to eat the Passover. So Pilate went out to them and said, "What accusation do you bring against this man?" They answered, "If this man were not a criminal, we would not have handed him over to you." Pilate said to them, "Take him yourselves and judge him according to your law." The Jews replied, "We are not permitted to put anyone to death." (This was to fulfill what Jesus had said when he indicated the kind of death he was to die.) (John 18:25–32 NRSV)

So scrupulous they are to avoid breaking any of the laws! Why, if a person were lying bleeding in a ditch alongside the road, they'd probably walk on the other side to avoid being contaminated by the blood; they'd rather see a person die than think that they might be defiled! So unlike Jesus, who taught us that the sabbath is a gift from God, not an excuse for avoiding helping your neighbor. I hear they wouldn't even enter Pilate's house last night because then they would have to go purify themselves for the sabbath. All careful to avoid the ritual dirtiness of being under the roof of a Roman, but quick enough to call on a Roman to do their dirty work!

> Then Pilate entered the headquarters again, summoned Jesus, and asked him, "Are *you* the King of the Jews?" Jesus answered, "Do you ask this on your own, or did others tell you about me?" Pilate replied, "I am not a Jew, am I? Your own nation and the chief priests handed you over to me. What have you done?" Jesus answered, "My kingdom is not from this world. If my kingdom were from this world, my followers would be fighting to keep me from being handed over to the Jews. But as it is, my kingdom is not from here." Pilate asked him, "So you are a king?" Jesus answered, "You say that I am a king. For this I was born, and for this I came into the world, to testify to the truth. Everyone who belongs to the truth listens to my voice." Pilate asked him, "What is truth?"
>
> After he had said this, he went out to the Jews again and told them, "I find no case against him. But you have a custom that I release someone for you at the Passover. Do you want me to release for you the King of the Jews?" They shouted in reply, "Not this man, but Barabbas!" Now Barabbas was a bandit. (John 18:33–40 NRSV)

Pilate! Roman scum! He's never had the backbone to stand up for anything! And he refused to stand up to the priests, though he suspected they hadn't any right to have Jesus arrested. Keep the order! Keep the peace! But what kind of peace is this? One based on lies. What kind of order is this? Simply how people act when they're afraid. Pilate tried to worm his way out of responsibility, tried to turn the decision over to the crowd. But they just wanted to be entertained, just wanted the spectacle of another crucifixion. Didn't they know the things that Jesus had done for people? The things that Jesus could continue to do for people? They didn't care any more about the truth than Pilate did! "Give us Barabbas!" they shouted. A thief, a liar, an anarchist! So he's loose on society again by their own fickle desire. And the kindest, most caring, most wonderful person that I've ever known is . . .

Then Pilate took Jesus and had him flogged. And the soldiers wove a crown of thorns and put it on his head, and they dressed him in a purple robe. They kept coming up to him, saying, "Hail, King of the Jews!" and striking him on the face. Pilate went out again and said to them, "Look, I am bringing him out to you to let you know that I find no case against him." So Jesus came out, wearing a crown of thorns and the purple robe. Pilate said to them, "Here is the man!" When the chief priests and the police saw him, they shouted, "Crucify him! Crucify him!" Pilate said to them, "Take him yourselves and crucify him; I find no case against him." The Jews answered him, "We have a law, and according to that law he ought to die because he has claimed to be the Son of God." (John 19:1–7 NRSV)

The Son of God? I don't know. He was certainly human enough to get hungry and to feel pain. But if Jesus wasn't *the Son of God, then how did he bring Lazarus back to life? Oh, I don't know. These questions are too big for me. Look, the point is, he never hurt anybody, only helped people, did wonderful things. Certainly more than* King Herod *ever did, that pompous Roman puppet.* Herod *cares for no one but* Herod. *There isn't* anyone *that* Jesus *didn't care about. There isn't* anyone *that Jesus didn't . . . love. Is there some law against love?*

Now when Pilate heard this, he was more afraid than ever. He entered his headquarters again and asked Jesus, "Where are you from?" But Jesus gave him no answer. Pilate therefore said to him, "Do you refuse to speak to me? Do you not know that I have power to release you, and power to crucify you?" Jesus answered him, "You would have no power over me unless it had been given you from above; therefore the one who handed me over to you is guilty of a greater sin." From then on Pilate tried to release him, but the Jews cried out, "If you release this man, you are no friend of the emperor. Everyone who claims to be a king sets himself against the emperor."

When Pilate heard these words, he brought Jesus outside and sat on the judge's bench at a place called The Stone Pavement or in Hebrew Gabbatha. Now it was the day of Preparation for the Passover; and it was about noon. He said to the Jews, "Here is your King!" They cried out, "Away with him! Away with him! Crucify him!" Pilate asked them, "Shall I crucify your King?" The chief priests answered, "We have no king but the emperor." Then he handed him over to them to be crucified. (John 19:8–16a NRSV)

No king but the emperor? A fine lot of Jews are these children of Abraham! They complain that Jesus blasphemed by calling himself the Son of God, committed treason by calling himself the king of the Jews, and then they pledge all their allegiance to a Roman emperor who calls himself a god! They should have been on trial, not Jesus. They should be facing the ultimate punishment, not Jesus. And if Pilate really thought the charges were baseless, or petty, the Roman swine, he could have let Jesus go—or at least let Jesus live. But no. He handed Jesus over to the rabble. And he washed his hands of the whole affair. The world has gone insane.

> So they took Jesus; and carrying the cross by himself, he went out to what is called The Place of the Skull, which in Hebrew is called Golgotha. There they crucified him, and with him two others, one on either side, with Jesus between them. Pilate also had an inscription written and put on the cross. It read, "Jesus of Nazareth, the King of the Jews." Many of the Jews read this inscription, because the place where Jesus was crucified was near the city; and it was written in Hebrew, in Latin, and in Greek. Then the chief priests of the Jews said to Pilate, "Do not write, 'The King of the Jews,' but, 'This man said, I am King of the Jews.'" Pilate answered, "What I have written I have written." When the soldiers had crucified Jesus, they took his clothes and divided them into four parts, one for each soldier. They also took his tunic; now the tunic was seamless, woven in one piece from the top. So they said to one another, "Let us not tear it, but cast lots for it to see who will get it." This was to fulfill what the scripture says,
>
> > "They divided my clothes among themselves,
> > and for my clothing they cast lots."
>
> And that is what the soldiers did. (John 19:16b–25a NRSV)

I wasn't there. But those who were say that they tried to strip every bit of Jesus' dignity away from him, humiliated him in every way possible. They mocked the notion that he was the king of the Jews, with that sign, with that robe, with that crown of thorns. Then they left him naked on the cross for hours while they gambled for his clothes. I can't image the pain, the blood, the flies, the insults. How could God have allowed this to happen to such a good man? Why didn't he do something? Why didn't Jesus do something? He'd done wondrous things for others.

> Meanwhile, standing near the cross of Jesus were his mother, and his mother's sister, Mary the wife of Clopas, and Mary Magdalene. When Jesus saw his mother and the disciple whom

he loved standing beside her, he said to his mother, "Woman, here is your son." Then he said to the disciple, "Here is your mother." And from that hour the disciple took her into his own home.

After this, when Jesus knew that all was now finished, he said (in order to fulfill the scripture), "I am thirsty." A jar full of sour wine was standing there. So they put a sponge full of the wine on a branch of hyssop and held it to his mouth. When Jesus had received the wine, he said, "It is finished." Then he bowed his head and gave up his spirit. (John 19:25b–30 NRSV)

It's not possible to believe that he's dead. He can't be! But he is. I've heard that they didn't even bother to break his legs, like they do so cruelly to make victims die more quickly. He was already dead. And then they stabbed him in the side on top of that. But before he died, I understand, Jesus did one last kind deed— he made sure that his mother would be taken care of. Maybe he would have asked me to do that if I had been there. Of course, he knew that I wasn't *there. So he* knew *that I, too, had abandoned him. What must his last thoughts of me have been? I* should *have been there. I'm glad I* wasn't *there to see him in such pain and agony. But I* should *have been.*

Since it was the day of Preparation, the Jews did not want the bodies left on the cross during the sabbath, especially because that sabbath was a day of great solemnity. So they asked Pilate to have the legs of the crucified men broken and the bodies removed. Then the soldiers came and broke the legs of the first and of the other who had been crucified with him. But when they came to Jesus and saw that he was already dead, they did not break his legs. Instead one of the soldiers pierced his side with a spear, and at once blood and water came out. (He who saw this has testified so that you also may believe. His testimony is true, and he knows that he tells the truth.) These things occurred so that the scripture might be fulfilled, "None of his bones shall be broken." And again another passage of scripture says, "They will look on the one whom they have pierced."

After these things, Joseph of Arimathea, who was a disciple of Jesus, though a secret one because of his fear of the Jews, asked Pilate to let him take away the body of Jesus. Pilate gave him permission; so he came and removed his body. Nicodemus, who had at first come to Jesus by night, also came, bringing a mixture of myrrh and aloes, weighing about a hundred pounds. They took the body of Jesus and wrapped it with spices in linen cloths, according to the burial custom of the Jews. Now there was a garden in the place where he was crucified, and in the garden there was a new tomb in which no one had ever been laid. And so, because it was the Jewish day of Preparation, and the tomb was nearby, they laid Jesus there (John 19:31–42 NRSV).

Joseph—he is a good man. He did what all of us should have done, at least—to take care of Jesus' body, to give him in death the dignity that the soldiers took away from him in his last hours of life. And now, it's over. Our hopes, our expectations, our friendship, our purpose for living. And we still don't know but that they might come hunting for us. Yes, I'm still scared, and still feeling a coward. I guess I'll have to live the rest of my life with the knowledge that I let him down—the best person who ever lived. How I yearn to hear him say he had forgiven me for that! But now he's dead. And my spirit—it feels dead, too. I hear that Mary, the one from Magdala, is eager to go to the tomb as soon as the sabbath is over. I don't see what good that will do anyone. What could she possibly hope to find but a place full of death?

The Resurrection of the Lord (Sunrise)
First Presbyterian Church, Ponca City, Oklahoma
April 20, 2014

Jeremiah 31:1–6
Acts 10:34–43
John 20:1–18

"The Pilgrim Heart"

I am more familiar with sunsets than sunrises, not because I'm not up early enough to see the sun come up, but because, growing up in various houses, our back-yard patio always faced west. I especially remember sunsets in El Paso, where we lived during my elementary years. Almost every evening, my parents and I used to sit on the back patio of our home on the lower slopes of Mount Franklin, watching the sun go down behind the horizon of desert hills to the west across the valley of the Rio Grande. Against the red glow of the evening sky, we could see the silhouette of a little mountain that sits by itself on the place where the American states of New Mexico and Texas and the Mexican state of Chihuahua all come together. The mountain is called El Cristo Rey—"Christ the King"—and atop that mountain, clearly visible by day and perfectly outlined in the evening by the brilliant sunset behind it, we could see the giant cross that gave the mountain its name. On the cross, in relief, is a statue of Jesus with arms outstretched toward the great international city straddling the border—El Paso, Texas, and Ciudad Juárez, Mexico.

I remember walking up the trail that leads from the base of El Cristo Rey to the huge cross at its peak. At least twice, I have climbed to the top of that mountain—once with my father and once with a schoolmate. I remember standing at the base of that giant cross, looking to the east out across the city and to the north up the little ribbon of green along the Rio

Grande and west out across the desert stretching far away toward Arizona and California and southward toward the hidden mysteries of Mexico. I remember the flowers placed at the foot of the cross in little bunches or in baskets or vases, offerings of devotion left by pilgrims who made the ascent up to the monument, some of them walking, some of them on their knees, some of them in wheelchairs, some of them children, some of them young adults with babies in their arms, some of them quite old. How far had they come to make their gesture of piety? Many of them, undoubtedly, came from the squatters' shacks clustered at the very foot of the mountain. Some, I imagine, journeyed even hundreds of miles, moved by their love of Jesus and their hope in his promises.

There were *always* people going up and down the broad path to the statue, but at certain times of the year, clearly visible from our backyard, there were organized processions, sometimes groups of hundreds of people making their pilgrimage. Especially during Lent I remember them—a long column of the faithful, moving ever so slowly, it seemed, from the base toward the summit. Here and there, this line of devout would be hidden by a hillock, only to appear again *higher* on the mountain, a great human chain steadily winding toward its destination. And finally, they would appear at the top, and cluster at the base of the cross. There, on the peak of El Cristo Rey, they would look up at the face of Jesus carved out of stone, and kneel in prayer to their Lord and Savior.

For more than fifty springs, the wonderment of it all has remained in my memory—the simple love and gratitude and hope that year after year brought pilgrims to that lone desert mountain, parched and sunbaked even in the spring, commemorating *another's* climb up *another* desert hill half a world away, parched and sunbaked even that spring nearly 2,000 years ago when Jesus first stretched out his arms on the cross and looked out over a great city. There were no pilgrims then, of course. The hearts of a few in that crowd were *breaking*, for there were some *faithful* who had climbed the hill, tearful, dismayed—women who had been followers of Jesus, and also the disciple John, apparently. But most of the crowd either passed by, oblivious to the suffering one and the cosmic drama unfolding in their presence, or they ridiculed him, or cursed him.

Had we been there on Calvary that day, what would our hearts have felt? What would our faces have shown? What would our lips have said? We can never know. We can only examine our hearts *today*, in the light not only of Jesus' crucifixion, but in the light of God's raising him from the dead. Do the cross and the empty tomb and the appearances of the risen Lord to his disciples produce in us a faith that instills joy and love and thanksgiving and wonderment in our heart that sets *us* out on a pilgrim's journey through life marked by a spirit of humble devotion? Or do we simply pass by the cross once a year on Good Friday if we have time, and take a quick obligatory glance into the empty tomb on Easter Sunday, as we march along in our routine, without letting either the passion of the crucifixion or the promise of the resurrection work themselves into the recesses of our heart?

The crucifixion and resurrection were the center of early Christian preaching. Fantastic to some, a riddle to others, the testimony of a God who loves his creation enough to send his own Son to proclaim his love in words and in deeds, but whose love was rejected by nailing him to a cross, but then who would not permit such sin to *defeat* his love, but instead raised his Son from the grave as *guarantee* of the *stubbornness* of his love. That was the joyful message of the new Christian faith.

Some of those who heard it rejected it as *unbelievable*—the thought that God would allow his own Son to be born in poverty and lowliness and then to suffer and die for the salvation of the disobedient and the ungrateful, for the wretched and the unclean, and the thought that *anyone* could be raised from the dead, was an offense to the beliefs they had learned from childhood.

But for *many* who heard the story, it was good news, just what they most needed in their lives, and it was good news that was *confirmed* by the love and mercy and peace and belonging that they experienced in the *church*—a reality which had no other explanation than that Christ was alive again and working powerfully in the hearts of believers through his Spirit. They came to know firsthand the meaning of the stone rolled away and the empty tomb—a meaning that Mary and Peter and a second disciple could only *wonder* about that *first* Easter morning. For the resurrection on the third day, after the gloom and defeat of the crucifixion, unleashed upon the *whole world* the miracle of God's love and mercy and peace and belonging that until then had been felt only by the little band of followers of the earthly Jesus. Now, the truth that Jesus had declared in the villages of Galilee would reverberate around the *globe*. Now, even the *Gentiles* would experience the blessing of the covenant that God had made with Israel. Now, every person of every age in every corner of the world whose heart yearned for good news of acceptance and forgiveness and courage and hope had the promise of the power of Jesus Christ himself to defeat the despair and oppression and hatred and frustration of their lives and to transform the mundane minutes and hours and days of existence into life enriched with eternal meaning and consequence. And they had the assurance of scripture and the example of Christ's own resurrection as testimony that God's love in Jesus Christ would not end at the grave, but that death is merely a door to the loving embrace of Christ Jesus himself and to glorious reunion with all the saints seated around the throne of God.

The resurrection of Christ—the empty tomb, the appearance of the risen Lord to his followers—meant to the early Christians, and means to Christians today, that the love of God is steadfast, that the mercy of God is sure, that the peace of God is real, that the promises of God are trustworthy. God cares for each man and woman and child and all of creation, without distinction and without reservation. Nothing that anyone has done—not you, not you, not you, not me—can put us beyond the probing reach of God's loving care—not even the crucifixion of his own Son. And nothing that anyone has done—not you, not you, not you, not me—is able to wreck God's purpose of salvation, God's intention of restoring creation back to its right relationship of loving obedience and intimacy that God vowed from the beginning.

That is why Easter is a time for celebration. That is why every *other* day of the year is a time for giving thanks to God for what God has done for us in Jesus Christ. That is the message of Christ's church—the proclamation that sets its agenda for mission and ministry and the truth that gives urgency to its discipleship and substance to its fellowship. What more could God do to declare his love for us? And is not the least *we* can do to *thank* him and *praise* him and *glorify* him by offering our own lives in return, by becoming pilgrims on a life's journey of grateful devotion? So we must let our hearts be transformed from empty concern for self to passionate concern for others regardless of race or nationality or class, from being practiced in *pride* to being practiced in *repentance*, from vainly seeking security in the promises of the *world* to finding security in the promises of him who *made* the world, from the loneliness that comes when we suppose that no one in the universe can wipe away our bitterest tears to trust that he who gave up his own Son for our sake will never abandon us.

The procession up El Cristo Rey was an especially long one each Easter, and the pilgrims were all dressed in white—the color of the resurrection, the clothing of joy. Once again, the sober reflection of Good Friday had been succeeded by the unconditional triumph of Easter. Once again, the cross had pointed the way to the empty tomb. Once again, hundreds of people had trekked up that mountain to pledge grateful devotion to God and to his Son, the risen and living Lord of all. Those who knelt at the cross almost 2,000 Good Fridays ago did so in grief and fear. But the ones who have knelt at the cross ever since have been able to do so in joy and confidence. Is the proof of God's amazing and steadfast love good news for you? Then let the joyful song leap from your true pilgrim's heart into every ear and up to the highest heavens: "The Lord is risen! He is risen indeed!" Alleluia! Amen.

The Resurrection of the Lord

First Presbyterian Church, Ponca City, Oklahoma

April 20, 2014

Acts 10:34–43
Colossians 3:1–4
Matthew 28:1–10

"Whom God Raises Up"

"So if you have been raised with Christ . . . " (Col 3:1a NRSV). What do those words mean? We sometimes forget, so many years after the women found the tomb empty, so many Easters since they first told *their* story to the eleven, that it was not at *all* clear to those *first* followers of Jesus what the resurrection *was*. Certainly, Jesus had spoken now and then about being raised on the third day. They had puzzled over that. He had said that he must go to Jerusalem and be rejected and be tortured and be killed. They had resisted that. What it all meant, and what it meant for *them*, they had not understood. And it scarcely became any more clear when, "as the first day of the week was dawning, Mary Magdalene and the other Mary went to see the tomb. And suddenly there was a great earthquake; for an angel of the Lord, descending from heaven, came and rolled back the stone" (Matt 28:1–2 NRSV). But at least *perplexity* was not as numbing as *fear*. And their perplexity began to yield to understanding when "Jesus met them and said, 'Greetings!' And they came to him, took hold of his feet, and worshiped him" (Matt 28:9 NRSV).

Sometime later, the eleven met Jesus on a mountain in Galilee, and

> [w]hen they saw him, they worshiped him . . . . And Jesus came and said to them, "All authority in heaven and on earth has been given to me. Go therefore and make disciples of all nations, baptizing them in the name of the Father and of the Son and

of the Holy Spirit, and teaching them to observe all that I have commanded you. And remember, I am with you always, to the end of the age." (Matt 28:17–20 NRSV)

And they began to understand a little more, and with the Spirit of the risen Christ present and active among them, they embarked upon the great adventure of building the church and speaking and doing the gospel in every corner of the earth.

Christ's resurrection transformed them—this timid band of followers who had despaired of feeding the multitude with a few fish and loaves, who had trembled before wind and wave, who had pledged Jesus their loyalty but then scattered into the rat holes of Jerusalem when danger threatened. But now that the risen Jesus had appeared to them, they amazed themselves with the miracles they were able to perform, with the numbers of people who were coming to believe, with the forgiveness that was spoken more easily from their lips, with the love that flowed more readily from their hearts, day by day. It was almost as if the disciples were different people—still recognizable to each other and to those around them, but otherwise changed in almost every respect. Wasn't that the most convincing evidence of the resurrection?

Several years after Mary Magdalene and the other Mary made their way to the tomb in darkness and encountered the resurrected Christ, and some time after Saul on his way to Damascus had encountered the resurrected Christ and had been plunged *into* darkness, the apostles learned that the new Christians in the little town of Colossae in Asia Minor had *misapprehended* the *meaning* of the resurrection. They *spoke* in a spiritual way, they observed such pious duties as *fasting*, but for all the *trappings* of heaven-mindedness, they seemed just as interested in earthly wealth and security, just as entangled with common standards and values, as *non*-Christians, perhaps *more* so. They boasted of doing *without* physical comforts. But their aspirations were clearly all bound up with their expectation of material rewards.

They had mastered the vocabulary of the resurrection. They mimicked the discipline of Christ's followers. But their perspective and desires were no different from the mass of people around them. They wished for intimacy with the risen Lord, but their *horizons* were still earth-bound. They weren't concerned with the things of the *spirit*, but with the things of the *flesh*. Their behavior was indistinguishable from the *non*believers. They supposed that their *veneer* of *piety* would guarantee them health and wealth on *earth* and a jeweled crown in *heaven*. For *them*, the resurrection was yet an *external* thing; they talked much about it, but their relationships with each other were unchanged. It hadn't transformed their perspective on life. They still measured success by the first-century equivalents of big houses and expensive cars. They still sought security in insurance policies and retirement accounts. They still gave allegiance to ideologies and devotion to celebrities. They were still consumed with lust and enslaved to greed.

The apostle Paul questioned how this could be so—this false spirituality and idolatrous worldliness—among *any* folk who had been united with Christ by baptism into his death and into his resurrection. Resurrection means no longer being shackled by the yearnings of the flesh and the desires of the world. Not only was *Christ* raised up; anyone who is *united* with Christ in faith *is*, *must be*, raised up *with* him, must *die* to all that is earthly—fornication, impurity, passion, evil desire, covetousness,—must surrender the false wisdoms that people sometimes call "common sense" in favor of the wisdom of God that requires *uncommon sacrifice*, must starve off hunger for *human praise* and be willing instead to be *scorned* and *rejected*, must give up judging others on the basis of one's *own* notions of justice and right and instead seek to be a *servant* to others and to show them *mercy*. To *follow* the *risen* Christ is to live as someone who has been *raised up* with Christ. And "[i]f you have been raised with Christ," Paul declared, "seek the things that are above, where Christ is, seated at the right hand of God" (Col 3:1 NRSV). Every relationship must be governed by heaven's standard. Every thought must accord with the mind of Christ. Every word must be spoken in holy love. Every deed must be worthy of God's blessing.

What does it mean to seek the things that are above? It *doesn't* mean to turn one's back on *this* world and the *needs* of those who are *in* it; far from it. The truly *spiritual* person, the person who sets his or her mind on things that are *above*, the person who is *living* the resurrection, knows and honors God's great love for all creation, freely shares the bounty of its harvest, genuinely cherishes each of its inhabitants, no matter how wretched or how lowly, no matter how disreputable or how ungrateful. "[F]or you have died"—to all that is unChristlike,—"and your life is hidden with Christ in God" (Col 3:3 NRSV).

To die with Christ is to be no longer who we once were. Now our identity is bound up with the risen Christ in a union so close that the only true life we have is life in Christ. He has become our voice, our vision, our will, our hope, and our joy. Now we look at life and at one another through the eyes of Christ, whose vision God has endorsed in the most striking of miracles. So there is no longer any place for prejudice. There is no longer any cause for hatred. There is no longer anything to be gained by deceit. There is no longer anything to be won by vanity. Fear is no longer holy. Self-reliance is no longer a virtue. To injure any person is to injure someone for whom Christ died. To insult any person is to insult God his Father. Popular judgments, worldly notions, material successes, fleshly appetites—these are *no longer* our *standards* and *cannot* be our *goals*. "[F]or you," Paul proclaims, "have died, and your life is hidden with Christ in God" (Col 3:3 NRSV). And having died with Christ in the waters of your baptism, you must live as people who have been raised up with him by the power of the resurrection that God worked that first Easter long ago and that God is *still* working in the hearts and minds and spirits of Christ's followers *today*.

You see, Easter is a blending of *our* story into the story of *Christ*. Easter is a call to *unite* ourselves with the life and death of Jesus, and so allow God to raise *us* up to *new* life in eternal fellowship with the risen Christ. And unless and until *our* story intersects and intertwines and becomes one with the story of him who was born in humility, lived in obedience, taught, healed, and forgave, was rejected and scorned and scourged and mocked and crucified and buried, and then was *vindicated* by God's raising him up from the dead to live and reign in power and glory, we shall *remain* sealed in *our* tombs of darkness and decay. Unless and until *our* story intersects and intertwines and becomes one with the story of Jesus Christ, then Easter may be for us a beautiful thought, a tale of sentimental appeal and romantic satisfaction, but it won't really make any difference to us or to anyone else. Truly to believe in the resurrection is not merely to say that the power of God raised up Jesus from the cold and darkness of *his* grave 2,000 years ago. Truly to believe in the resurrection means that I can say that God raised *me* up from the cold and darkness of my fear and my prejudice and my lust and my greed and my pride and my self-centeredness *today*. The power that is able to do *that* is *surely* able to raise up my *body*, too, when Christ comes again.

Once, the disciple Peter made an effort to tear his mind from the things that are on earth. He answered Christ's call to follow him—reluctantly, we imagine, giving up his trade, his family, his home, and trusting to the security and hope that by *worldly* standards seemed to be *no* security and *no* hope at *all*—the word of a poor carpenter's son from Nazareth. He saw the carpenter's son flush out demons from the mind of a young man, saw him give sight to a man born blind and restore life to a dead little girl and even to a man who had been four days in the tomb, heard the carpenter's son speak words of mercy and forgiveness and hope that awakened countless spirits which had been cold and sullen, felt the carpenter's son's firm grip in moments of camaraderie and his gentle touch at times of discouragement, tasted the bread and smelled the wine given by the carpenter's son in anticipation of the breaking of his body and the pouring out of his blood. But when the carpenter's son was arrested and tried and ridiculed and executed, fear and despair pulled Peter back to the familiar landscape of *earthbound pleasures and cares*.

Then the Holy Spirit visited Peter with the power of the resurrection, and raised *him* up to be a witness to the risen Christ. Once unlearned and uncomfortable with strangers, Peter became eloquent and confident in his testimony. Once impressed with every practical objection, Peter became convinced that *no* obstacle could long stand in the way of the gospel. Once stubborn in opinion and narrow in perspective, Peter discovered that God is adventurous and surprising, opening minds and changing hearts. Once a strict legalist, judging others and prejudiced toward anyone who was different from himself, Peter became zealous that *everyone* should have the opportunity to experience the love and mercy of Christ.

Jesus, you see, was not the *only* one whom God raised up on Easter. And the power of the resurrection is still at work today, as testified to by every person who is willing to *die* with Christ and whom God raises *up* with Christ. "Do not be afraid," said the angel to the women; "I know that you are looking for Jesus who was crucified. He is not here; for he has been raised, as he said" (Matt 28:5–6a NRSV). "So if *you* have been raised with Christ, seek the things that are above, where Christ is, seated at the right hand of God" (Col 3:1 NRSV).

Do you believe in the resurrection? Everyone who *dies* with Christ, God promises to *raise up* with Christ. Have *you* been raised up with Christ? If so, you are experiencing newness of hope, and eternal life. And *Christ* is *alive* in *you*.

Second Sunday of Easter

Spanish Springs Presbyterian Church, Sparks, Nevada

March 30, 2008

Acts 2:14a, 22–32
1 Peter 1:3–9
John 20:19–31

"And Him Crucified"

"The music is so solemn," said the woman, a parishioner who had come to us from a rather different church background. "I like peppy music." "Well, it *is* Lent," I explained, as associate pastor of the church. "It's a time for remembering Jesus' suffering, and the weight and reality of sin, and our fellowship with him in suffering." "Maybe I'll just go someplace else until Lent is over," she concluded. "I'll be back for Easter."

Perhaps not in quite such a dramatic fashion, a lot of people see Lent and Eastertide as very alien from each other, not only in mood, but in the very substance of their faith. Aside from musical tastes, some people just don't think that *suffering—Jesus'* or their *own*—has much to do with Christianity, especially *Protestant* Christianity. The *Reformation*, they assert, was about getting beyond all that penitential stuff, not brooding on the wounds of Jesus whom Catholics insist on keeping on the cross!

True enough, the Christian faith is an *Easter* faith. It is the *resurrection* that propelled the church into motion as an evangelical body, that is, having to do with declaring the good news. And, to that degree, as Martin Luther proclaimed, *every* Sunday is a little *Easter*—a celebration of the resurrection on the first day of the week. But just as mountains are defined by the lower terrain that surrounds them, the Easter hope is carved out of the despair of the tomb. A faith that leaves Jesus on the cross is no true reflection of the whole gospel. But a faith that ignores the facts of the crucifixion has no substance in reality, and disregards much of scripture as irrelevant. And it leads to *misconceptions* about Jesus and who Jesus' *followers* are and what Jesus' followers are supposed to *do*.

When the apostle Paul heard that the Christians at the church in Corinth were asserting privileges over one another, failing to share what they had and treating the poor in the congregation inhospitably at mealtime, claiming that some were better than others or that *their* Christianity was superior or that *their* salvation was more sophisticated, Paul was moved to write to them, "When I came to you, brothers and sisters, I did *not* come proclaiming the mystery of God to you in lofty words or wisdom. For I decided to know nothing among you except Jesus Christ, and him *crucified*" (1 Cor 2:1–2 NRSV)—a testimony that Paul recognized as "a stumbling block to Jews and foolishness to Gentiles, but to those who are the called, both Jews and Greeks, Christ the power of God and the wisdom of God" (1 Cor 1:23b–24 NRSV).

Now, one might expect Paul, who so far as we know had never even *heard* of Jesus until *after* the disciples began to preach that he had been raised from the tomb, would have emphasized Christ's *resurrection*. It wasn't for teaching that Jesus had been *crucified* that *Paul*—then known as *Saul*—had persecuted the first Christians, but for teaching that Jesus was *alive* again. Then, of course, he underwent a miraculous conversion when he encountered the risen Christ on the road to Damascus. That God had raised Jesus from the dead would have seemed proof *enough* that he was God's Son, and that he should be *listened to* and *obeyed*. But Paul insisted that the Christians at Corinth needed to know that Christ had been *crucified*—a fact that made it harder for *many* people, Jew and Gentile *alike*, to put their faith in him, made it more difficult for many people to recognize him as "the power of God and the wisdom of God." After *Easter*, what's the *point*?

> When it was evening on that day, the first day of the week, and the doors of the house where the disciples had met were locked for fear of the Jews, Jesus came and stood among them and said, "Peace be with you." After he had said this, he showed them his hands and his side. Then the disciples rejoiced when they saw the Lord. Jesus said to them again, "Peace be with you. As the Father has sent me, so I send you." When he had said this, he breathed on them and said to them, "Receive the Holy Spirit. If you *forgive* the sins of any, they are *forgiven* them; if you *retain* the sins of any, they are *retained*." (John 20:19–23 NRSV)

John seems to say that it was by the marks of the *passion* that Jesus' disciples were able to identify the resurrected Christ as the Jesus they had known. And Thomas, who wasn't present at that *first* appearance of Jesus to the disciples, insisted,

> "Unless I see the mark of the nails in his hands, and put my finger in the mark of the nails and my hand in his side, I will not believe."
>
> A week later his disciples were again in the house, and Thomas was with them. Although the doors were shut, Jesus came and stood among them and said, "Peace be with you." Then he said to Thomas, "Put your finger here and see my hands. Reach out your hand and put it in my side. Do not doubt but believe." Thomas answered him, "My Lord and my God!" (John 20:25b–28 NRSV)

We often read this account as having its point in the next verse: "Jesus said to [Thomas], 'Have you believed because you have *seen* me? Blessed are those who have *not* seen and yet have come to believe'" (John 20:29 NRSV). Clearly, the evangelist wanted later Christians to understand that they were at no disadvantage for not having actually seen the resurrected Christ with their own eyes. You and I, in Eastertide of the year 2008, may have just as strong and valid a faith as the *original* disciples did that *first* Easter.

But notice the repeated stress on what it was that *convinced* the disciples of the fact that it was indeed *Jesus* who had been raised from the dead and was now standing in their midst and granting them peace and breathing upon them the Holy Spirit and proclaiming their role in forgiving sins: it was the evidence of the *crucifixion*. It was the evidence of Jesus' *suffering*—his *persecution* and his *death*—that convinced them that the person standing before them was not a *counterfeit* savior, but was *Christ*, and *that* led Thomas to proclaim him Lord and God. And Peter, in his speech to the crowd gathered in Jerusalem, made the point that the one who had been *raised* from the *dead* was the *same* one whom they had *crucified* and *killed*. For *anyone* to have been *raised* from the *dead* would surely have been regarded a startling event pointing to that person's special favor with God, but it *wasn't* just *anyone*. It was *Jesus*, whom the Jews had put to death for performing "wonders and signs" for sick people and discouraged people and abused people and forgotten people with which they had found *fault*, who was brought forth from the tomb to life again, and power.

Like it or not, and whether it fits the temper of the times or not, the Christian faith has something to do with suffering, even with dying. When people became Christians in New Testament times, life did not turn into a bed of roses. Frequently, it became more challenging, more difficult, more dangerous, often more lonely. By the time 1 Peter was written, probably as a sermon on the occasion of baptism, followers of Christ were sometimes finding themselves rejected by friends, cut off from family, perhaps even threatened by the government. None of those possibilities was exactly a publicist's dream: "Become a Christian and be ridiculed. Become a disciple and go to jail." Nobody in their right mind goes looking for testing and trial. But the preacher of 1 Peter reminds the baptized, "In this you rejoice, even if now for a little while you have had to suffer various trials . . . for you are receiving the outcome of your faith, the salvation of your souls" (1 Pet 1:6, 9 NRSV). In some inevitable sense, faith is refined by adversity, does not deny or ignore suffering, but faces it squarely—not just the crises and disappointments that everyone experiences in the course of a lifetime, but trials that come about specifically *because* of their faith—and finds in such suffering something "more precious than gold" (1 Pet 1:7 NRSV).

The risen Christ is the same Jesus who was put to death for his faithfulness to God—for what he did on the basis of what he believed, for what he said on the basis of the truth he knew. And it is vitally important for us to remember, at Easter, both that Jesus had been *crucified*, and *why*. He had fed people who had been made hungry through others' gluttony. He had healed people who had been kept sick by other people's indifference. He had forgiven people who had been denied God's grace by others' self-righteousness. He had befriended people who had been excluded by others' purity. *That* was his *ministry*. And that was what he commissioned his *followers* to do. *For* that ministry, he was arrested and put on trial and sentenced to death and crucified. For *continuing* that ministry, his *disciples* could expect to face arrest and trial and sentence and even death. *Some* of them, by the time the Gospel of John was written, had *done* so. For being *faithful* to that ministry, despite the dangers and the threats and ultimately the world's punishment, Jesus was *raised* from the dead by God. For being faithful in *continuing* his ministry, despite the dangers and the threats and ultimately the world's punishment, scripture declares that *we* are receiving the *outcome* of our faith, the salvation of our souls.

Thomas's doubt seems not to have been so much that God could raise someone from the *dead*. Indeed, Jesus, by the power of God, had raised *Lazarus* from the dead just days or weeks before, as Thomas knew full well. *His* specific problem was in believing that God had raised *Jesus* from the dead, the Jesus who had been condemned and executed as a criminal and a traitor for blasphemy and sedition, for disrupting the established order and the status quo that favored the moneyed and the privileged and the well-connected, that kept the powerful in power and the self-righteous on their thrones of judgment, that prayed confidently to hear God's blessing and was deaf to the cries of the needy. "Unless I see the mark of the nails in his hands, and put my finger in the mark of the nails and my hand in his side, I will not believe," (John 20:25b NRSV) Thomas stubbornly insisted. And yet, when he *did* see the evidence that it was the same person who had been *crucified*—who had been taken into custody, who had been convicted, who had been executed,—he leapt ahead of all the others in understanding who Christ *was*, who Jesus *had* been *all along*—"My Lord and my God!" (John 20:28 NRSV)—the one who indeed expects, gives, and commands mercy, even if one must *suffer* for it.

You and I cannot inspect the wounds in the body of the resurrected Christ. But as people who have *not* seen and yet *believe*, it is up to us today to testify that the resurrected Christ *is* the crucified Jesus. It is up to us today to authenticate, by way of our own ministry and the ministry of the church, that it was for faithfulness in showing *mercy to others* that Jesus was *crucified*, and it was for faithfulness in showing *mercy to others* that Jesus was *raised from the dead*. It is up to us today to demonstrate that it was for a suffering love, a love willing to take risks, a love willing to put the interests of the loved above the safety of the lover, a love willing to pour itself out completely and hold nothing back in reserve, that many found *fault* with Jesus, *objected* to Jesus, could not *bear* Jesus. It is up to us today to give witness through our *own* loving deeds that this Jesus is *not* dead, but *lives* and *continues* his ministry through the disciples upon whom he *still* breathes the Holy Spirit and who, in countless deeds of sacrificial and suffering love, proclaim the living Lord Jesus Christ, and him crucified.

Third Sunday of Easter

First Presbyterian Church, Dodge City, Kansas

April 21, 1996

Acts 2:14a, 36–41
1 Peter 1:17–23
Luke 24:13–35

"The Guest"

The clock in the hallway chimed seven o'clock. The man was standing inspecting the place settings on the dining room table when his thoughts were interrupted by a knock at the door. His heart began to beat with anticipation as he went to the front hallway and, after a hurried attempt to compose himself, put his hand on the knob and swung the door open. As quickly as his hopes had risen, they fell again. Standing before him was a person in the threadbare clothing of a vagabond and carrying a worn satchel. "Yes?" the man asked, making no effort to hide his impatience. "What is it?"

"Pardon me," said the other, "but I am looking for 1217 Fairview Drive. Could you direct me?"

"This is 1217 Fairview Drive," the man responded, somewhat surprised.

"Well," said the other, "I had received a message asking me to come here tonight."

"A message? A message from whom?"

"Well, it was a note that came to me—"

"There's obviously been some mistake," the man cut off the other in mid-sentence. "Look, I really haven't time for this. I'm expecting some very important company for dinner at any moment; in fact, he should already have been here by now."

The other drew out a scrap of paper from his coat pocket, consulting it briefly. "1217 Fairview Drive."

"Of all the impertinence," the man thought to himself. "Look here, I'm afraid that someone has played a very poor joke on the both of us. Either that, or you have the wrong address. I'm sorry, but I must prepare for my guest."

The other nodded slightly, looking at the man as he closed the door.

The clock in the hallway chimed the quarter-hour, and then the half-hour. "Seven-thirty," the man muttered to himself. "I distinctly said seven. Well, I'm sure that he's a busy man. And yet—"

He went to the door and opened it to see whether his guest's car might be pulling into the long driveway. To his surprise, he saw only the cloaked back of the vagabond figure, who was sitting on the porch step and facing away from the house, illuminated by the porch light. "What? You're still here?" he said in amazement which quickly turned to anger. "I told you, this is not the place you're looking for."

The other turned around slowly and looked up at him. "This is the address I was given," he said simply. "I don't have anywhere else to go. I believe this is where I'm supposed to be."

The man was exasperated. What would his guest think if he were to drive up to the house this very minute? A transient parked on his doorstep! "Look," said the man, "shall I have to call the police?"

"All I could do is show them this address," answered the other, referring to the slip of paper.

The man slammed the door in frustration. He had never had to deal with someone like this before, though he had seen plenty of them the day that he spoke at the dedication of the new night shelter, all crowded around the entrance.

The clock chimed again. "Seven-forty-five," the man thought. "The meal will be spoiled." He went back to the front door and stood on tiptoe to look through the little window and down at the step. The vagabond figure was still sitting there, only now the porch light revealed that the shoulders of his cloak had turned white. It was snowing lightly. "Great!" the man said to himself.

He opened the door and the other turned his face up to him questioningly. "You are putting me in a very awkward position," said the man.

"Am I?" asked the other.

"It's snowing."

"Yes, it is."

"And you've nowhere else to go? What about the homeless shelter?"

"I'm supposed to be here."

The man gave a frustrated grunt. "Have you eaten today?"

"No."

"Well," said the man, "come in, then, and I'll make you a sandwich or something. But then you're going to have to leave." He hoped that he was not doing something foolishly dangerous.

The other got up and followed the man into the house.

"Careful to—" the man started as he looked down toward the other's feet, and stopped in mid-sentence when he saw not shoes, as he expected, but sandals.

The other finished the sentence for him by wiping his sandaled feet on the mat that said "Welcome."

The man cleared his throat. "Follow me to the kitchen," he said brusquely.

As they passed the opening into the dining room, the other remarked, "I see that you are ready for a fine dinner."

"Yes, though I suppose I might as well blow out the candles," the man answered, and he went to the dining room table and did so. "It appears that my guest has been detained," he said, as he resumed walking toward the kitchen. The clock chimed eight o'clock. "Or perhaps he's not coming at all," he added in an uncharacteristic tone of reproach.

"You must be disappointed," said the other as they reached the kitchen and the man motioned him to sit down at the kitchen table.

"Yes, frankly, I thought that he would be courteous enough to be on time." Then he added, "Or to let me know not to expect him." The man's anger had been transferred now from the vagabond figure to the expected guest. In fact, he began to be impressed by the other's quiet manners and simple dignity and even his calm persistence on the porch step. "Would you like some roast beef? Standing rib."

"I don't wish to impose," said the other. "I appreciate your hospitality, but you needn't do that. A piece of bread would do nicely."

"You might as well have it," said the man, drawing the roasting pan from the oven. "I assume now that he's not coming. It would be a shame to waste this."

The other smiled a bit. "Perhaps you should call him," he suggested.

"The funny thing is," said the man, "I wouldn't even know how to reach him. I just met him a few days ago—didn't even meet him, actually. It was a dinner to kick off a fund-raising campaign for the new children's hospital. He gave the grace before the meal and then said a few inspirational words about caring for children and so forth. I began to think that he would be a great person to write a motivational book about successful living and all that. I'm a publisher, you see, and I was told that he is quite popular among some people—has even done some rather miraculous things. I had to get to another appointment immediately after dinner, so I had a friend take him my card and a note inviting him to dinner tonight at 7:00. He apparently travels around quite a bit and I didn't have any other way of getting in touch with him, but I thought, since I didn't hear back to the contrary, that he would come tonight. I wanted to pose the book deal to him." The man donned an apron and pulled out a carving knife and fork and looked at the other. "I don't know why I'm telling you all this, it being a rather private thing, but I guess it doesn't matter now."

The other looked at him with a slight smile. "Many people tell me their frustrations," he said quietly. "They seem to find comfort in that."

The man set down the knife and fork and turned directly toward the other, studying his face. "Yes, I believe they do," he said slowly. "Have we ever met?" He shook off the question and turned back to the roast beef before the other had a chance to respond. "Our self-help titles haven't been doing so well lately, and I thought this fellow had a fresh approach that might sell. But if he's not any more responsible than this, I don't think we could do business anyway. So, where are you from?" he asked, changing the subject.

"I travel around quite a bit," the other answered.

"A drifter, eh? Well, I guess this economy's got a lot of people wandering around. Seems to be the price of making a profit." He paused and then returned to his earlier train of thought. "But listen, this guy was really good. Everybody at that dinner was mesmerized by him. I could've listened to him go on all night. About getting back to basics, you know? Loving your fellow human beings—the standard topics at an affair like that, but really compelling, you know? No gimmicks. No programs. Taking the Ten Commandments to heart, and stuff like that, but in a way that made it seem that it was the way that everyone should *want* to live. Gratitude for what we have. And when he spoke about reaching out to help the sick, and especially the children, I don't mind telling you that I had tears in my eyes. I think that he could be a real seller."

"You seem hungry for such words yourself," said the other.

"Yes," the man said, "I know that my attention has been diverted by business lately." He paused a few seconds. "Or at least that's what my wife told me when she left," he added, more to himself than to the other.

"How long has 'lately' been?" asked the other.

The man looked at him, pursed his lips, and nodded reflectively.

"Perhaps you need to read your own books."

"No," said the man, sitting down now across the table from the other. "I've read them. My rise in publishing circles is everything that they point to as 'success.' I'm on every social list, a guest at every charity fundraiser. My kids went to the best colleges. They're all executives," he gestured, then sighed and looked at his lap. "I don't even fool around with other women."

"What about love?" the other asked.

"I care about my fellow human beings, if that's what you mean. That's why I was at that dinner. I've got letters of appreciation from every civic organization in town."

"That seems to be a part of your *being* in the social circles," responded the other. "What about love? Love that doesn't *get* you something but love that *costs* you something?"

The man suddenly shoved himself back from the table. "You can eat at my table, but I won't take your prying into my life," the man blurted out indignantly, and went back to the kitchen counter. He unceremoniously flopped a slice of roast beef onto a plate and banged it down in front of the other. "Here," he said curtly as he set a basket of bread and a bowl of steamed broccoli with cheese sauce down on the table. He walked back over to the counter and picked up the evening newspaper, making an effort to ignore the other. The other sat and looked at the man, not so much with shock as with compassion.

Suddenly, the man uttered an expression of surprise and dismay. "Well, that explains it," he said. "Listen to this: 'Out-of-Towner Arrested. A man who had raised a popular following in the city in recent days by speaking about the importance of living according to the principles of love and compassion and mercy was arrested yesterday when he was discovered in the company of known drug users during a police raid. The others present, who were also arrested, claimed that the man was simply talking to them about the importance of treating their bodies with respect and dealing honestly with life's problems.' Oh, sure!" the man slapped the paper down on the counter. "And to think that I fell for that fraud? Eat up, friend," he said to the other. "He fooled me once. But that loser will never be served dinner in this house!"

"Why do you think he's a fraud?" asked the other.

"You can't tell me that someone hangs out with dope addicts just to preach to them!" said the man.

"Was he acting differently in doing so from the way he spoke at your dinner? Did he not say to you that a person must be willing to go among people who are hurting and in pain and in difficulty of any sort, and minister to them? Did he not tell you that reputation and riches and even virtue must not stand in the way of responding in love to those who are in need?"

"No *respectable* person would be mixed up in something like this," the man insisted.

"No," responded the other quietly, looking into the man's eyes. "But a *faithful* person might."

"Well, he can tell that to the judge."

"Listen," said the other, "there is only one who can read the motives of the human heart. And the only motive that is acceptable to him is the motive of love."

The man came back to the table and slowly sat down again, his eyes fixed on the eyes of the other. "I know you," he said. "I've heard those words before."

"Why don't you join me for dinner?" the other said. He cut the slice of meat in half and placed a piece on a butter dish, and pushed the larger dish across the table toward the man. "Have some bread," he said, as he held the bread basket and the man took a slice, still looking at him with a bewildered expression. Then the other bowed his head and said, "Our Father, we ask your blessing upon this meal and we give you thanks that you nourish us to be faithful in doing your will." He raised his head and smiled gently at the man sitting across the table.

"My God," the man exclaimed.

Fourth Sunday of Easter

Spanish Springs Presbyterian Church, Sparks, Nevada

May 15, 2011

Acts 2:42–47
1 Peter 2:19–25
John 10:1–10

"Ecology"

A few weeks ago, the secular calendar noted the observance of Earth Day. Some years ago, April twenty-second was designated as an annual occasion to focus on the importance of preserving the earth for future generations and to advocate the conservation and restoration of natural resources. Recognizing that scripture testifies to the goodness of the earth as God created it, and recalling that God commissioned humankind to till it and keep it, and remembering that the psalmist testifies to the fouling effect of human sin upon even plants and animals, and rejoicing that Revelation promises a renewal not just of Jerusalem but of the entire planet, many Christians have embraced Earth Day as an opportunity to emphasize that faithful Christian stewardship includes, emphatically, proper care for the natural order with which God has entrusted us, and requires the attention of God's people upon the increasingly dire effects of greed and waste upon the environment—a situation, by the way, that always has its first and most serious impact upon the poor, whom Jesus and the prophets before him testified are a special concern of God. This year, Earth Day fell on Good Friday, the day of *another* important observance which, for Christians, must take liturgical priority even over the subject of *stewardship*, as do the stories of the empty tomb and the appearance of the risen Lord to his disciples. But today, well into Eastertide, the lectionary opens an opportunity for us to think together about the fullness of the meaning of ecology.

"They devoted themselves to the apostles' teaching and fellowship, to the breaking of bread and the prayers," Luke proclaims in the book of Acts.

> Awe came upon everyone, because many wonders and signs were being done by the apostles. All who believed were together and had all things in common; they would sell their possessions and goods and distribute the proceeds to all, as any had need. Day by day, as they spent much time together in the temple, they broke bread at home [or it might be translated "from house to house"] and ate their food with glad and generous hearts, praising God and having the goodwill of all the people. And day by day the Lord added to their number those who were being saved. (Acts 2:43–47 NRSV)

The dictionary defines "ecology" as "the branch of biology that deals with the relations of organisms to one another and to their physical surroundings."[1] The word itself comes from two Greek words—*oikos*, which means "house," and *logos*, which means "word." Ecology is literally words about where we live, or, more accurately perhaps, words about the *relationships* in *which* we live. "House" here has to be understood more in the sense of "household," not so much a *building* as a matter of active *interdependence*, not so much a *biological* unit as a set of mutual *responsibilities*. We see that same Greek word, *oikos*, "house," in our English word "economy," which literally means "household management" and clearly relates to the work of the steward of the house, and even in the word "ecumenical," having to do with the whole inhabited world, expanding our stewardship horizon beyond our own walls to encompass the entire planet and all who live on it.

The early Christians in Jerusalem continued to worship in the temple, and Christians in outlying communities continued to worship in the synagogue. But both inside and outside of Jerusalem, Christians also began to meet in houses, in the homes of various members of the church, for worship and a meal and fellowship on the first day of the week. Luke, very likely, was never in Jerusalem, probably never visited the Near East at all. Gentile in background, his experience of the Christian life was centered in the *house church*, not in the temple or in synagogues. Indeed, when *Luke* thought of church, it would have had nothing to do with cathedrals and basilicas, not even storefront churches in little shopping centers, probably not really any *building* at all, as much as *people* and their activities, bound together in a relationship with each other and with the risen Lord Jesus Christ. The Christian ecology, if you will, was tied up with the apostles' teaching, fellowship, breaking bread together—that is, having meals together, of which the

---

1. *New Oxford American Dictionary*, 2nd ed., 536.

eucharist was a part—and praying, including the Lord's Prayer and perhaps other prescribed prayers in addition to prayers offered up extemporaneously. And one of the principal characteristics of this ecology, or contributors to it, or results of it, was that "[a]ll who believed were together and had all things in common; they would sell their possessions and goods and distribute the proceeds to all, as any had need" (Acts 2:44–45 NRSV). Their mood was one of joy and gratitude. Their habits were those of generosity and mercy. Their experience was that of peace and acceptance. And, inevitably, "day by day the Lord added to their number those who were being saved" (Acts 2:47b NRSV). See how this is really a description of the relationships among believers, and between believers and Christ, and between the believing community and the world that lay beyond the walls of the house of the church.

"What does all this have to do with ecology?" some of you may be asking. How does any of this fit in with caring for the environment, with such things as clean water and clean air and healthy forests and healthy fisheries and protecting wildlife and halting and reversing global warming? Inasmuch as the environmental movement borrowed the word "ecology" from its broader context, the better question for us *Christians* would be, how does caring for the *environment* fit in with the relationships and responsibilities of the people who constitute the household of *faith*? As important as living in proper relationship with the natural order is simply as a matter of *survival*, the *Christian* has an even more *important* reason for being concerned with the health of the planet—because faithfulness to *Jesus Christ* requires us to be good stewards of all that God has entrusted to us.

This passage from Acts has famously sparked needless debates about capitalism and communism. What the early church, as Luke describes it, was doing had nothing to do with political ideology or economic theory. "All who believed were together and had all things in common; they would sell their possessions and goods and distribute the proceeds to all, as any had need" (Acts 2:44–45 NRSV) is not a biblical endorsement of this philosophy or that. It is a description of the believers' response to the gospel. And it was the result of the believers' devotion to the apostles' teaching and fellowship, and to eating together and praying together. As simply as Luke puts it, it sounds like it was a spontaneous act of faith, without debate and even without vote. It just happened. Everyone saw that it was the thing to do, because they were no longer in competition with each other, were no longer interested in private gain. They no longer gauged success in terms of possessions, no longer regarded personal desires as paramount. That freed them to give up any ambition for claiming a hunk of real estate or amassing worldly wealth, and instead to look to the well-being of the *whole*, a way of living that insured that *everyone's* needs were met. *Food* was *important*, but maintaining *fellowship—relationship—*was *equally* important. "Me and mine" was no longer the driving motive of life, but *Christ*, who called his followers to think in terms of "we and our" as the pattern for serving "them" and caring about "theirs."

It's a simple extension of our concern for the neighbor next door whom we see *every day* to our concern for people we *don't know* and for generations *yet unborn*. As stewards of the household of believers, we can understand the summons to be caretakers of the earth, our home, so that there will continue to be green pastures and still waters, free of the pollutants and toxins that are the residue of human ingratitude and greed. Yes, all of nature is eventually and inevitably tainted by human sin. And all of faithful living has to do with proper relationships—between individuals, between communities, between human beings and God, between humankind and the world that God has created as good and has entrusted to us to maintain.

Did the apostles teach about the greenhouse effect and pesticides and ozone and contamination of the soil and the water? No. But they taught how Jesus said to love one's neighbor as oneself, and to love God with all one's heart and mind and soul, reserving nothing from God's sovereignty, exempting nothing from Christ's Lordship. And it takes not much connecting of dots to understand that sending poisoned water downstream is not showing love to our downstream neighbor, that melting the icecap is not being good parents and grandparents and great-grandparents, that eliminating the habitats required for fragile species to survive is tantamount to making God out to be a liar who declared that everything he created was good, very good. The focus on God and God's goodness, the habits of community and sharing, the attitude of cooperation and self-denial that characterized the believers' response to the good news of the resurrection, are the foundation for an ecology of living that embraces God's call, way back in Genesis, to till and keep what God created for the well-being of all. God did not ordain that *some* would *have* and that *others* would *not* have. God did not designate *some* parts of creation as *expendable* and *other* parts of creation *reserved* for the privileged *few*. God did not grant absolute ownership of *anything* to *anybody*. Understanding that, the early Christians who rejoiced at God's total self-giving in Jesus Christ happily gave everything they had for the good of all, and devoted themselves to the things of God, including very prominently worship and study. The Christian way was not to grab and monopolize and compete and exhaust, but to share "with glad and generous hearts." That was something of what it meant to praise God. And, as a result, they gained the goodwill of others. "And day by day the Lord added to their number those who were being saved."

Sharing food and other resources "with glad and generous hearts" is really the bigger picture of stewardship, including stewardship of the natural order—curtailing the indulgence of *our* desires so that the needs of *others* can be met, shortening the extent of our reach for affluence so that the earth is a blessing for all and so that consumption and waste *now* does not leave *future* generations to wonder what that passage in Genesis about God seeing that everything he made was "very good" was all about. Sharing food and other resources "with glad and generous hearts"—and disciplining ourselves to do what is required to manage those resources so that they can *continue* to be shared—is the *basis* of ecology, which means the responsibilities and relationships about all of us living in the "house" God has given us and has invited us to care for as our "home," demonstrating the interdependence that defines us as "community." Those first Christians didn't *know* that what they were doing was practicing an "ecology." *They* just thought they were *praising God.*

Fifth Sunday of Easter

Spanish Springs Presbyterian Church, Sparks, Nevada

May 22, 2011

Acts 7:55–60
1 Peter 2:2–10
John 14:1–14

"Who We Are"

Every time I hear this morning's epistle reading, I am astounded. "But you are a chosen race, a royal priesthood, a holy nation, God's own people" (1 Pet 2:9a NRSV). Whenever I think of my own actions and inactions, thoughts and attitudes—my failure to match my deeds more closely to my convictions of faith, my silent assent to falsehoods and deceptions, the injustice of my prejudices, and the carelessness of my desires—and then read or hear this passage, I am positively astounded. For Peter is speaking not only to the *first*-generation Christians of *Asia Minor*; he is also speaking across the ages and miles to *me*.

Most of the time, frankly, I don't feel very holy and I don't consider myself as being regal. And there are a lot of occasions on which I don't seem to be acting or thinking like God's chosen, like God's own possession. But then I hear the voice of God speaking through scripture, declaring as a *fact* that I am part of a chosen race, a royal priesthood, a holy nation, God's own people, declaring as a *fact* that I am part of God's new Israel elected by divine decree to bear good tidings of love and mercy and forgiveness and peace and joy and hope. The scripture does not say to me "you should be," or "you should try to be," or "you can be," or "you will be." The scripture says boldly, "you *are*." Now. *This moment.*

Whenever I think of the church, and the darker episodes of its history—its frequent complicity with oppressive governments, its numerous failures to confront inhumanity and hatred, the inquisitions which sought to *bind* the soul rather than *free* it, and its tendency to save itself as an *institution* rather than risk its existence so that others can have abundant life—and then read or hear this passage, I am positively astounded. For Peter is speaking not only to the *first-century* church; he is speaking to the church of our *own* day and in our *own* nation and community.

Much of the time, frankly, it is difficult to detect the separateness of the church from the values of the culture around it, and its message often seems more judgmental than priestly. And there are a lot of occasions on which we must wonder about God's wisdom in choosing the church as his own possession, for putting so much trust in it and depending so much upon it. But then I hear the voice of God speaking through scripture, declaring as a *fact* that the church is the new Israel elected by divine decree to be the *embodiment* of love and mercy and forgiveness and peace and joy and hope. The scripture does not say to the church, "you should be," or "you should try to be," or "you can be," or "you will be." The scripture says boldly to the church, "you *are*." Now. *This moment.*

Scripture declares that, long centuries before Christ, God called to himself a band of scruffy, uncouth, nomadic herdsmen and brought them down into Egypt, where they multiplied and prospered until the jealousy of a king forced them into slavery. But they were still God's possession, and God eventually brought them up out of Egypt and tested them in the wilderness and then finally gave them a land of their own to possess, where they would be a light to the peoples of the world, declaring and demonstrating the will of God—a chosen race, a royal priesthood, and a holy nation. There were many times when the Jews individually and as a society did not seem to live *up* to their high calling, but they remained God's own, nevertheless; God would not be unfaithful to them, God would not abandon them, even though they were unfaithful to *him*, and ran after *other* gods.

With the resurrection of Christ, and the unleashing of the Holy Spirit, the mantle of the royal priesthood devolved onto the shoulders of all those who profess belief in God's own Son, whether in Israel or in countries far away, and the holy nation expanded beyond boundaries of geography and the chosen people of God spread beyond the lines of genealogy to include Samaritans and Syrians and Greeks and Romans and even you and me, and all of us in the church of every time and place, despite the fact that we often do not feel or act particularly holy or royal or priestly. And yet, according to *God's* perspective, that is who we *are*—a chosen race, a royal priesthood, a holy nation, God's own people. Not "should be," not "should try to be," not "can be," not "will be," but "are."

The Gospel of John is noted for what biblical scholars call "realized eschatology." Eschatology is the theological word for the study of the end times, and in the Christian understanding it refers especially to the events that will occur at the second coming of the Lord and to the way things will be when the kingdom is established. To say that John is written from a perspective of *realized* eschatology is to observe how *that* Gospel frequently speaks of life with Christ in its total fullness as an *existing fact*, rather than a blessing which will come only at some *future* date, something which is *not yet*, something for which we still must *wait*. In John's Gospel, the promise was already *fulfilled*.

What could prompt such a bold assessment? The community within which the Gospel of John was written, somewhere around the turn of the second century, was evidentiary proof of Christ's presence within his followers and they in him. The fellowship of believers with their risen Lord was not mere theory; the miracles that could and would take place when Christ returned were not simply speculation. Reflection on the life of the community showed that the fellowship already existed; the miracles were already happening. For Christ already ruled. The living presence of Christ was already in every Christian. With Christ's death and resurrection, the conditions were right for God to send the Counselor, the Holy Spirit, to comfort and to empower, to dwell within the believer and prompt even greater works than Jesus himself had done. This was not a promised event to be realized in the unspecified *future*; it was a promise already *fulfilled*, being realized in the *present*, in the community of believers who had faith in Jesus Christ and recognized the presence and power of the Holy Spirit at work within them. They observed almost daily, within themselves and the other members of the community, how God in Christ was changing people and investing their lives with meaning and purpose. The new life available within the church was not a dry theological doctrine; it was the everyday experience of believers. So many people who lived in an otherwise brutal and uncaring environment discovered within the church meaning and forgiveness and wholeness and hope, that Christ's presence was beyond question. Men and women were hearing the gospel, responding in faith, growing in grace, being equipped for service in the world, and thanking God for their salvation—not something that was to happen at death or at the end of time, but something that was happening right now, miracles beyond number and joy beyond description.

The spiritual community of the Gospel of John recognized for themselves what 1 Peter had earlier expressed: that they had been built into a "spiritual house" (1 Pet 2:5 NRSV), a holy priesthood offering sacrifices not of sheep and goats, but of prayers and praise, of righteousness and mercy, of love and obedience. The risen Christ was the cornerstone of this community, on which its design and appearance and stability were established, and the members of the community were themselves living stones cemented and fused together as a temple, resting on Christ as their foundation. It was not a matter of waiting for it to happen—for these *early* believers, it already *was*.

Some of us look back on the early Christians and wonder how thinking men and women could abandon their jobs and possessions and, in some cases, their families, for the sake of the faith. Others of us assume that their rather carefree approach to living was the result of their being an unsophisticated people living in an unsophisticated age. *They* did not have to plan how to get their kids through college, *they* did not have to worry about the threat of terrorism, *they* did not have instant news reports of natural disasters and human atrocities, *they* did not even know how fragile the ozone layer is.

But if we regard these men and women so intoxicated with the joy they found in the church of Jesus Christ as being mere simpletons, or if we think that these early believers obviously did not have to put up with Christians like the ones *we* know, or if we suppose that they were all either so independently wealthy or so hopelessly poor that they had nothing to *lose* by joining the community of faith, we would be doing them a great injustice and we would be missing entirely the message of scripture. It is not that these people were oblivious to the imperfections of the world in which they lived or the personalities of the folks within their community; they were aware that innocent youth were dying on battlefields, that diseases still killed the physical body, that fear and hatred and pride still ruled in many a human heart, and influenced many a *Christian* heart as well. They could see what was happening around them, and they lived under a constant threat of persecution. Any one of them could end up like Stephen, martyred because of his bold faith in Jesus Christ.

But the imperfections of the world and of the church did not mean that Christ's absolute lordship was merely a dream or only a wish. For these Christians, Christ was *present* and his lordship was *real*; the things that he had promised had become true for *them*. They were already experiencing eternal life—they could see it in their acts of service, they could hear it in their words of love, they could even taste it whenever they worshiped together and partook of the bread and the wine. The reign of Jesus Christ was not in some dim future which never seems to be quite yet; even at that moment, Jesus Christ was enthroned and ruling over his kingdom. When they became followers of the risen Christ, they stepped out of the darkness of their previous existence and into the marvelous light of God. And anyone looking at them could hear in their words and see in their actions what Jesus

Christ is like, and what God himself is like. For they believed that whoever has seen the *Son* has seen the *Father*, and that whoever has observed the *church* has witnessed the body of *Christ*. Jesus had told a fearful and uncertain band of disciples on the night before his crucifixion: "Very truly, I tell you, the one who believes in me will also do the works that I do and, in fact, will do greater works than these, because I am going to the Father" (John 14:12 NRSV). No wonder the members of John's spiritual community knew that they were witnesses to miracles, to signs and wonders of their own doing, or rather, of the Holy Spirit's doing *through* them.

Peter called the church, and all of us, a chosen race, a royal priesthood, a holy nation, God's own people. That is who we are. God has made us so, for the purpose that we may declare the wonderful deeds of him who called us out of darkness into his marvelous light, and that we might do even greater works than those of our Lord. We—you and I, and the church—are what other people see of Jesus Christ and of God the Father. Our lives, not only what we *preach*, but even more importantly what we *do*, are the visible testimony of the way and the truth and the life. Does any of us feel uncomfortable in such a calling? Does any of us feel out of place in such company? If our eyes and hearts are open wide enough, we will soon *see* the miracles happening and perceive *that eternal life* which is present for us even now.

Once, there was nothing extraordinary about us. But then Christ was raised from the dead, and the Holy Spirit was sent into our midst. Once, we were dependent upon our own efforts and upon the ways of the world. But then Christ came to dwell within us and free us from selfish desires and earth-bound horizons. Once, we were scattered individuals, each of us striving vainly to justify him- or herself. But now we are knitted together in love and prayer for each other in the church of Jesus Christ. Once, we were no people. But now we are God's people.

Sixth Sunday of Easter

Spanish Springs Presbyterian Church, Sparks, Nevada

May 1, 2005

Acts 17:22–31
1 Peter 3:13–22
John 14:15–21

"To Suffer for the Good"

When I was the age that my children are now, anything seemed possible. Childhood, adolescence, young adulthood all ought to be the age of exuberance and opportunity, and they were for me. But in addition to the breadth of horizon that is a normal part of the psyche of youth, the times *themselves* seemed hopeful, particularly for the rise of the dignity of people. Bob Dylan reminded us that times were "a-changin'," old ways of doing things were being questioned, and were found sometimes to be unworthy; old truisms were being exposed to penetrating light, and were discovered to be false; old prejudices were being confronted with objective facts, and were shown to be the products of fear and pride.

    A century after the Civil War, there was still hateful resistance to desegregation and equal rights in both the North and South, but the trend was clear and the progress was inexorable. And even in the throes of an unpopular war, there seemed to be the seeds of recognition that armed conflict is futile and peace is the proper destiny for humankind. There were differences of opinion about the details of process, but there seemed to be a broad consensus about the goals. And events such as the assassination of Dr. Martin Luther King Jr., devastating as they were, seemed clearly to be the desperate deeds of a worldview and a bigotry doomed to ultimate failure and rejection. There was no real possibility that the progressive tides of social justice could be turned back and America could descend again to the unholy ways of segregation, or that poverty and hunger would ever again be considered acceptable, or that the nation would ever again stumble into someone else's war.

And in the wake of the Second Vatican Council, it even seemed that there was a new possibility of peace and cooperation within Christianity; ancient distrust and mutual suspicion seemed to be in retreat, and in the very act of marching together prophetically against the social and personal scourges of racism and poverty and hunger and war, Christians of many variant traditions were discovering a shared calling and a common vision, so that a return to the days of slander and insult among people of faith was finally past, and *differences* would now be valued as *gifts* to the *whole* rather than cited as a *mandate* for perpetual *disunity*. Spirits were high. There was no place for cynicism in such a time.

It was in such an environment that my sense of justice was formed, and my intolerance for *in*justice. But they did not yet have the theological underpinning of the fullness of the Bible; they were yet more political, less spiritual. In particular, my sense of justice and my intolerance for injustice were not yet informed by the clear and constant call of the Old Testament prophets that the justice of God requires special concern in legislative halls and courtrooms for those easily overlooked and forgotten and pushed out of the way, by the clear and constant reminder of the Old Testament prophets that those who are blessed materially in this world easily succumb to the temptation of thinking that their prosperity is something they have earned for themselves rather than something given graciously by God, by the clear and constant testimony of the Old Testament prophets that Jesus himself quoted and referred to not as a truth that his coming had displaced and superseded, but as a truth that his coming had reiterated and confirmed. To love *him*, he told his disciples, meant to do for *others* the sorts of things that *he* did for others. He was the fulfillment of the *prophets* as well as the *law*. And every nutritious morsel he gave to someone who was hungry, every hopeful word he spoke to a beggar, every healing touch he laid on a sick person, every generous pardon he granted to a sinner, was an instance of God's will and God's command and God's justice. And it dismays me, absolutely enrages me, when people whose Christianity is spread famously across the headlines of the newspapers these days ridicule those who call for mercy and peace and care of the environment and preference for the poor, and when they insinuate that people who *do* champion such values are *un*-Christian or *anti*-Christian.

It must have greatly dismayed early Christians that their attempts to follow Christ by living as he taught, ministering as he demonstrated, should earn them the enmity and scorn of the people around them. Worldly speaking, people's turning to Christ the Son of God as their Lord and Savior, their authority and their hope, often *increased* their troubles and left them *less* secure. In Asia Minor, for one, baptism seemed to set people on a road to earthly abuse and persecution. Their neighbors tended to criticize their new ways, their families tended to criticize their new friends, their rulers tended to criticize their new loyalties. The joy that the news of the empty tomb and the many appearances of the risen Christ had instilled in their hearts, the lilt that the good news of the resurrection infused in their spirits, must have been difficult indeed to maintain in the face of the insults and slander and threats of persecution heaped upon them by people who were hostile to the gospel of Jesus Christ—people who thought that the status quo was just fine, either because they *benefited* from it or because they couldn't *imagine* anything *different*.

We don't know the exact circumstances that prompted the writing of 1 Peter. Most probably it was a sermon delivered to a congregation on the occasion of baptism, and therefore quite possibly around Easter, when the sacrament of baptism was generally administered. The story of the cross and the empty tomb and the appearances of the risen Christ to his disciples would have been not only fresh in mind—that was the substance of preaching *every* Sunday—but newly reenacted by immersion in the water and the rising up out of the water and the welcome into the community of believers and admission to the sacred meal with the risen Christ himself that was reserved for people who had symbolically *died* with Christ and been *raised* with Christ. Not only would they have experienced the ritual of baptism, they would have voiced their commitment to this Christ in whose name the water was poured over their heads. They would have given witness to the power of the Holy Spirit whose presence was thought specially to come at baptism. They would have surrendered their own program for life to the will of God whom they acknowledged as the only *true* God. And for *this*, neighbors and friends and relatives judged them, ridiculed them, abandoned them, turned them over to the authorities.

The list of martyrs is lengthy. It began long ago with Stephen, it included eventually Paul and Peter himself, it contains names from the early church like Bishops Ignatius and Polycarp, pre-reformers in the Middle Ages and reformers in the 1500s, Dietrich Bonhoeffer and Martin Luther King and Oscar Romero, a teenage girl at Columbine High School and, just last week, a young American woman working for peace and wholeness in the streets of Baghdad. Less dramatically, it includes people who lose or give up their *jobs* for the sake of God's truth and justice, people who refuse to trade what is *right* for some *advantage*, people who consider *integrity* to be more important than *popularity*.

The words of the preacher long ago are just as important to us who strive to be faithful in a culture of faddish consumerism twenty centuries after the crucifixion and resurrection as they were in an ancient culture of imperialism and paganism. Sadly, Christianity itself from time to time has adopted the manners and goals of both consumerism and imperialism, has allied itself with them, so that those who speak prophetically against such accommodations are criticized by fellow Christians. In all of this, and through the cynicism and despair of contemporary politics and economics and entertainment, you and I need to hear and believe this assurance: "Now who will harm you if you are eager to do what is good? But even if you *do* suffer for doing what is right, you are blessed. Do not fear what they fear, and do not be intimidated, but in your hearts sanctify Christ as Lord" (1 Pet 3:13–15a NRSV). Jesus himself told his disciples not to dread whatever human hands could do to them, cruelly and unjustly, but rather to dread the consequences of surrendering one's soul. And he told them that, in their continuing endeavor to do what he had taught them, whether amidst people who were *ir*religious or people who were *super*religious, they would not be alone in the struggle; they would have a Comforter, an Advocate, who would help them *keep* Christ's commandments and make their witness to the right—the Spirit of truth, whom the world would never recognize, but who would *abide* with Christ's followers and in fact dwell *within* them. He promised the Holy Spirit as *their* strength and *ours*, reminding, prompting, defending, empowering—the same Holy Spirit that descended upon those believers of old to whom 1 Peter was addressed at their baptism, at their *dying* with Christ and being *raised* with Christ. The gift of the Spirit would not keep them from persecution—indeed, speaking the truth of God as the Spirit would prompt them, would likely *expose* them to persecution. But wasn't it better to suffer, if suffering should come, for doing what was *right* and *good* rather than doing what was *wrong* and *evil*? For testifying to *truth*, rather than being silent in the presence of *falsehood*? The preacher wasn't encouraging the Christians of Asia Minor to go out looking for martyrdom. The preacher was telling them that they must never doubt the salvation of God, so that they would never be afraid to speak and do the truth in the face of threatening evil. To suffer for doing what is *wrong*—even the *world* accepts *that* principle, agrees with *that* kind of justice. But the follower of *Jesus Christ* is called on to suffer for doing what is *right*.

The world still does not acknowledge or practice the justice of God; too often, even *Christians* do not, impressed with the arguments and assertions of popular wisdom or even our own selfish desires. But none less than the Son of God suffered unjustly in the world, to the point of being put to death on the cross for befriending the friendless and forgiving the unforgiveable and all the other good and right things he did and said to fulfill what the prophets had testified long before. *We* can expect no *easier* time of it in the world. Perhaps that is the knowledge that has helped the black majority of South Africans to respond to the white minority, since the end of apartheid, with an offering of generous forgiveness and a call for mutual repentance rather than an attitude of revenge and a new wave of tyranny. Theirs is a model of Christian patience in suffering that *all* of us would do well to emulate—not submission to injustice, but patience in hope. And as Jesus articulated God's will in both speech and silence, as appropriate, so *we* are to be ready to give an accounting of the patient hope that is in us—to testify that Jesus Christ taught and healed and forgave and ministered to all who believed in him, for which he was put to death, but then God *raised* him from the dead and he appeared to many, and then he was raised up to heaven and seated in the place of honor and authority, and he abides *today* with his followers in the power of the Holy Spirit so that *they* can give *witness* to *him* as Lord of all. And he experiences *and blesses* the pain and suffering of each of his followers in a world where justice too often must be *hoped* for. But at least it is a *hope*, and one that is based on the dependable promise of God, who worked a great miracle to vindicate his own innocent Son, who was put to death unjustly on the cross.

I regret any part that my own attitudes of dismay and occasional rage over various injustices in our world may have played in the cynicism that my children sometimes express about motives and values in today's political and social and religious debates. As any parent, I would like to *shield* my children from the world's injustices, even the ones in which I unwittingly may have taken part (may God forgive me). On the other hand, I am pleased that they have developed a deep sympathy for the poor, the neglected, the oppressed, the powerless. I hope that they will find ways to channel their own beliefs and convictions into constructive change that enhances the dignity of all people. And I hope that they can resist the sting of the inevitable comments from those at school and elsewhere who will criticize and ridicule their beliefs and values. That is a part of growing up, learning to live in a world that is not yet the kingdom of God, but which one day *will* be.

Ascension of the Lord

Spanish Springs Presbyterian Church, Sparks, Nevada

June 2, 2011

Acts 1:1–11
Ephesians 1:15–23
Luke 24:44–53

"No More Good Old Days"

Many people come to church, so I am told, that is, to *worship*, in order to escape the chaos of modern life. That is a large part of why attendance swells at Christmas and Easter—many people, whatever the condition of their faith, feel drawn by a sense of nostalgia to a *place*, to an *activity*, that they associate with simplicity and calm and stability, often seeking a return to the security they felt in childhood. They want a *haven* from the dizzying changes in the world and the confusion in their own lives, if only for one candle-lit night each year, if only for one trumpet-hailed morning. And, looking for refuge from the burden of responsibility for playing the game of life whose rules seem continually to be changing on a field that seems constantly to be shifting, they turn to the church, where the words are familiar, where the people are congenial, and, classically anyway, where even the *architecture* speaks of solace and permanence, and where the passages and crises of life—birth, marriage, death—are enfolded into a mantle of comfortable normality.

So it is little wonder that when, instead of offering a *retreat* from the ground-shaking changes and strident debates of the world outside, the changes we dread and the debates we shun end up invading the church *itself*, the result is *tumult* in church councils and *unrest* in the pews, and factions form and people threaten this and that and ministers and other church leaders scramble to hold the flock together. Just utter the words "Angela Davis" or "Reimagining Conference" or "Amendment B" in Presbyterian circles, for instance, and any picture of simplicity and calm and stability is replaced immediately by the fresh recollection of shrill headlines, angry protests, and enflamed debates. Despite the subject of the controversy *du jour*, a lot of people leave not so much because of the denomination's specific position on this or that issue, but because they simply don't want to have to deal with it in the *church* as well as in the *society* from which they always thought the church was supposed to be a *sanctuary*. If a particular church won't allow them to return to the good old days of not having to deal with complex questions public and personal, then they'll look for something else.

But if the church now and then, here and there, *has* offered itself as an *escape* from the challenges of life, that certainly was *not* the destiny the New Testament forecasted back in the beginning. The church was *born* in *crisis*. Jesus had *died*. And not only *died*, but had been *put* to death as a *blasphemer* and a *traitor*, meaning that his *followers* were under suspicion and had to fear for *their* lives, as well. He had appeared to them after the resurrection, which had filled them with joy, but the *world* seemed not to have changed *at all*, and Jesus kept talking about having to *leave* them *again*. They desperately wanted things to be like they had been *before* as they accompanied Jesus hither and yon when he was teaching the crowds and healing the sick and everything seemed like it was going to be all right, despite the murmurings of the Pharisees and the scribes.

The disciples had come so to *rely* upon Jesus, and then he was crucified and buried, and their world fell apart, but then he had returned to them in his resurrection body, and for a few weeks it was like the good old days, but now he was talking with them in ways that they didn't understand about baptism and the Holy Spirit, and so they just finally ignored all that and asked about what would really make them feel calm and secure: "Lord, is this the time when you will restore the kingdom to Israel" (Acts 1:6b NRSV)? "Are you now going to make everything all right? Are things going to be the way we always hoped they would be? Are all of our troubles going to be over now? Are the Romans going to be gone? Are the oppressive rich going to get their comeuppance? Are the Pharisees and scribes going to be knocked off their pedestals for what they did to you, and for what we fear they want to do to *us*?" Their vision of the *future* was a reversion to the *past*. They supposed that what *God wanted* was something that had *already been*. Paul hadn't yet written his letters to the Thessalonians about his understanding of what the end of history would be like. The book of Revelation didn't exist yet, nor even any of the less apocalyptic writings of the New Testament. Their standard of creation's perfection was what *had* been, but that was idealized beyond all semblance of fact. They weren't at all comfortable with uncertainty. They weren't really looking for any new adventure, certainly not for a future that would be very much shaped by what *they* would *dare* to do in the name of their crucified and risen Lord, what *they* would *risk* on the strength of their *faith*, what *they* would give *witness* to in their *own* words and deeds based on the promises of God and the instructions of Christ.

As far as Jesus was concerned, the disciples were posing the wrong question. Their focus was in the wrong place. Their vision of the future God was planning was really a wistful glimpse in their own rear-view mirror.

> [T]hey asked him, "Lord, is this the time when you will restore the kingdom to Israel?" [Jesus] replied, "It is not for you to know the times or periods that the Father has set by his own authority. But you will receive power when the Holy Spirit has come upon you; and you will be my witnesses in Jerusalem, in all Judea and Samaria, and to the ends of the earth." (Acts 1:6b–8 NRSV)

Their thoughts were all on a scale far more limited than what God intended. Their hopes for the days ahead were much too shackled by their memories of the past. Were everything to return to the good old days, merely a restoration of what *had* been, no matter how "golden" it appeared in *their* estimation, they would never go where God *wanted* them to go—not geographically, beyond Israel to the ends of the earth, not interpersonally, beyond the Jews to the Gentiles, not powerfully and mercifully, beyond the sorts of people Jesus had healed and befriended and forgiven, to additional categories of the sick and the outcast and the sin-burdened. To return to the good old days would be to draw a circle around their faith, a line beyond which they would not venture, a boundary beyond which, so they thought, God could not possibly be interested in curing and welcoming and pardoning.

When people sometimes claim that everything would be better if we just went back to the way things were, it always begs the question, "Better for whom?" Better for *women*, who were required to play one role in life, and only one, and didn't even have the right to vote? Better for *children*, who worked in factories twelve and more hours a day and had no schools? Or *men* who worked in dangerous conditions and could be fired for no cause? Better for the *disabled*, whose physical condition in the era before legislation required accommodation to their limitations isolated them from other people and afforded them little or no ability to travel, to work, or even to shop for themselves? Better, perhaps, for *African-Americans*, who were barred from voting in many states, and, before that, were slaves to be bought and sold? Everyone's *golden days* were someone *else's* days of leaden misery, inequality, injustice, abuse.

But Jesus had already promised that those who believed in him would do even greater works than he himself had done, because he was going to the Father. So, when, having also promised the disciples that they would receive power when the Holy Spirit came upon them, Jesus was "lifted up, and a cloud took him out of their sight" (Acts 1:9b NRSV), the die was cast. There would be no going back to the puny glories of the past. God's future was *more* than just about *Israel*. God's future involved *more* than the Jews *only*. God's healing was to be *broader* than just those whom *Jesus* had healed. God's forgiveness was to be more *liberal* than pardon for the sins *Jesus* had addressed. God's hospitality was to be more *inclusive* than even the outcasts *Jesus* had scandalously welcomed. And the *source* of the disciples' confidence in continuing and extending the work of Jesus in the world was their faith that God, honoring all that Jesus had said and done, had raised him to the very place where God rules—had established him in the position of power and authority as Judge of all, King of all, Lord of all. And the promise that the Holy Spirit would come rest upon them until Christ himself would return one day was guarantee that they had *not* been abandoned, were *not* left to their own devices and without the same resources that *Jesus* had had during his earthly ministry. Yes, they would have to make their own decisions about the work of the church. No, they would not be relieved of the struggle and responsibility to discern God's will and discern the faithful path toward God's future among all the possibilities, many of which might appear reasonable, some of which might be fraught with danger. But *always*, they would have the authority of Christ's own commission and the hope of Christ's own approval and the comfort of Christ's own forgiveness as they encountered and wrestled with issues old and new on the road to the salvation of the whole world. Their task was *not* to *restore* the *past*, but to *transform* the *present*, making low the hills and lifting up the valleys so that the way of Jesus, when he returned, would be made smooth, and every knee bend and every tongue proclaim him Lord and Savior. If *nostalgia* ruled the hearts of Jesus' followers, they would never do any more than *he* had done, and probably not even *that*. If their expectations of the *future* went no further than their experience of the *past*, God's redemption of the whole world would never be accomplished. If new cases of illness were not healed, if more classes of outcasts were not embraced, if additional categories of sinners were not forgiven, Jesus might as well have stayed in the tomb. For Christ's resurrection would not have been good news for non-Jews. It might have been interesting, but essentially irrelevant. It would have had no effect on future generations. Its blessings would not have been known beyond Israel. Its promise of salvation would not have been experienced by any but the few to whom Christ personally appeared.

The freeing of the disciples from nostalgia for what *had* been was the prerequisite for the church's mission. The ascension of Christ to the right hand of God and the bestowal of the Holy Spirit days later propelled the church across borders of nation and race and custom and respectability to become Christ's agent at work in the whole world and in every generation. The followers of Christ *could* have stood looking up toward heaven longingly, wistfully, nostalgically, and the church of Jesus Christ would have *died* before it was ever *born*. The story of Jesus would never have been *told*, because there wouldn't be any *present* work of Jesus through the *church* that would cause anybody to be *interested* in stables and mangers and parables, much less a cross and a tomb and an upper room.

One of the great issues that has faced the church throughout the ages is whether it will be paralyzed into inaction, into a failure to witness meaningfully in new situations and contemporary settings, by its longing for the good old days. But however *good* they were, they were *not* the fullness of God's purpose for creation. There were large classes of people excluded from the fellowship in which God's grace is to be demonstrated. There were whole races and nationalities that were considered beyond God's interest. There was an entire gender that was excluded from full participation in Christ's church. Even now, there are people who are being told "You don't belong," "You can't come in," "God doesn't care about you." And when the *next* barrier is broken down, there will *still* be *others* who are waiting not only to *hear,* but to *experience* the good news of Jesus Christ, the gospel of his life, death, and resurrection, in their *own* lives, in their *own* circumstances, and to be enfolded into the fellowship of believers and come to have eternal life in the kingdom of God. And they, too, like the first witnesses to the Lord's ascension to his heavenly throne, will worship Jesus Christ, and will have great joy, and will continually be blessing God.

Seventh Sunday of Easter

Spanish Springs Presbyterian Church, Sparks, Nevada

May 5, 2005

Acts 1:6–14
1 Peter 4:12–14; 5:6–11
Luke 17:1–11

"God's Gift to Christ"

Our Gospel reading comes from that part of John's Gospel that Bible scholars refer to as "the high priestly prayer." As the hour for the glorification of Jesus approached—as *John* saw it, Jesus was *glorified* when he was lifted up on the *cross*—our Lord, with his disciples listening, prayed that the Father *would* glorify him. He prayed, too, that the Father would watch over and keep the disciples, whom Jesus was sending out into the world. He knew that the disciples would be tempted, would be persecuted, would be menaced with doubts and fears. As his friends, as his followers, as his partners in ministry, as his church, Jesus naturally thought of *their* needs as his death approached. He cared deeply for this band of men and women who had come to trust him and to depend upon him and to love him.

Based upon the Gospel record, *outsiders* might judge the disciples to be bunglers, to be slow of wits and sluggish in feeling, unreliable, unsteady, now timid, now brash, easily swayed in opinion and irresolute in action. But in *Jesus'* eye, they were rare jewels, a precious treasure, worth surrendering his life, even, not a *one* of them *less* than a lavish gift from the Father to the Son. In his earthly life, Jesus had carefully protected and guarded them each one. Now, in the disciples' hearing, and as the shadow of the cross was lengthening toward him, Jesus commended them to the Father's gracious care.

This prayer of Jesus, tender as it is, would have little meaning for *us* were it not for the fact that John meant for it to be understood not simply as Christ's prayer for those *original* disciples, but for all the *subsequent* Christians across the centuries, including each of us, as well. John knew that *later* followers of Christ would be listening to Jesus' prayer: "I have made your name known to those whom you gave me from the world. They were yours, and you gave them to me, and they have kept your word" (John 17:6 NRSV).

Probably, none of the people in the community of faith for which John wrote his Gospel had personally known Jesus. But, threatened by persecution, troubled by divisions, they could read themselves into Jesus' prayer and find a deep and abiding solace in Jesus' words, and courage too for persisting in spite of dangers and disappointments. They all, and each one of them, were in the mind of Jesus on the eve of his crucifixion. They all, and each one of them, were the very ones for whom Christ himself prayed only hours before God raised him up in glory. They all, and each one of them, were God's own gift to his beloved Son.

The wise men, so we are told, brought the baby Jesus gifts costly and rare—gold, frankincense, myrrh. On the scale of gifts that *human* hands can bear, those were lavish offerings, very impressive. But here in the seventeenth chapter of John, we learn what *God himself* had given to Jesus—you and me.

Have you ever thought of yourself as God's gift to Christ? Or that, if you *were* God's gift to Christ, God must have lost the receipt, or else you would have been exchanged for something more suitable long ago? It may be difficult enough to think of Peter, the hothead, the misconstruing, the sleepy, as God's gift to Christ. Or Thomas, the doubter, the questioner, the uncertain. Or Judas Iscariot, the revolutionary, the greedy, the betrayer. But those of us whose names are not chiseled into history—we who make jokes about being "God's gift to women," or "God's gift to men," or "God's gift to learning," or "God's gift to art"—have we ever seriously considered that *we* are God's gift to *Christ*? That is what scripture indicates.

Suddenly, do our flashes of temper seem monstrous, does our indifference seem blasphemous, does our self-reliance seem heretical, does our self-contentment seem ludicrous? Are we ashamed of the stains on our moral clothing, and wonder how they ever got there? Do we nervously try to brush off the lint and dust from our spiritual wardrobe and pull ourselves erect in attentive salute? Or do we chuckle or scoff and say to ourselves, "Surely Jesus can't mean *me*?"

But Jesus, John is saying to us, in fact means just that. We are his valued possession, given to him by God, no less, and, conscious of his approaching absence from the world in which the disciples must *continue* to live, he anxiously beseeched the Father to accept and care for us and protect us fragile beings of spirit and flesh, that we might not simply continue to *exist* in the world, but *thrive* as witnesses to Christ and the eternal life which is only in him. That *all* believers might participate in Jesus' *own* glory is the ultimate aim of the entire prayer.

There have been times in the life of each believer, and times in the life of the whole church, when God's love and care, God's acceptance and protection, have seemed uncertain. The death of a loved one, the loss of a job, the failure of health, the abandonment of a spouse, the ingratitude of a child, natural disaster, human cruelty all have taxed human certainty in God's safekeeping. What of God's *answer* to Christ's prayer at times of *loss* and *pain*? Persecution that threatens to stamp out the faith, bitter words and mistrust that divide denominations and congregations, have cast deep doubt on whether God has in fact blessed the enterprise we call the church. What of God's answer to Christ's prayer at times of *schism* and *suspicion*?

Faith in Jesus as the Son of God means that we know in fact God has *not* abandoned us and *will not* abandon us. Those Christians who have lived through such experiences, not least among them being the saints addressed in 1 Peter, can testify that where there is pain, where there is suffering, where there is anxiety, where there is hurt and anger, God is not *absent* from Christ's own, but is faithfully brooding over them, and God can be counted on not to abandon those God considered a worthy gift to his own Son, and whose protection God pledged to his own Son. God is never far from us in time of great need; the only time God is far away is when we *push* God far away in moments of great self-satisfaction and great comfort, great self-congratulation and great reputation. Then, perhaps, the gift has lost its luster, has turned sour, has gone rank.

But even in such cases, God does not give up, but remembers and remains faithful to answer Christ's prayer even though we are too proud or too dense to pray for ourselves. God remains anxious for our well-being, and is moving mountains to save each one of us from being thrown or throwing ourselves headlong over the precipice. Though our pedigree says we are not of this world, yet the habits of the world still have sway over us. But having been given to Christ in baptism, and Christ at his crucifixion having entrusted us to the eternal care of God, the stamp of our true ownership has been engraved indelibly on our brow: we belong, body and soul, to Jesus Christ. For so God has ordained. And God does not forget that.

All those who *believe* in Christ *belong* to Christ. We are not our own, but Christ's. We are not to set our own agenda; that is *Christ's* prerogative, as God has decreed. So, even in the *absence* of Jesus, Luke tells us in Acts, "[a]ll these were constantly devoting themselves to prayer, together with certain women, including Mary the mother of Jesus, as well as his brothers" (Acts 1:14 NRSV). "All these"—just as Jesus had asked God to protect them in his name, "'so that *they* may be one, as *we* are one'" (John 17:11b NRSV). The gift that God gave to Christ was not to be a *broken bauble*, a *fractured knickknack*, but a single body of believes, *whole* and *united*, able to give encouragement and comfort to one another, able to demonstrate a consistent witness to the lordship of Jesus Christ, able to sing together in a hundred different languages one beautiful song of praise in perfect harmony.

Was Jesus' prayer unrealistic? Was the gift given by God—even believing human beings—so inherently unstable and fractious that it began to break into hundreds and thousands of pieces the instant that Pentecost was past? Were the forces of human pride and human prejudice so strong that even *Christ's great hope* and *God's best effort* could not avail to keep the church united?

From one perspective, the history of Christianity is a history of constant debate and division. No sooner had Jesus ascended to the Father, it seems, than difference of opinion and difference of expression overshadowed the church's progress of single-minded mission and ministry. Within decades, councils were denouncing those with whom they disagreed and congregations were excommunicating those who questioned their theology. Purity of doctrine and faithfulness of practice were frequently at stake, but pride and prestige equally so. And nearly five hundred years after the Reformation, the landscape is not crowned with the church of Jesus Christ, disciples mutually seeking to give honor to the one true Lord, but rather is walled off into denominations and so-called "independent" churches. Even our own Presbyterian denomination has a history of division and contention.

Is this the gift that God gave to Christ? Folk who busy themselves with arguing side issues and who are quick to draw lines in the dirt and who denounce each other whom Christ called to be a family as tightly knit as the Trinity of Father, Son, and Holy Spirit? Surely not. And *all* sides are complicit in tarnishing the gift who are unwilling to sit with and discuss with and pray with and laugh with and weep with *another* who professes faith in Jesus Christ.

That is why our ecclesiastical ancestor John Calvin spent so very much time working for ecumenical reconciliation, and why the Presbyterian Church (U.S.A.) today continues to work with and support the efforts of state, national, and international ecumenical councils of churches and alliances of churches and Churches United in Christ. This is a part of our *witness*—that Jesus Christ desires his church to be one, and *prayed* for that and *continues* to pray for that—not that all other Christians in the world come to see things just like *we* do, but that *all* of us *together* rise *above* our differences to affirm the absolute lordship of Jesus Christ and humbly and sensitively and in a spirit of obedient servanthood seek the mind of Christ in matters of worship and witness, daily living in home and school and office and shop and marketplace and government hall as well as sanctuary, that we may *glorify* God the Father and his Son Jesus Christ.

Each of us needs to ask him- or herself, "What sort of gift to Christ am I?" Am I everything that God intended his gift to be? I know that I am precious in his sight—*so* precious, that Christ gave his life for me, and on the eve of his sacrifice, gave me over in prayer to the loving care of God his Father. And I know that Christ expects me to be united in genuine love and visible caring to every other believer, that Christ might be glorified in a church harmonious and united. How can I live my life, how can I live my faith, how can I live my love for Jesus Christ so as to be a worthy gift? How can I live in harmony and unity with other believers so as to glorify him?

Pray for this congregation, and for the Presbyterian Church, but also for the whole church of Jesus Christ, that all of us together, by our unity, by our harmony, by our faith, by our words, by our deeds, might be known to all people as truly God's gift to his Son, a gift that is beautiful and worthy and precious.

Appendix

The Week of Prayer for Christian Unity, January 18–25, is an annual ecumenical observance of Christ's prayer that his church should be one. Using scripture passages chosen by an international ecumenical committee, worship materials are provided through the Graymoor Ecumenical & Interreligious Institute.

Week of Prayer for Christian Unity
Holy Cross Catholic Community, Sparks, Nevada
January 25, 2008

Isaiah 55:6–9
1 Thessalonians 5:12a, 13b–18
John 17:6–21

"If Jesus Prayed for It . . ."

In the Presbyterian Church, ministers are called by a congregation. We are not assigned to particular parishes, but, after a long process that relies much on prayer and discernment, we are voted into the position by the members of the local church after being recommended by the congregation's pastor nominating committee and being approved by the presbytery, which is our area-wide governing body. Before a pastor nominating committee will ever have met with a candidate for the position of pastor, the church will have filled out an information form designed to describe the character and needs of the church, and specifying the skills and interests they are seeking in a pastor, and the minister will have filled out an information form specifying the skills and interests and experiences that the minister has to offer, along with the sort of church for which she or he is looking. Either on their own, or with the aid of the national office, the churches that are looking for a pastor and the ministers who are looking for a church get in contact with each other. That usually happens on the basis of a close match between the sort of pastor the *church* says *it's* seeking and the sort of *church* the minister says *he* or *she* is seeking.

I haven't filled out such a form in ten years now, and I understand that it has changed in several ways, but there used to be a ranking of pastoral interests and skills on both forms. In reciprocal fashion, the church was supposed to indicate, from among twenty or so potential pastoral tasks, in order, the half dozen that it considered most important in a pastor, and the minister was supposed to rank, in order and from that same list, the half dozen that she or he was most interested in performing. As you might expect, the list on both forms included things like preaching, worship leadership, teaching, pastoral counseling, administration, congregational communication, mission programming. It was fairly common knowledge in the denomination, and in its seminaries, that anyone seeking to be a senior pastor would be foolish not to rank preaching and worship leadership high on their list, because that was invariably what churches were most concerned about when seeking a pastor. Identifying *other* skills and interests on the list as priorities would likely delay the candidate's finding a church, if ever.

Among those other skills and interests on the list was "ecumenical relations." Apparently, the people at our vocations agency considered that it was a valid pastoral task, and that some church somewhere might be so zealous about ecumenism that its search committee ought to be helped to identify a similarly zealous *pastor*. But I have never yet been involved with, or known, a congregation that considered ecumenical relations one of the half dozen priorities it wanted its pastor to emphasize and spend her or his time on. In *Protestant* churches, anyway, the popular image of a pastor pictures him or her in the *pulpit*, not sharing coffee and cookies at an interfaith conference.

On the night before the crucifixion, according to John's Gospel, Jesus, after washing the feet of his disciples—the lowliest form of servanthood, an unpleasant task usually assigned to a slave—and declaring that *they* must be willing to do the same thing for *each other*, went on to speak to them about his relationship with *them* and his relationship to *God*. He encouraged the disciples to be faithful in the face of the opposition they would encounter in the world. And then "he looked up to heaven" (John 17:1 NRSV) and voiced a prayer to the Father. And as soon as he had *finished* his prayer, he went out across the Kidron Valley to a garden, and there he was arrested by the soldiers and police and chief priests and Pharisees whom Judas had led out from the city to find him.

In all of his long speech to the disciples that night, Jesus said not a word about preaching or worship leadership or administration, discussed nothing about proper techniques of pastoral counseling or things to remember in preparing church budgets or photocopying or even mimeographing church newsletters. Instead, he spent those last precious hours with his closest friends and followers talking about serving each other in the most menial and thankless tasks, of loving each other, of remaining firmly rooted in their Lord, of expecting the Holy Spirit, of weathering the gales of hatred and opposition that they would encounter, and, miraculously, of their receiving his peace in the midst of it all. And then, in a most intimate conversation between the Son and the Father, which the disciples were privileged to overhear—and we, now, *with* them—Jesus prayed for his friends and followers and entrusted them to God's care.

Many of us, over the years, have become very familiar with the prayer or parts of it, may even take it rather for granted. But if we stop and think about it, it is absolutely *extraordinary* that when Jesus was about to be betrayed and arrested and tried and executed, he prayed not about his *own* situation, but about *theirs*—his *disciples'*: that they be "sanctified," that is, set apart for the task for which Jesus had been preparing them. And at the *climax* of his prayer was this petition: "I ask not only on behalf of these"—that is, the eleven disciples who, having accompanied him during his ministry, were still gathered with him in the dining room,—"but also on behalf of those who will believe in me through their word, that they may all be one" (John 17:20-21a NRSV). Jesus' prayer "that they may all be one" was *not* just a request for some nice sentimental chumminess, but for a particular relationship that was the very underpinning of his life and ministry, the very purpose of the incarnation: "As you, Father, are in me and I am in you, may they also be in us, so that the world may believe that you have sent me. The glory that *you* have given *me* I have given *them*, so that *they* may be *one*, as *we* are *one*, I in them and you in me, that they may become completely one, so that the world may know that you have sent me and have loved them even as you have loved me" (John 17:21b-23 NRSV).

Careful attention to Jesus' words here discloses that the unity of the church is *not* a *given*. Already, by the time the Fourth Gospel was written, the church was divided by theological disagreements, racial and ethnic differences, very likely by variations in worship. If not quite *inevitable*, such division was nevertheless *natural*. We know that Paul warned against teachers whom he believed were not accurately portraying the gospel, or at least feared that their teaching was leading to misunderstandings that he thought were very important to correct, many years before John wrote down Jesus' prayer. Perhaps John wanted *his* church to know that unity was not *automatic*, on the one hand, nor a purely *human* achievement, on the other. It was something for which even *Jesus* had to *pray*, but *for* which Jesus *did* pray, and for which Jesus was able to pray *confidently*.

But it is also something that was so *important* to Jesus, a vital testimony to his very relationship with the Father, that it was an urgent concern on the last night of his earthly life. For John, the idea that Jesus reveals the Father in his words and work and in his whole person is fundamental. So the *church* must reveal *Jesus* in *its* words and its work and its whole *life*. If it is *divided*, if it is *squabbling* and *bickering*, if it is *denying* the validity of any of its parts as really *being* the church, it *scandalizes* its Lord by casting doubt on his authentic oneness with God. But it cannot *manufacture* its unity as just another program option on the list of possible tasks that the *pastor* can perform if and when he or she gets *around* to it. It is a gift of *God*, but it is only *manifest* to the extent that the whole community of faith does in *its* life what Jesus did in *his* life, even to the point of his death on the cross: proclaiming the gospel, serving without reservation the person in need, healing the sick and the broken, forgiving the sinner and welcoming the outcast, and teaching the faithful.

Why did Jesus speak of unity explicitly only at the *end* of his earthly life? Because as long as he was with his disciples, everyone could see that *he* was their bond of unity. But now that he was departing from them, their unity could no longer be presumed. Both *before* the crucifixion and *after* it, the unity of his followers *was* and *is indeed* the sign and expression that Jesus is the Son of God, that the two of them are *one*. All that Jesus said, all that Jesus did, all that Jesus commanded his followers to say and do, we believe to be the truth of God. But the world will not *receive* it as truth if it doesn't believe that Jesus is the Son of God the Father, and the world won't *do* so—will remain a place of fear and greed and disparity, susceptible to sin and overshadowed by death—so long as Christ's followers avoid, insult, deny, anathematize, and demonize those with whom they *disagree*, or those with whom their *ancestors* disagreed.

Christ's followers are to be "sanctified in truth" (see John 17:17 NRSV)—"holy"—which means to be set apart for a special purpose. But if those who are seeking to be Christ's followers are far apart from *each other*, it is not a sign that some of us are more holy than *others* of us. Rather, it is a sign that we are in fact separated from *God*. As we come closer together, in worship, in mission, in fellowship, in prayer, allowing ourselves to be drawn nearer in the Spirit's tether, we will more and more find our *differences* to be a mutual embarrassment and a shared scandal. We will recognize our divisions to be relics of a shameful past or obstacles to a faithful future, which must be discarded or overcome because they make the church a false witness to its Lord.

The church exists to testify to the mutuality and reciprocity of the relationship between the Father and the Son, and in fact to *share* in it, to find its *life* in it. The church's *unity* has to do with the very *character* and *identity* of *God* that has been revealed to us in the life and death and resurrection of Christ, and attested to in scripture. If the *church* does not demonstrate in its *own* life the unconditional and reconciling love of God, how will the world ever *believe* it? Do *we* really believe it *ourselves*? If *so*, how can any difference be allowed to divide? How can any disagreement be declared irreconcilable? How can any practice be made exclusionary? How can any tradition be allowed to reinforce within the *church* the contentious and competitive and prideful ways of the *world*?

Among the very oldest words in the New Testament are these from Paul to a church where dispute and disunity were threatening the witness to the oneness of the Son and the Father:

> Be at peace among yourselves. And we urge you, beloved, to *admonish* the idlers, *encourage* the faint hearted, *help* the weak, be *patient* with *all* of them. See that none of you repays evil for evil, but always seek to do good to one another and to all. Rejoice always, pray without ceasing, give thanks in all circumstances; for this is the will of God in Christ Jesus for you. (1 Thess 5:13b–18 NRSV)

Christ desires that, in prayer to God as in interactions with each other, we do his will, which is what happens when we follow his example. And the example that he left his disciples on the very night of his arrest—the very last thing that he showed his followers how to do at his final meal with them before the crucifixion—was to pray "that they may all be one. As you, Father, are in me and I am in you, may they also be in us, so that the world may believe that you have sent me" (John 17:21 NRSV). Shouldn't working for the unity of the church, not on *our* terms, but on *God's*, be at the very *top* of any priest's or minister's list of things to do, as well as *each* member of the church? After all, if *Jesus* prayed for it . . .

List of Sources Cited

Bonhoeffer, Dietrich. *Christ the Center*. Translated by Edwin H. Robertson. San Francisco: Harper & Row, 1978.
———. *The Cost of Discipleship*. Rev. ed. Translated by R. H. Fuller. New York: Collier, 1963.
———. *Creation and Fall: A Theological Interpretation of Genesis 1–3, Temptation*. New York: Macmillan, 1959.
Foster, Richard. *Celebration of Discipline: The Path to Spiritual Growth*, 3rd ed. San Francisco: HarperSanFrancisco, 1998.
Leibholz, G. "Memoir." In *The Cost of Discipleship*, Rev. ed., by Dietrich Bonhoeffer, translated by R. H. Fuller, 11–35. New York: Collier, 1963.
Luther, Martin. *Career of the Reformer IV*. Edited by Lewis W. Spitz. Vol. 34 of *Luther's Works*. Philadelphia: Muhlenberg, 1960.
Schweizer, Eduard. *The Good News According to Luke*. Translated by David E. Green. Atlanta: John Knox, 1984.
Schweitzer, Albert. *The Quest of the Historical Jesus*. Translated by W. Montgomery. New York: Macmillan, 1968.
Shields, Carol. *Small Ceremonies, The Box Garden, Swann*. New York: Quality Paperback Book Club, 1996.
Tennyson, Alfred, Lord. "The Charge of the Light Brigade." https://poetryfoundation.org/poems/45319/the-charge-of-the-light-brigade.

www.ingramcontent.com/pod-product-compliance
Lightning Source LLC
Chambersburg PA
CBHW070254230426
43664CB00014B/2527